D0367221

Paris—A Musical Gazetteer

PARIS

– *A Musical Gazetteer*

Nigel Simeone

Yale University Press
New Haven and London

Designed by Thomas Whitridge
Set in Monotype Fournier by Ink, Inc., New York, New York.
Printed in the United States of America by Edwards Brothers, Ann Arbor, Michigan.

Library of Congress Cataloging-in-Publication Data
Simeone, Nigel, 1956–
Paris – a musical gazetteer/Nigel Simeone.
p. cm.
Includes bibliographical references.
ISBN 0-300-08053-0 (cloth) – ISBN 0-300-08054-9 (pbk.)
1. Music – France – Paris – Directories. 2. Musical landmarks – Paris. I. Title.
ML21.F7S56 2000
780'.944'361 – dc21   99-054362

A catalogue record for this book is available from the British Library.

The paper in this book meets the guidelines for permanence and durability of the Committee on
Production Guidelines for Book Longevity of the Council on Library Resources.

10 9 8 7 6 5 4 3 2 1

For Libby

Contents

Acknowledgements

I owe a particular debt of gratitude to John Tyrrell for his patient and characteristically generous advice when this book was at an embryonic stage. From the start, my wife, Jasmine, provided many helpful ideas; she was of great support during the writing of the book, as well as a companion on several trips to Paris. Reginald and Josephine Simeone, both expert and devoted francophiles, helped with a number of detailed enquiries. Several friends and colleagues read all or part of the manuscript at various stages, or discussed aspects of the book with me; I am most grateful for their comments and suggestions. They include James Briscoe, Roy Howat, Libby Jones, Robert Pascall, and Philip Weller.

Many of the photographs were newly taken by Stephen Cornell and Karen Sturt. Their generosity, skill and determination deserve thanks of a special kind. A wide range of biographies, catalogues, collections of correspondence, and dictionaries have been of assistance in assembling the information presented in the gazetteer, as have works on the history and topography of Paris. It is a pleasure to acknowledge my debt to all these sources here, and to refer readers to the bibliography for details. Individuals and institutions that have helped with specific enquiries include Felix Aprahamian, David Cannata, Roy Howat, Rex Lawson, Robert Threlfall, and the Fondation Singer-Polignac.

The gazetteer would not have been possible without several visits to the city that is its subject. I am particularly grateful to the staff in the Music Department of the Bibliothèque Nationale who have always enabled my visits there to be useful.

At Yale University Press Harry Haskell was the most generous and encouraging of editors, taking a lively interest in the project from the start, and making a number of helpful suggestions at later stages; Susan Abel edited the typescript with immense care and skill.

This book is dedicated to Libby (Elizabeth-Louise) Jones, who has been its constant inspiration.

The Scope of the Gazetteer

As far as I am aware, this is the first gazetteer to the musical monuments of Paris, though a brief account of some major landmarks was written by Guy Ferchault in 1937. Information about where musicians lived and worked in the city is often hard to find, and it was curiosity about such biographical details that led me to write the present book. My intention has been to chart the Parisian activities of some of the great musical personalities who lived in the city: where they had their homes, where their works were performed, where they received their education, where they are buried, and where they are commemorated.

Paris occupies a unique position as a musical capital. As well as being the home (though less often the birthplace) of almost every great French composer in the last four centuries, it is the city where Chopin, Donizetti, Liszt, Mozart, Prokofiev, Rossini, Stravinsky, Verdi, Wagner, and many others spent extended periods of their lives.

This book is not intended as a guide to the present-day musical life of the city; its purpose is rather to provide documentation on historic musical locations, to set musical events into the context of the city itself, and to direct the reader to sites of musical interest (including those no longer extant). Two points should be stressed: first, many of the locations listed in the gazetteer (including almost all the private addresses) are not open to the public; second, some entries are a record of what was once at a particular location rather than of what is there now.

The musicians in the first, and longest, section of the book include many of the most significant French composers of the past two hundred years (with a few from earlier periods), as well as some of the most celebrated foreign musicians who spent parts of their working lives in the French capital. The lives of all these personalities were, to a greater or lesser extent, bound up with the history, the politics, and the wider artistic life of the city itself.

An apology is due to readers who seek, but do not find, a particular composer in the gazetteer. Limitations of time and space have been significant factors. I must take full responsibility for the process of selection, though the decision to omit musicians was made only with the greatest reluctance, or when adequate documentation proved impossible to find. To give one example, Manuel de Falla, Debussy once joked, "moved more often than Beethoven" during his years in Paris, and I found it no easier to track Falla's Parisian dwellings half a century after his death than it was during his lifetime. Occasional visitors to the city, such as Bruckner, Grieg, Mahler, Puccini, Rimsky-Korsakov, Sibelius, and Johann Strauss the younger, are not included in the directory of musicians (though several are mentioned elsewhere in the gazetteer).

Churches with significant musical traditions, theatres, and concert halls where important premières took place, some important musical institutions and orchestras, and a selection of music publishers and instrument makers are described in separate sections. There is also a list of libraries, museums, and galleries with holdings of material relating to music in the city, especially from the period since around 1750 which is the gazetteer's principal concern. The large number of present-day street names commemorating musicians in Paris are listed, and the gazetteer is completed with an index of locations arranged by arrondissement and by street.

Using the Gazetteer

Buildings listed as private addresses in the gazetteer are not open to the public unless otherwise stated. Many older buildings have been demolished or rebuilt beyond recognition. Locations are given on the basis of Michelin grid references for Paris (used in all Michelin maps of the city, for example, *Paris Plan*, nos. 11 and 14, and *Atlas: Paris et Banlieue*, no. 25). The grid reference is followed by the nearest Métro, RER, or SNCF station(s); for example, in the entry on Bizet, "22 rue de Douai, 9e (D13, Métro: Blanche)" indicates that the address is in the ninth (9e) arrondissement, at Michelin grid reference D13, and that the nearest Métro station is Blanche.

It will be necessary for the prospective visitor intending to use the gazetteer for locating addresses to have a street atlas such as the Michelin *Paris Plan* (no. 11 or no. 14) that includes Métro and bus maps. Seasoned visitors to Paris will already know that travelling by bus is one of the most interesting ways of seeing the city, and many of the locations listed can easily be reached by bus. Tickets for the public transport system may be used on the Métro, the bus, the RER, and SNCF trains within the specified zones. For visitors wishing to follow a trail around districts with strong musical connections, the index by arrondissements should be of use for planning itineraries. Though it has not been my intention to write a travel guide, the four walks around areas of musical interest will, I hope, be of use to a visitor less familiar with the city. For those with limited time, a list of ten outstanding musical landmarks follows the walks.

Four Musical Walks

Paris is, of course, a wonderful city to see on foot. The four walks included here take in some of the most significant musical landmarks, and several sites of more general interest. The longest of the walks is Walk 1, which would take most of a day, with appropriate stops at some of the many cafés en route. Walks 2 and 3 explore parts of Paris which are not always on the itinerary of visitors to the city but which have some fine musical associations. Allow most of a day for the longer version of Walk 2 (or less than two hours for the short version). Walk 3 can be done in half a day, though it is worth taking longer to spend time in the Opéra, the Trinité, and Montmartre Cemetery. Walk 4 includes a stroll up the Champs-Elysées, one of the most famous of all Parisian avenues. For specific locations, readers are referred to the appropriate entries in the gazetteer.

Walk 1: A Circular Walk from les Invalides

Michelin *Paris Plan* maps 29, 30, 31, and 43

Begin at Invalides Métro station and walk towards the Hôtel des Invalides onto the esplanade des Invalides. This was the scene of the displays of oriental music which so astonished Claude Debussy, Erik Satie, and others at the 1889 exposition. Turn left onto the rue Saint-Dominique. Opposite the Ministry of Defence, the fine basilica of Sainte-Clotilde can be seen behind a small park. The first organist at this lovely nineteenth-century church was César Franck, and his successors included Charles Tournemire and Jean Langlais. After visiting the church, walk down the rue de Martignac for about a block and turn left onto the rue de Grenelle. You will pass the Musée Maillol on your right. On reaching the carrefour de la Croix-Rouge, cross over onto the rue du Vieux-Colombier, and the mighty towers of Saint-Sulpice soon loom into view. The church has a wonderful musical tradition—for instance, Charles-Marie Widor was organist there for more than half a century and his assistants included Gabriel Fauré. The Cavaillé-Coll organ is one of the finest in Paris, and the church as a whole is an architectural marvel of the first importance. From here, walk along the rue Saint-Sulpice, and at the end turn right onto the rue de Condé; then bear left onto the rue Crébillon, which comes out into the place de l'Odéon with its magnificent theatre, the scene of so many important musical events, including many of the concerts of the Domaine Musical. Walk along one side of the square down the rue Corneille onto the place Paul-Claudel, perhaps taking time out for a short stroll in the nearby Jardin du Luxembourg (in the footsteps of Jean Valjean and Cosette in *Les Misérables*); then (from the place Paul-Claudel) walk along the rue de Médicis, where Francis Poulenc lived for many years at no. 5. On reaching the place Rostand, angle left, take the first (sharp) left onto the rue Monsieur-le-Prince, where Camille Saint-Saëns lived at no. 14 from 1877 until 1889. On reaching the carrefour de l'Odéon several blocks on, cross the boulevard Saint-Germain to the rue de l'Ancienne-Comédie, which in due course becomes the rue Mazarine. This comes out at the back of the Institut de France, where many celebrated French composers attended performances of their cantatas composed for the Prix de Rome. Walk left along the quai Malaquais, which becomes the quai Voltaire. Wagner stayed at the Hôtel du Quai Voltaire (plaque outside). From here it is a short walk to the glorious Musée d'Orsay, with its many exhibits relating to music, and to the RER station there. Alternatively, continue along the quai Anatole-France (and then the quai d'Orsay), past the Assemblée Nationale and the Foreign Ministry, and finish at Invalides Métro just down the rue Robert-Esnault-Pelterie, the first turning on the left.

Walk 2: Passy

Michelin *Paris Plan* maps 27–28
This is a peaceful walk through a very distinguished residential area of the city. The *seizième* was home to several great French composers, including Debussy, Fauré, and Dukas, as well as to some of the most important patrons of the arts, notably the princesse de Polignac and the vicomtesse de Noailles.

Begin the walk at Trocadéro Métro station. From the place du Trocadéro, walk up the avenue Georges-Mandel, a broad road boasting some impressive private houses—including no. 36, where Maria Callas spent her last years. At the intersection with the rue du Pasteur-Marc-Boegner you will see the glorious Polignac mansion on the left, now home to the Fondation Singer-Polignac. Walk along the side of the house, noting the magnificent windows of the music room. Turn left onto the rue Scheffer, where you will pass the house where the vicomtesse de Noailles had her salon (plaque outside). On reaching the major intersection of this hilly street, you have a choice:

a) If time is limited, turn left onto the avenue Paul-Doumer, and as you near the Trocadéro, you will see the walls of Passy Cemetery on the left (the entrance is on the rue du Commandant-Schloesing). The cemetery is just a few metres from the Trocadéro and a short walk across the Seine from the Eiffel Tower (from the cemetery there are fine views of it). Though Passy Cemetery has rather fewer visitors than several larger cemeteries in Paris, it includes the graves not only of two of the giants of French music—Debussy and Fauré—but also of one of the greatest French painters, Edouard Manet. From here, return to Trocadéro Métro, or walk through the Palais de Chaillot and its gardens before crossing the Seine to the Eiffel Tower.

b) For a longer walk, continue along the rue Scheffer (crossing the avenue Paul-Doumer), and turn right onto the rue Vineuse. This runs down to the place de Costa-Rica and a fascinating part of the district. Walk down the rue Raynouard, take the steps on the left down the avenue du Parc-de-Passy, and turn right onto the avenue Marcel-Proust. On the left is the rue d'Ankara, where Dr. Blanche had his famous clinic, visited by Charles Gounod on several occasions. Continue along the rue Berton, passing the gardens of the Maison de Balzac (a beautiful house, well worth a visit; the main entrance is on the rue Raynouard). If you do not have time to visit, continue along the rue Berton and rejoin the rue Raynouard. Almost immediately on the right is the rue des Vignes, where Fauré lived for many years at no. 32. Continue until reaching the top. Turn right onto the avenue Mozart. La Muette Métro station is ahead of you, and the Jardin du Ranelagh on the left. It was in these gardens that Rossini's Passy villa stood (in the avenue Ingres). Unless you are visiting the Musée Marmottan (with its outstanding collection of Monets), walk back up the chaussée de la Muette to La Muette Métro. If you are feeling energetic, continue along the rue de Passy until you reach the place de Costa-Rica once more; then either walk up the rue Vineuse to Trocadéro and Passy Cemetery or turn down the rue de l'Alboni to Passy Métro station. From here, the Métro (line 6, direction Nation) is an astonishing experience, an aerial journey across the Seine, with marvellous views.

Walk 3: From the Opéra to Montmartre Cemetery

Michelin *Paris Plan* maps 6, 18, and 19

The Palais Garnier is perhaps the most famous of the musical landmarks of Paris, and a visit to the inside of the theatre is not to be missed. The auditorium is closed when rehearsals are in progress, but even so there is plenty to see. Once you have left the Opéra, it is worth walking around the building, to get a real impression of its epic scale. From the place de l'Opéra, turn left onto the boulevard des Capucines, which becomes in due course the boulevard des Italiens. Turn right down the rue de Marivaux and follow it along the side of the Opéra-Comique onto the place Boieldieu, where this historic theatre can be seen to best advantage. Walk back along the other side, via the rue Favart, and retrace your steps along the boulevard des Italiens until you reach the rue de la Chaussée-d'Antin. Rossini's residence in central Paris was on the corner (an almost invisible plaque celebrates the fact, on a building which has been altered beyond recognition). Continue right, up the rue de la Chaussée-d'Antin, where Chopin, Mozart, and others stayed.

The imposing facade of the Sainte-Trinité can be seen at the top. This splendid nineteenth-century church, with its recently restored interior, was where Messiaen served as organist for more than sixty years. To the right of the Trinité find the rue Blanche, where Franck lived as a young man at no. 45, and then, when he was newly married, at no. 69. Walk up it for several blocks and turn left onto the rue Ballu, where Lili and Nadia Boulanger lived. Their house is now in the place Lili-Boulanger (plaque outside). Turn right onto the rue de Vintimille, where both Debussy and Berlioz lived for short periods (at nos. 11 and 17, respectively). The next intersection is with the rue de Calais, where Hector Berlioz had his last address, at no. 4. Across the aptly named square Berlioz is the rue de Douai. Here, at no. 50, Pauline Viardot lived for many years and held her celebrated salons. Other famous musical residents of the street were Georges Bizet at no. 22 and Maurice Ravel at no. 40 bis (the latter for a few months in 1901). From the rue de Douai, rejoin the rue Blanche and go left along it until it reaches the boulevard de Clichy. This busy and noisy thoroughfare was home to

Arthur Honegger (at no. 71) and, for many years, Darius Milhaud (at no. 10). Walk left along the boulevard until you come to the avenue Rachel. Cross the boulevard and go right on the avenue Rachel to the entrance to Montmartre Cemetery, where some of France's greatest musicians and dancers are buried, including Berlioz, Lili and Nadia Boulanger, Delibes, Nijinsky, Offenbach, Taglioni, and Viardot.

Walk 4: From the Place de l'Alma to the Etoile

Michelin *Paris Plan* maps 17, 16, and 29

From the place de l'Alma, walk up the avenue Montaigne. The magnificent Théâtre des Champs-Elysées soon appears on the left-hand side. Perhaps the most notorious first night in twentieth-century musical history took place here on 29 May 1913 with the première of Igor Stravinsky's *Le sacre du printemps*. Continue up the avenue Montaigne to the rond-point des Champs-Elysées, where Meyerbeer died (at no. 2). Turn left up the avenue des Champs-Elysées, and a few hundred yards up on the left-hand side is no. 67, the site of a house where the ballerina Fanny Cerrito lived and where Verdi stayed in 1865. Continue to the Arc de Triomphe, and take the avenue Carnot. Ravel lived at no. 4 from 1908 until 1917 and composed several of his greatest works here, including *Ma mère l'oye*, *Daphnis et Chloé*, and the *Valses nobles et sentimentales*. The Hôtel Splendide (no. 1 bis avenue Carnot) counted among its guests Stravinsky at the time of the première of *Le sacre du printemps* in 1913, and Kurt Weill in 1933.

To extend this walk, return to the Etoile and take the avenue Foch (formerly the avenue du Bois de Boulogne) on your right, and walk some distance until you reach the entrance to no. 80. Debussy lived for many years in the seclusion of the private square here (his house was at no. 24 in the square). Porte Dauphine Métro station is nearby.

Ten Parisian Musical Landmarks

For the visitor with limited time who wishes to see perhaps one or two musical sites, the following is the author's selection of ten personal favourites. The list—arranged in the order in which places appear in the gazetteer—includes three houses (not open to the public), two churches, three theatres, one museum, and one cemetery.

12 place Vendôme (*see* Chopin under "Musicians"): The place Vendôme is an opulent square worth visiting on any pretext, but its musical associations are particularly poignant, in that it was the site of Chopin's last house, where he died in 1849.

43 avenue Georges-Mandel (*see* Polignac under "Musicians"): Set in a broad and imposing avenue, the mansion built by the prince and princesse de Polignac was visited by many of the great figures in the early years of the twentieth century. Though the building is not open to the public, the large music room eloquently described by Marcel Proust, the scene of several remarkable first performances, can be seen from the side of the house.

4 avenue Carnot (*see* Ravel under "Musicians"): Situated a stone's throw from the Arc de Triomphe, Ravel's apartment for a number of years was at this address. He completed several of his most famous works here, including *Ma mère l'oye* and *Daphnis et Chloé*.

La Madeleine (*see* La Madeleine under "Churches"): This well-known church has wonderful musical associations, as both Saint-Saëns and Fauré served as organists here. Fauré composed his Requiem for the funeral of a parishioner at the church. The interior is particularly fine; Stravinsky described the Madeleine as his favourite building in Paris.

La Trinité (*see* La Trinité under "Churches"): This is one of the finest Parisian churches from the second half of the nineteenth century; its interior was recently restored. The organist here from 1931 until his death in 1992 was the great composer Olivier Messiaen.

Opéra (*see* Opéra under "Theatres and Concert Halls" [Palais Garnier]): A magnificent building, much of which is open to the public. A visit is very strongly recommended, especially if the auditorium (with its ceiling painting by Marc Chagall) is open. After you have explored the theatre and its surroundings—especially the fabulous staircase and the mirrored foyers—it is also worth discovering whether there is an exhibition in the Bibliothèque-Musée de l'Opéra.

Opéra-Comique (*see* Salle Favart under "Theatres and Concert Halls"): The site of an opera house since 1783, the present theatre (the third) was opened in 1898. Two of the famous premières given in this building were Debussy's *Pelléas et Mélisande* in 1902 and Ravel's *L'heure espagnole* in 1911. The second theatre (destroyed by fire in 1887) witnessed the première of Bizet's *Carmen* in 1875. The first theatre (also destroyed by fire, in 1838) had been home for many years to the Théâtre Italien. Rossini lived for a time in a tiny room in the eaves. The première of Bellini's *I puritani* was given here in 1835.

Théâtre des Champs-Elysées (*see* Théâtre des Champs-Elysées under "Theatres and Concert Halls"): This was the scene of the premières in May 1913 of Debussy's *Jeux* (the first ballet in modern dress) and, two weeks later, of Stravinsky's *Le sacre du printemps*. The building, a fascinating example of early twentieth-century architecture in excellent condition, is well worth a visit, ideally for a performance.

Musée de la Musique (*see* Musée de la Musique under "Museums and Libraries"): Part of the astonishing Cité de la Musique, this museum is one of the newest and most remarkable in Paris. Though it is a little way from the centre of the city, the museum is easily reached by Métro. No musically inclined visitor should miss this stunning museum, and parents of older teenagers may be interested to know that the present author spent three enjoyable hours here with a musical seventeen-year-old who was completely captivated by the place.

Passy Cemetery (*see* Passy Cemetery under "Graves and Monuments"): Near the Trocadéro (and just across the river from the Eiffel Tower). Two of the greatest French composers—Debussy and Fauré—are buried in this small cemetery.

Four Centuries of Music in Paris
A Brief Outline

Before 1715

The Bourbon Louis XIII became king in 1610, in succession to Henri IV, though after 1629 Cardinal Richelieu was effectively the ruler of France. During Louis XIII's years in power the Académie Française was founded (1635). Following the accession of the young Louis XIV in 1643 (with Mazarin and Louis XIII's wife, Anne of Austria, as regents), the cultural life of the city developed rapidly. The king was a good dancer and in 1661 established the Académie Royale de Danse. Eight years later the Académie Royale de l'Opéra was founded, then reconstituted under Lully's direction in 1672, from which date it was known officially as the Académie Royale de Musique (and informally as the Opéra). Much of the city's musical activity at the time took place in the bustling district from the Louvre to the present-day Forum des Halles. Following the completion of the Palais Royal in 1634, the district around the rue de Richelieu became a centre for musical and theatrical activity (Richelieu's own theatre in the Palais Royal opened in 1641). Several of the outstanding composers of the French Baroque lived in the area, among them Lully, Delalande, D'Anglebert, Destouches, François Couperin, and Rameau. The nearby district of the Marais was among the most sought-after areas for large private hôtels, and here André Campra and Marc-Antoine Charpentier were both active as composers to the aristocracy.

During the seventeenth century, concert life began to develop, not only in public buildings, but also in private houses: Chambonnières and Clérambault were among the musicians who gave concerts in their own homes. This was also the era when several of France's greatest dramatists flourished—Corneille (1606–84), Racine (1639–99), and Molière (1622–73).

The long reign of Louis XIV came to an end in 1715, when he was succeeded by Louis XV, initially under the regency of Philippe d'Orléans. During the eighteenth century, the population of Paris grew to more than a million, and the city became a magnet for visitors from abroad, including such diverse characters as Casanova, Mozart, and the eminent music critic Charles Burney. Organ recitals began to attract large audiences, and such was the popularity of some of the concerts that the church authorities felt obliged to intervene: Claude-Bénigne Balbastre's recitals in Saint-Roch were banned by the archbishop. The most important concert series was the Concert Spirituel, founded by François-André Philidor and inaugurated on 18 March 1725. Here Parisians could enjoy virtuosi such as Leclair and Balbastre, as well as a wide repertory of Italian music (the first concert included Corelli's "Christmas" Concerto), which led Diderot to describe Philidor as the "founder of Italian music in France." Other concert-giving societies were the Concert Français, the Concert Italien, and the Concert des Amateurs, founded in 1769 with François-Joseph Gossec as its conductor. This ensemble changed its name in 1780 to the Concert de la Loge Olympique and subsequently commissioned Haydn to compose his "Paris" symphonies (nos. 82–87). Mozart first visited the city in 1763 and returned in 1766 and 1778, when the Concert Spirituel gave the first performance of his "Paris" Symphony. Meanwhile, literature also flourished, and among the leading writers and thinkers were Voltaire (1694–1778), Rousseau (1712–78), and the "Encyclopédistes," notably Diderot (1713–84) and D'Alembert (1717–83). In 1774, Louis XVI acceded to the throne, following the fifty-nine-year reign of Louis XV.

1789–1815

The fall of the Bastille on 14 July 1789 marked the effective start of the Revolution. From this time onwards, church property was systematically destroyed or expropriated, with a consequently devastating effect on some aspects of musical life, most obviously in churches and aristocratic houses. The Concert Spirituel ceased in 1791, and the Chapel Royal was closed down. Louis XVI was guillotined on 21 January 1793; musicians did not escape the brutality of Robespierre's Reign of Terror in 1793–94:

the most celebrated musician-victim of the guillotine was Jean-Frédéric Edelmann, whose music had attracted praise from distinguished critics, among them the young Mozart. Despite the suppression of churches, music flourished during the years of the Revolution. Claude-Joseph Rouget de Lisle composed "La Marseillaise" in 1792, one of many revolutionary songs which enjoyed immense popularity, especially in theatres, where the audience regularly broke into fights over which song to sing. (A decree of 1796 stated that "songs dear to Republicans" should be played by theatre orchestras "before the rising of the curtain.") In 1793 a school was established to train musicians for military bands. It was renamed the Conservatoire National Supérieur de Musique in 1795 and its educational purpose broadened; the teaching staff included Cherubini, Le Sueur, and the violinists Pierre Baillot and Pierre Rode. The public performance of music—often in the open air—was a prominent part of many revolutionary celebrations, much of the new music being written by Gossec. Napoléon became first consul in 1799 and was crowned emperor in 1804. The Chapel Royal reopened in 1801 (under the direction of Paisiello, Paer, and then Le Sueur), and concert and operatic life was dominated by composers such as Méhul, Cherubini, Le Sueur, and Spontini (Napoléon was particularly fond of Italian music).

1815–1870

Louis XVIII had come to the throne in 1795, but his reign became effective only with the restoration of the Bourbon monarchy following the fall of Napoléon (1814) and his defeat at Waterloo (1815). Cherubini was appointed director of the Conservatoire in 1822, and Alexandre Choron formed a new school for church musicians. The enthusiasm for Italian opera, already evident during Napoléon's time, became all the more fanatical with the arrival on the Parisian scene of Rossini and later of Bellini, Donizetti, and Verdi. When Charles X succeeded Louis XVIII in 1824, Rossini's *Il viaggio a Reims* was commissioned to celebrate the occasion. On 27–29 July 1830, the Bourbon monarchy was toppled in the July Revolution, and a new king, Louis-Philippe, came to the throne. During this period Paris welcomed some of its most celebrated musical visitors, including Chopin, Liszt, and Wagner. The city had by now become a place where almost every composer of international importance felt the need to make a name, particularly at the Opéra. Sensational recitals by Chopin, Liszt, Alkan, Gottschalk, and others satisfied a seemingly insatiable appetite for piano music, while the transcendental playing of Paganini cast an extraordinary spell over musicians and public alike.

Sung by the likes of Malibran, Grisi, Sontag, Lablache, Nourrit, and Tamburini, the operas of Rossini and Meyerbeer dominated the repertoire at the Opéra and the Théâtre Italien, but this was also a productive time for such French opera composers as Adam, Auber, Boieldieu, and Thomas.

In February 1848 the monarchy was overthrown and a republic declared. The first French election with universal male suffrage took place in April. During the civil disturbances in June, barricades were erected all over the city (César Franck and his bride were obliged to clamber over such a barricade to reach Notre-Dame-de-Lorette for their wedding), and thousands of Parisian protesters were gunned down by the army. Louis-Napoléon, nephew of Napoléon I, won the election in December 1848 and declared the Second Republic. In 1852 he took the name Napoléon III and established the Second Empire. The next two decades were notable for the expansion and comprehensive rebuilding of central Paris under the guidance of Baron Haussmann. The urban landscape was transformed by the construction of the *grands boulevards*, and on 1 January 1860, with the absorption into the city of the villages surrounding Paris (such as Montmartre and Passy), the 13e through 20e arrondissements were created and the city's boundaries extended outwards to the fortifications constructed by Thiers in 1841–45.

Visits to the city by instrumentalists gave Parisians the opportunity not only to hear the most glamorous virtuosi of the day, but also such novel visitors as Anton Bruckner, who gave an organ recital in Notre-Dame that was admired by Franck and Saint-Saëns. The musical theatre was dominated by the stage works of Bizet, Gounod, and Delibes, performed to varying degrees of public acceptance, as well as by the spectacularly popular operettas of Jacques Offenbach, whose earliest theatrical triumphs were during the first Exposition universelle in 1855. Berlioz, perhaps the greatest French genius of the age, had lived through most of the century's constitutional upheavals, and his lasting influence was due not only to his musical compositions but also to some of the most vibrant and entertaining writing ever devoted to music. Verdi wrote *Les vêpres siciliennes* and *Don Carlos* for the Opéra (and was much frustrated by the experience on both occasions). The Paris première of Wagner's *Tannhäuser* provoked one of the nineteenth century's more shocking displays of audience participation when members of the Jockey Club arrived at the Opéra with whistles, which they blew throughout the three performances. Thereafter, Wagner withdrew the work.

Paris was also a centre for instrumental innovation during this period: Sax, Vuillaume, Erard, and Cavaillé-Coll produced new or vastly improved instruments, which opened up exciting possibilities for composers and performers. In midcentury a resurgence of organ playing took place in Paris churches with the advent of organists who were able to exploit Cavaillé-Coll's new instruments to the full, among them Franck, Guilmant, Widor, and Saint-Saëns. Public orchestral concerts reached a wider audience, especially following the establishment of Pasdeloup's Concerts Populaires at the Cirque d'Hiver, while chamber music flourished thanks to Alard's Société de Musique de Chambre and more recondite societies, such as that devoted to the late quartets of Beethoven.

1870–1871: Siege and Commune

By 1870, the population of Paris had reached two million, three quarters of them born elsewhere. These were largely skilled workers, and a remarkable 95 percent of Parisians at this date could read and write. The Franco-Prussian War (declared by Napoléon III on 19 July 1870), the subsequent siege of Paris (during the winter of 1870–71), and the Commune (18 March–28 May 1871) were traumatic events for residents of the city. Few French composers left the country altogether, though Gounod moved to England in 1870 and remained there until 1874. The Third Republic had been proclaimed at the Hôtel de Ville on 1 September 1870, but within weeks Paris was besieged by Prussian troops. Bizet, Duparc, Fauré, Massenet, and Saint-Saëns were among those who joined the National Guard or other regiments. Franck also volunteered and helped to maintain food and fuel supplies; Henri Duparc later recalled the sight of his teacher stumbling from street to street with buckets of coal for the elderly. As a civil servant, Chabrier was obliged to follow Thiers's itinerant administration. After the Prussian siege, the Commune led many to flee the city, among them Bizet, to Compiègne (then to his estate at Le Vésinet); Fauré, to Cours-sous-Lausanne via Rambouillet (with the help of a forged passport); Massenet, to Biarritz; and Saint-Saëns, to London, where he made his debut as a pianist. An apprehensive Franck remained in Paris during this alarming time, which culminated in *la semaine sanglante* (the Bloody Week), when Parisian fought openly against Parisian and thousands were killed. Following Auber's death, Salvador Daniel was appointed director of the Conservatoire by the Communards, only to be shot ten days later by Thiers's Versailles troops. Surprisingly, perhaps, there were even a few "patriotic concerts" in the Tuileries gardens and elsewhere during these chaotic weeks, though theatres and halls were closed.

1871–1900

After a humiliating defeat and what amounted to a period of civil war, Parisians were in no mood for patriotic flag-waving, but a reawakening of national self-esteem was vital. In music this had already begun with the establishment in February 1871 of the Société Nationale de Musique, whose affirmative motto was "Ars Gallica." The activities of the new society were suspended during the Commune. Founding members and those present at the first meetings included Bizet, Duparc, Franck, Saint-Saëns, Massenet, and Fauré. By the mid-1880s, Vincent d'Indy had become heavily involved in the society's activities, and in November 1886 he and Ernest Chausson became secretaries, with Franck as honorary president. After the turn of the century, many younger composers (especially Ravel) became disenchanted with the society, but for more than three decades its importance was very considerable. In direct response to the Société Nationale, French composers in the later years of the nineteenth century wrote a great deal of instrumental music: Saint-Saëns, Franck, and Fauré, among others, composed works of major significance. In the early years of the society, composers usually performed their own works, and Saint-Saëns, Fauré, Chabrier, Chausson, d'Indy, and others made regular appearances.

Music for the stage after 1871 encompassed the greatest works of Bizet (*L'Arlésienne* and *Carmen*) and Delibes (*Sylvia* and *Lakmé*), as well as operas by Gounod and Massenet. The French controversy over Wagner raged for most of the period, and Parisians also began to encounter music from Spain, Russia, Scandinavia, and further afield. The revitalising of church music continued unabated, thanks to organists such as Fauré, Tournemire, and Vierne, while orchestral concerts reached a new level of excellence and enterprise with the establishment of series by Lamoureux and Colonne.

The semiprivate salon continued to be an important factor in Parisian musical life, and it was in such salons that many of Fauré's songs and some of the earlier works of Debussy and Ravel were first performed. The musical evenings at Pauline Viardot's house in rue de Douai and, later, at the princesse de Polignac's mansion in Passy were among the most remarkable.

The *Expositions Universelles*

Expositions universelles (world fairs) were held in Paris in 1855, 1867, 1878, 1889, 1900, 1925, 1931, and 1937 and were intended principally as spectacular showcases for industry and technology, usually with a dash of exotic colour added. These prestigious and immensely well-attended events brought a vast influx of visitors to the city, with a consequent upsurge in musical activity. The 1855 exposition provided Offenbach with the impetus to open his temporary summer theatre on the Champs-Elysées; its success led directly to the establishment of the Bouffes-Parisiens the following winter. During the 1867 exposition, Verdi's *Don Carlos* was first performed at the Opéra. During the exposition of 1878, Parisians could hear concerts—such as those of Russian music conducted by Nikolai Rimsky-Korsakov—in a vast new hall, the Trocadéro. Ironically, this was demolished to make way for a new building (the present Palais de Chaillot) for the 1937 exposition. Rimsky-Korsakov was back for the 1889 exposition, for which Gustave Eiffel built his famous tower. At this exposition, there was more music from around the world than ever before: the colonial pavilions, situated on the esplanade des Invalides, included musicians and dancers from Java and elsewhere who exerted a powerful influence on young composers, notably Debussy and Dukas, who visited the exposition together. Music was again well represented at the 1900 exposition, with a visit by Gustav Mahler and the Vienna Philharmonic Orchestra, and the first performance of Fauré's Requiem in its full orchestral version. The 1937 exposition featured spectacular light shows on the Seine, accompanied by works composed especially by leading French musicians—

Honegger, Milhaud, Ibert, Koechlin, and Messiaen, among others. Messiaen's *Fête des belles eaux* was first performed on 25 July 1937 at the "Fêtes du son, de l'eau, et de la lumière," by an ensemble of six Ondes Martenot, and the performance was relayed to the riverbank through loudspeakers.

1900–1918

In 1900, the first Paris Métro line opened, between Maillot and Vincennes. During the years before the outbreak of World War I, several of the most glittering events in the city's musical history were staged: first performances of towering works by Debussy (*Pelléas et Mélisande, La mer*) and Ravel (*Gaspard de la nuit*, the String Quartet), as well as the dazzling arrival of Diaghilev's Ballets Russes. This period brought together an extraordinary array of musicians (Stravinsky, Ravel, Debussy), dancers, choreographers (Nijinsky, Karsavina, Fokine), and artists (Bakst, Benois, Roerich) to create theatrical experiences which were original, beautiful, and unmistakably contemporary: Stravinsky's *Firebird* and *Petrouchka*, Ravel's *Daphnis et Chloé*, and Debussy's *Jeux* were all first performed in the years 1910–13. Perhaps the most famous riot in musical history, at the première of Stravinsky's *Le sacre du printemps*, took place at the brand-new Théâtre des Champs-Elysées in 1913.

Though the Société Nationale de Musique had been an important spur to national renewal in the aftermath of the Franco-Prussian War, younger composers began to find its programmes dull and its values outmoded. Ravel tendered his resignation to the Société Nationale in January 1909, and he wrote to Charles Koechlin as follows: "Societies, even national, do not escape from the laws of evolution. Only, one is free to withdraw from them. This is what I am doing by sending my resignation as a member. I presented three works of my pupils, of which one [by Maurice Delage] was particularly interesting. Like the others, it too was refused. It didn't offer those solid qualities of incoherence and boredom, which the Schola Cantorum baptises as structure and profundity.... I am undertaking to form a new society, more independent, at least in the beginning. This idea has delighted many people. Would you care to join us?"

In addition to Ravel himself, the founding committee of his new society, the Société Musicale Indépendante, included André Caplet, Florent Schmitt, Louis Aubert, Roger-Ducasse, and Charles Koechlin, who responded positively to Ravel's invitation. Fauré was elected president. At the first concert, which took place on 20 April 1910 in the Salle Gaveau, *Ma mère l'oye* received its first performance, Ravel played Debussy's *D'un cahier d'esquisses,* and Fauré accompanied Jeanne Raunay in his song cycle *La chanson d'Eve.* Just over a year later, on 9 May 1911, the new society put on a concert at which the audience had to guess the identity of the composers. The première of Ravel's *Valses nobles et sentimentales* was given on this occasion (by Louis Aubert, its dedicatee), and the audience chose Satie, Kodály, and Ravel as likely composers.

Musical education in the city was in a healthy state, helped by the appointment of Fauré as director of the Conservatoire and, through him, the arrival of teachers such as André Messager, Paul Dukas, and Maurice Emmanuel. Among the students at d'Indy's Schola Cantorum were Albert Roussel (later on the staff), Edgar Varèse, and Erik Satie, a most unusual mature student (his exercises were often corrected by Roussel, three years his junior). Musicians from abroad who came to study or to work included Alfredo Casella, Manuel de Falla, and Ralph Vaughan Williams, all of whom came to know Ravel. Musical life continued in the city following the outbreak of World War I, though concerts, operas, and ballets were severely curtailed and many theatres closed. The war years marked the melancholy but productive final period of Debussy's life, the composition of works such as Ravel's Piano Trio (completed just after the declaration of war) and *Le tombeau de Couperin,* and the flowering of Lili Boulanger's astonishing but short-lived talent, as well as the première of Satie's *Parade* in 1917. Ravel and Roussel both served as lorry drivers in the French army.

1918–1939

Stravinsky, Prokofiev, Villa-Lobos, and others spent extended periods in Paris during the interwar years. A new generation of French composers emerged during this period, among them Poulenc, Milhaud, Honegger, and the others who were to be grouped together by Cocteau as Les Six, as well as two of the most original composers of the time, Varèse and Messiaen. During this period also, Fauré produced his last great works, Ravel wrote much of his later music (such as *La valse,* the two piano concertos, *L'enfant et les sortilèges,* and *Bolero*), and Serge Diaghilev died (in 1929). Satie had not lost his power to shock: the première in 1924 of his last major work, *Relâche*, caused a sensation. The city continued to attract and to inspire composers from overseas. Many of them, like Aaron Copland, came to study with the legendary Nadia Boulanger. George Gershwin collected examples of the motor horns he needed for *An American in Paris* during visits in 1926 and 1928 and composed much of the work in the city. After the rise of Hitler, some visitors to Paris were motivated by necessity: Kurt Weill was among those who settled in Paris for a few years before emigrating to the New World.

1939–1945

Perhaps the most influential figure in Paris during World War II was Olivier Messiaen. Following his release in 1941 from a prisoner-of-war camp in Silesia, he started to teach privately and at the Conservatoire (his earliest pupils included Pierre Boulez and Yvonne Loriod), published *Technique de mon langage musical,* and composed the *Trois petites liturgies de la Présence Divine, Visions de l'Amen,* and *Vingt regards sur l'Enfant-Jésus.* Concert life, and especially the performance of French music, suffered greatly under the German Occupation (1940–44), but thanks to the courage of Denise Tual, André Schaeffner, Gaston Gallimard, and others, series such as the Concerts de la Pléiade encouraged the performance of new French works—for example, Poulenc's Violin Sonata (played by Ginette Neveu and Poulenc) and Messiaen's *Visions de l'Amen* (played by Loriod and Messiaen). Claude Delvincourt was an enlightened appointment as the new director of the Conservatoire in 1941, and he became a courageous irritant to the occupying forces, protecting his students with great tenacity when they were threatened, and outwitting the enemy by founding L'Orchestre des Cadets, a remarkable symbol of an institution's resistance and of its director's determination.

Casualties of the war included Maurice Jaubert (1900–40), who composed a number of outstanding film scores during the 1930s, such as *Zéro de conduite* (1933) and Marcel Carné's *Hôtel du Nord* (1938), one of the most starkly evocative films set in Paris. Jaubert was killed in action at Azerailles, Meurthe-et-Moselle, on 19 June 1940. One day later, on 20 June 1940, Jehan Alain (1911–40) was killed in action near Saumur at the age of twenty-nine. He was later acclaimed by Messiaen as one of the most original musical minds of the period.

Since 1945

Following the end of the Occupation, the provisional government proclaimed the Fourth Republic in Algiers on 3 June 1944. On 20 August the collaborationist Marshal Pétain left Vichy under a German escort, and five days later, on 25 August, General de Gaulle arrived at the Gare Montparnasse; he made a triumphal procession from the Arc de Triomphe to Notre-Dame the following afternoon. The election of de Gaulle as president in 1958 marked the start of the Fifth Republic. The postwar years were the setting not only for some of the greatest works of Messiaen but also for the emergence of such composers as Maurice Duruflé and André Jolivet, along with younger musicians—Pierre Boulez, Marius Constant, and Yvonne Loriod. In 1950 Pierre Henry established his Groupe de Recherche de Musique Concrète, and a new generation of composers came from abroad to study, Karlheinz Stockhausen and Iannis Xenakis among them.

Orchestral playing in Paris was variable in the years after World War II. Conductors such as Charles Münch, André Cluytens, and Jean Martinon did much to revive flagging standards. Boulez began to emerge as a figure of immense significance, not only as a composer and conductor but also as a commentator on music and a visionary planner: his establishment of the astonishingly enterprising Domaine Musical concerts at the Théâtre de l'Odéon (1954) and of the Institut de Recherche et de Coordination Acoustique-Musique (IRCAM) at the Pompidou Centre (1975) kept Paris at the forefront of musical exploration.

Rolf Liebermann's reign as director of the Opéra (1973–80) did much to inject fresh imagination and energy into an institution which had become complacent or becalmed. More recently, the move of the Conservatoire to its new premises at the Cité de la Musique (La Villette) has enabled musical education at the highest level to enjoy something of a renaissance in Paris. The Musée de la Musique, on the same site, places historical instruments in a vital historical context. These major buildings were among the *grands projets* of François Mitterand's government, as was the new Opéra-Bastille, which opened on Bastille Day in 1989.

1.1 Carlotta Grisi in Adam's *Giselle*,
Act 2 (Paris Opéra, 1841).
Lithograph by Haguenthal.

1 · Musicians

Adolphe Adam (24 July 1803–3 May 1856)

In 1838 Adam was living at 5 rue de Louvois, 2e (G13, Métro: Quatre-Septembre), the same building in which Donizetti lodged at the time (see entry on Donizetti). On 24 September 1840 Adam wrote to his friend Samuel Heinrich Spiker that he was moving to a new apartment, at 95 rue Neuve-des-Mathurins (now rue des Mathurins), 9e (F12–F11, Métro: Havre-Caumartin), in a newly developed area just behind the Madeleine. In the space of three weeks during spring 1841, Adam composed his most famous work, the ballet *Giselle*, first performed at the Opéra on 28 June 1841, with Carlotta Grisi in the title role (figure 1.1). Adam took great care over the work and was delighted with the results; before the première he wrote to Spiker on 12 June: "I am very happy with some parts of it and hope that the public will give credit for the efforts I have made to raise ballet music to a higher level than is usually expected" (Adam 1996, 98). It was a considerable success from the first production. According to some sources, Adam was living in 1848 at 30 rue Faubourg-du-Temple, 11e (G17, Métro: République). Towards the end of his life, from about 1850, he lived at 24 rue Buffault, 9e (E14, Métro: Cadet), and it was here that he died. Adam was buried in Montmartre Cemetery.

Jehan Alain (3 February 1911–20 June 1940)

Like Debussy, Jehan Alain was born at Saint-Germain-en-Laye. He came from an intensely musical family: his father was the composer and organist Albert Alain, and Jehan's younger brother Olivier and younger sister Marie-Claire both became musicians. He studied at the Paris Conservatoire from 1927 to 1939, where his teachers included Dukas and Roger-Ducasse for composition, and Marcel Dupré for organ (Alain won a first prize for organ in 1939). A delightful illustrated letter (undated, figure 1.2) gives Alain's address as 87 rue Péreire, Saint-Germain-en-Laye, 78100 (RER: Saint-Germain-en-Laye).

voila une longue épître!
le facteur parviendra-t-il à
vous l'ap-
porter.
je l'ex-
pôre

votre vieux piton

1.2 An undated cartoon by Jehan Alain showing his address at 87 rue Péreire, Saint-Germain-en-Laye.

After his marriage in 1935, Alain moved to Le Pecq. The same year he was appointed organist at Saint-Nicolas, Maisons-Laffitte (a town 20 kilometres to the northwest of Paris; RER and SNCF: Maisons-Laffitte); he remained there until 1939. Alain also worked as organist for the synagogue at 15 rue Notre-Dame-de-Nazareth, 3e (G16 Métro: Temple). Here he recorded an improvisation, based on a written sketch, later entitled *L'année liturgique israélite* (it was transcribed by his sister Marie-Claire Alain and published in 1993).

In October 1939, Alain was drafted into the French army and in a letter of 2 February 1940 he described himself as being in the 1st squadron of the 8th armoured regiment. By May, Alain was at Dunkirk. On 20 June 1940, while defending Saumur at Petit-Puy, he was hit by an enemy bullet and died, at the age of twenty-nine, leaving a widow and three children. Alain's most remarkable work as a composer was his organ music. His best-known pieces are probably *Litanies* and *Le jardin suspendu*, both first performed at the Trinité (at Messiaen's instigation) in a concert on 17 February 1938.

Duruflé wrote a *Prélude et fugue sur le nom d'Alain* for organ, published in 1943, which bears the dedication "à la mémoire de Jehan Alain, mort pour la France." Messiaen described Alain as "an excellent composer who unhappily died before his time.... I only met him once. Without really knowing each other, we followed near enough the same path, and it's possible that, if he'd lived longer, he would have gone in the same direction as myself" (Messiaen 1976, 80).

Charles-Valentin Alkan (30 November 1813–29 March 1888)

Alkan was born at 1 rue de Braque, 3e (H16, Métro: Rambuteau). He was one of six children, all of whom became musicians. Alkan's early years at the Conservatoire were extraordinary: Cherubini considered the nine-year-old Alkan to be "astonishing," and at the age of eleven he won a first prize for piano. Ten years later, in 1834, he was awarded a first prize for organ. As a young man, he admired Chopin, and the two became friends. In the 1840s he lived at 40 (and later at 34) rue Saint-Lazare, 9e (E13, Métro: Trinité), and during this decade he attracted considerable critical acclaim from Liszt and others. In 1848 he was one of the two candidates for the piano professorship at the Conservatoire following the retirement of Zimmermann. Antoine-François Marmontel was appointed instead, and Alkan never held a full-time post at the Conservatoire. He spent many years away from the concert platform, living as a recluse. From 1852, Alkan lived at 11 rue La Bruyère, 9e (E13, Métro: Saint-Georges). In 1853 he emerged from seclusion to give two concerts of music by classical masters, then gave no public concerts for twenty years. He moved in 1854 to 51 rue de Londres, 8e (E12, Métro: Europe), where he remained until 1859. Alkan's address during the 1860s is uncertain, but in about 1869 he moved to 29 rue Daru, 8e (E9, Métro: Courcelles), where he lived for the rest of his life. In 1873 he began regular concerts at the Salle Erard and the Salle Pleyel and took a number of private pupils. A man of astonishing diffidence, Alkan had a very small circle of friends and received few visitors. Brought up in a strict Jewish household, Alkan remained a religious man all his life. The much-repeated story that his death resulted from a bookcase falling on top of him as he reached for the Talmud is, however, a myth, as medical reports following his death make clear. He was buried in the Jewish division of Montmartre Cemetery.

George Antheil (8 July 1900–12 February 1959)

George Antheil arrived in Paris, with his girlfriend Boski Markus, on 13 June 1923, and the very same evening they went to the première of

Stravinsky's *Les noces* at the Théâtre de la Gaîté-Lyrique. They were based in Paris for the next five years, having taken a small apartment above Sylvia Beach's famous bookshop, Shakespeare and Company (figure 1.3), at 12 rue de l'Odéon, 6e (K13, Métro: Odéon). It was here that Antheil composed his most celebrated (and notorious) work, the *Ballet mécanique*. The original title was "Message from Mars"; in 1924 Antheil intended the work to accompany a film by Fernand Léger,

1.3 George Antheil climbing into his rooms above Shakespeare and Company, 12 rue de l'Odéon, circa 1925.

but this plan was later abandoned. Ezra Pound became interested in Antheil's music, and soon the young composer was mixing with many of the literary giants who called at Sylvia Beach's bookshop, including James Joyce, Ernest Hemingway, T. S. Eliot, and Wyndham Lewis. His music also attracted the friendly interest of the ageing Satie. In 1925 Antheil travelled to Tunisia, then to Budapest to marry Boski. On returning to Paris, he discovered a story in the newspaper reporting that he had been eaten alive by lions in the Sahara. In 1926 the couple became friendly with George Gershwin when he was visiting the city (see entry on Gershwin), and the *Ballet mécanique*, scored for eight pianos, pianola, and a vast array of percussion instruments (including electric doorbells, and the sound of aeroplane propellers) was given its riotous public première under the baton of Vladimir Golschmann on 19 June 1926 at the Théâtre des Champs-Elysées.

Daniel-François-Esprit Auber (29 January 1792–12 or 13 May 1871)

In about 1830, Auber was living at 50 bis rue Saint-Lazare, 9e (E13, Métro: Trinité). By 1839, his address was 22 rue Saint-Georges, 9e (E13, Métro: Notre-Dame-de-Lorette), where he lived for the next thirty-two years; he died there at the age of eighty-nine, during the Commune. After an immensely successful career in the theatre (most famously with *La muette de Portici*, *Fra Diavolo*, and *Le domino noir*), Auber was appointed Cherubini's successor as director of the Conservatoire in 1842. From this time on, his stage works became more overtly lyrical; among them is a setting of *Manon Lescaut*. Like almost all Auber's operas, this had a libretto by Eugène Scribe. At the Conservatoire he appointed Halévy and Adam to teach composition and did a good deal to improve standards in every department. Auber was a witty but extremely shy man who was admired by many of his contemporaries, including Rossini and, remarkably, Wagner. He was buried in Père-Lachaise Cemetery.

Vincenzo Bellini (3 November 1801–23 September 1835)

In mid-August 1833, Bellini lodged in the group of buildings known as the Bains chinois (opened in 1792 and demolished by 1853). This architectural curiosity was on the site of the present 27 boulevard des Italiens,

2e (F13, Métro: Opéra), at the corner of rue de la Michodière. Two pagoda-style apartment buildings, decorated with lacquered columns, were linked by a covered arcade housing restaurants, baths, and a beauty parlour (figure 1.4). Bellini took rooms here, ideally situated to allow him to cultivate his operatic contacts. At the time, Rossini was lodging in the

1.4 The Bains chinois in the boulevard des Italiens, where Bellini had an apartment.

eaves of the Théâtre Italien, around the corner from 69 rue de Richelieu, where Giuditta Pasta lived with Stendhal when she was in Paris. Bellini, perhaps the only person to be surprised that he did not receive treatment equal to Rossini's, soon became frustrated in his dealings with Parisian operatic managements. Bellini's inadequate grasp of French did nothing to help his case, and early in 1834 he suffered what one of his letters described as "a sort of crisis." He longed to escape from the city, and in May 1834 he went to stay with Solomon Levy at 19 bis rampe de Neuilly, Puteaux (SNCF: Puteaux), just to the northwest of the city. Having begun *I puritani* on 15 April, Bellini composed most of the work at Puteaux. Bellini wrote to Francesco Florimo on 26 May 1834: "As you see, my dear Florimo, I am in the country near Paris, a half hour by road. I am well lodged in the house of an English friend of mine. I compose without being disturbed by anything, and therefore hope to complete my opera more carefully" (Weinstock 1972, 162–63). In October 1834 he travelled into Paris by horse-drawn omnibus to rehearse a revival of *La sonnambula* at the Théâtre Italien, and he returned to the Bains chinois on 1 November. On 24 January 1835 *I puritani* was given its première with a cast which included four of the greatest singers of the age: Giulia Grisi, Luigi Lablache, Antonio Tamburini, and Giovanni Battista Rubini. Early in September 1835 Bellini fell ill at Puteaux, and, fearing that the composer had cholera, his hosts the Levys left the house. Medical treatment was of no avail, and he was found dead in the house on the afternoon of 23 September by Auguste Aymé.

Hector Berlioz (11 December 1803–8 March 1869)

Berlioz arrived in Paris in November 1821 and found lodgings with M. Drouault at 104 rue Saint-Jacques, 5e (K14, Métro: Cluny-Sorbonne). At the start of the next academic year (October 1822), he moved first to 71 rue Saint-Jacques, then to no. 79. He had come to Paris to study medicine, but as Berlioz recalled, he was wholly unsuited to such a career: "On arriving in Paris…with my fellow-student Alphonse Robert, I gave myself up wholly to studying for the career which had been thrust upon me, and loyally kept to the promise I had given my father on leaving. It was soon put to a somewhat severe test when Robert, having announced one morning that he had bought a 'subject' (a corpse), took me for the first time to the dissecting room at the Hospice de la Pitié. At the sight of that terrible charnel-house—the fragments of limbs, the grinning heads and gaping skulls, the bloody quagmire underfoot and the atrocious smell it gave off, the swarms of sparrows wrangling over scraps of lung, the rats in their corner gnawing the bleeding vertebrae—such a feeling of revulsion possessed me that I leapt through the window of the dissecting room and fled for home as though Death and all his hideous train were at my heels. The shock of that first impression lasted for twenty-four hours. I did not want to hear another word about anatomy, dissection or medicine, and I meditated a hundred mad schemes to escape from the future that hung over me" (Berlioz 1969, 46).

Berlioz began to visit the opera and to look at scores in the library of the Conservatoire, copying out passages which he particularly liked. By the start of 1823 he was studying composition with Jean-François Le Sueur, but he met with implacable opposition and hostility from his parents when he returned to La Côte-Saint-André in spring 1823 to announce his plan of becoming a composer.

On Sunday 10 July 1825 Berlioz enjoyed his first musical success with a performance of the *Messe solennelle* at the church of Saint-Roch. Berlioz moved in autumn 1825 to 27 rue de Harlay, 1er (J14, Métro: Cité), just off the quai des Orfèvres. In the summer of 1826 he entered the competition for the Prix de Rome for the first time and was eliminated after the first round. In September of that year, Berlioz was living back on the left bank at 58 rue de la Harpe, 5e (K14, Métro: Cluny-Sorbonne); the following month he finished his opera *Les francs-juges*. His Prix de Rome entry in summer 1827 was more successful: he passed beyond the first round and wrote the cantata *La mort d'Orphée*, which the jury judged to be "not susceptible of performance."

On 11 September 1827 Berlioz saw Harriet Smithson for the first time, playing the role of Ophelia in *Hamlet*, and, on seeing her in *Romeo and Juliet* a week later, he apparently told his friends: "That woman will become my wife, and on this play I shall write my grandest symphony" (Holoman 1989, 46). The same month, Berlioz moved to 96 rue de Richelieu, 2e (F13, Métro: Richelieu-Drouot), across the street from Schlesinger's shop (figure 1.5). He lived here for three years, until the end of 1830. The quest for the Prix de Rome continued to absorb Berlioz's time in the summer; he composed the cantatas *Herminie* (1828), *Cléopâtre* (1829), and *Sardanaple* (1830), the work with which he was, at last, to win first prize. In April 1830 he completed an altogether more important work: the *Symphonie fantastique*, first performed at the Conservatoire on 5 December 1830. After a few weeks with his family, Berlioz travelled to Rome, arriving in early March

1.5 The entrance to Berlioz's home at 96 rue de Richelieu.

1831. On returning to Paris in November 1832, he discovered that his old lodgings in rue de Richelieu were occupied, and he moved across the road to 1 rue Neuve-Saint-Marc (now rue Saint-Marc), 2e (F13, Métro: Richelieu-Drouot), where he rented the same rooms that Harriet Smithson had vacated the previous week. In December, Harriet finally succumbed to Berlioz's passionate advances, and by January 1833 there was talk of marriage, but otherwise it was a dismal year for Berlioz: as a composer he produced little, relations with his family reached a new low, Harriet had an accident (she fell from her carriage and broke her leg), and her theatre company was in chaos. The only high point of 1833 was the marriage of Berlioz and Smithson at the British Embassy, 35 rue du Faubourg-Saint-Honoré, on 3 October.

In January 1834, he began work on *Harold en Italie*. The couple moved in April to a cottage in Montmartre (figure 1.6), at 10 rue Saint-Denis (now rue du Mont-Cenis; the original building was demolished in 1925), 18e (C14, Métro: Lamarck-Caulaincourt).

1.6 Berlioz's Montmartre cottage at 10 rue Saint-Denis (now rue du Mont-Cenis). The building was demolished in 1925.

Berlioz finished *Harold* here during the summer. In October, with their baby son Louis (born on 14 August), Berlioz and Harriet moved to 34 rue de Londres, 9e (E12, Métro: Saint-Lazare). They returned briefly in October 1835 to the Montmartre cottage, where Berlioz worked on *Benvenuto Cellini*. In 1836 the family was back in rue de Londres, this time at no. 35, where Berlioz wrote the *Grande messe des morts*, completing it in June 1837 (for Berlioz's amusing account of the première, see Churches: Saint-Louis-des-Invalides). In October of that year Berlioz and Harriet moved a few doors down the street to 31 rue de Londres, and it was here, in September 1838, that Berlioz finished the first version of *Benvenuto Cellini*. In 1839, he wrote *Roméo et Juliette*, and the following year the *Symphonie funèbre et triomphale*. In 1841 he began his relationship with Marie Récio (later to become his second wife) and completed *Les nuits d'été*.

Berlioz separated from Harriet Smithson in 1844 and set her up in a small apartment at 43 rue Blanche (which he also used as his own legal address; by 1846 he was also using Adolphe Sax's showroom at 10 rue Neuve-Saint-Georges for the same purpose). By May 1844 he was living with Marie Récio at 41 rue de Provence, 9e (F13, Métro: Le Peletier); here he composed *La damnation de Faust*, which had its calamitous première on 6 December 1846. Berlioz set off early in 1847 for a tour of Russia and a series of concerts in London.

On returning to Paris in June 1848, Berlioz and Marie took a year's lease on an apartment at 15 rue de La Rochefoucauld, 9e (E13, Métro: Trinité), where he began composition of the Te Deum. On 16 July 1849 they moved to 19 rue de Boursault (now rue La Bruyère), 9e (E13, Métro: Saint-Georges). It was here (figure 1.7) that Berlioz wrote *L'enfance du Christ*.

Harriet Smithson died on Friday 3 March 1854, and she was buried in Saint-Vincent Cemetery (her body was later moved to Montmartre

1.7 Rue La Bruyère,
where Berlioz
wrote *L'Enfance
du Christ.*

Cemetery). On 19 October 1854, Berlioz married Marie Récio. The successful première of *L'enfance du Christ* took place at the Salle Herz on 10 December 1854. In 1856 Berlioz's landlord demanded a hefty rent increase, and the composer decided to buy a property outright. The search proved fruitless, however, and on 16 April Berlioz, Marie, and her mother, Madame Martin, moved to a fourth-floor apartment at 17 rue de Vintimille, 9e (D12, Métro: Place de Clichy). Here he began his grandest masterpiece, *Les Troyens*.

By 16 October 1856 Berlioz had moved round the corner to his last address (figure 1.8), 4 rue de Calais, 9e (D12, Métro: Blanche or Place de Clichy). It was a spacious apartment. According to Holoman (1989, 484–85), it was "a large dwelling of some five or six rooms. The furnishings belonged to Marie and her mother; Berlioz paid Madame Martin a small rent for them each month. An inventory taken after Berlioz's death suggests that his home was well equipped with pieces of furniture, draperies and linens, though short on cooking utensils and place settings." Berlioz completed *Béatrice et Bénédict* in March 1862. Three months later, on 13 June, Marie died suddenly while visiting friends in Saint-Germain-en-Laye. Berlioz died in his house at 4 rue de Calais on 8 March 1869. His funeral was at the newly finished Trinité on 11 March. Thomas, Auber, and Gounod served as pallbearers; among the mourners

1.8 Berlioz's last
Paris address at 4
rue de Calais.

was Bizet, who is said to have wept uncontrollably. Berlioz was buried in Montmartre Cemetery. A century later, in 1969, he, Harriet, and Marie were moved to a new site near the entrance to Montmartre Cemetery, and the path there was renamed avenue Hector-Berlioz.

Georges Bizet (25 October 1838–3 June 1875)

Bizet was born at 26 rue de La Tour-d'Auvergne, 9e (E14, Métro: Cadet), a building which was replaced by the present one in about 1850. Bizet's birth certificate recorded his name as Alexandre-César-Léopold. He was baptised Georges on 16 March 1840 at Notre-Dame-de-Lorette, and this was the name he used throughout his life, in preference to the names of the three emperors that had been bestowed on him at birth. Prodigiously gifted as a child, Bizet enrolled at the Conservatoire in October 1848 and soon became a close friend of Gounod; the friendship was to encompass many difficult moments during the years to come. After hearing the older composer's first opera, *Sapho*, Bizet became a passionate enthusiast of Gounod's works and made several piano arrangements of them while still a teenager. In 1852 he won a first prize in Marmontel's piano class, and in 1855 first prizes for organ and fugue. He joined Halévy's composition class in 1853, and during his time as a student Bizet wrote the sparkling Symphony in C: it was finished in November 1855, when Bizet was seventeen years old. The first time he attempted to win the Prix de Rome, in May 1856, no first prize was awarded; Bizet was given a second prize, which entitled him to free tickets at the various opera theatres in Paris. He had greater success a few months later, when he was awarded joint first prize in a competition for a one-act opera organised by Offenbach: *Le docteur Miracle* was first performed on 9 April 1857, and the same year, at one of Offenbach's Friday soirées, Bizet was introduced to Rossini, who gave him a signed photograph as a good-luck token for Bizet's second attempt at the Prix de Rome. On 3 October 1857, the jury (which included Berlioz) formally presented Bizet with the first prize, and he spent most of the next four years in Rome. During his last few months there, Bizet met Ernest Guiraud, who was to become one of his closest and most devoted friends. He returned to Paris in September 1860, longing for independence, but the illness of his mother obliged Bizet to live in the family apartment at 18 rue de Laval (rue Victor-Massé since 1887), 9e (E13, Métro: Pigalle).

The première of *Les pêcheurs de perles* was given at the Théâtre Lyrique on 30 September 1863, and on 3 October Bizet's father bought a plot of land at 8–10 route des Cultures, Le Vésinet (RER: Le Vésinet–Centre), where he built two cottages as summer residences for himself and his son. Bizet moved to this peaceful new address and found it conducive to composition. It was here that Saint-Saëns, unable to find Bizet's house, decided to attract his friend's attention by whistling a tune from *Les pêcheurs de perles*. Bizet worked on *Ivan IV*, meanwhile earning a meagre living by making piano arrangements of works by Gounod, Mozart, and others. During the mid-1860s he was invited to perform at several fashionable salons, but for much of the time his future seemed bleak. His meeting with Céleste Vénard (known as La Mogador) raised his spirits considerably. She bought a property close to Bizet's in Le Vésinet, and her company ensured that he was no longer bored there. He travelled to Paris only on Tuesdays and Saturdays, teaching, playing poker with his friends, and making preparations for *La jolie fille de Perth*, eventually given its première, after several delays, on 26 December 1867. The following year, he was much encouraged by a new friendship, with the singer Marie Trélat and her husband.

Bizet's address in 1868–69 was 32 rue Neuve-Fontaine-Saint-Georges (now rue Fromentin), 9e (D13, Métro: Blanche or Pigalle), where he wrote the unpublished opera *La coupe du roi de Thulé*. On 3 June 1869, Bizet married Geneviève Halévy (Fromental Halévy's daughter), whose traumatic early life and nervous disorders were to cause him a great deal of anguish. (After Bizet's death, she married Emile Straus; Proust said that she was the model for his Duchesse de Guermantes.) In autumn 1869, the couple moved to an apartment at 22 rue de Douai, 9e (D13, Métro: Blanche), a building later described by Daniel Halévy as having been constructed by an architect who wished "to demonstrate the highest art of his industry by covering the facade with columns, scrolls and angels so that it looked like the work of a delirious mason who had passed through Rome" (Curtiss 1959, 183–84). This was Bizet's Paris address for the rest of his life, the house in which he composed some of his greatest music, notably *Carmen*. Bizet's near-neighbours included Ernest Guiraud, Pauline Viardot (at 50 rue de Douai), Gounod, and Degas. Parisian life was disrupted by the outbreak of the Franco-Prussian War in July 1870, and in August, Bizet joined the 6th battalion of the National Guard (figure 1.9). All the

1.9 Bizet in National Guard uniform, photographed in 1870 or 1871.

while, Geneviève was in a state of mental instability, and Bizet wrote her numerous affectionate and reassuring notes while he was away on sentry duty. During the Commune, Bizet and his wife fled to Compiègne, then to Le Vésinet. Like so many Parisians, Bizet was confused and angered by the Communards, describing them in a letter to a friend as "scoundrels, madmen, or cowards!," at the same time denouncing Thiers's Versailles government as "unspeakably foul" (283–84).

By 28 May 1871, much of Paris lay in ruins, but the Bizets returned in early June to find their apartment undamaged. Later in the year he completed *Jeux d'enfants* (sold to Durand on 28 September for six hundred francs). In 1872, he composed the opera *Djamileh*, and his son Jacques was born on 10 July.

Despite the happy distraction of fatherhood, and the increasingly stressful presence of his mother-in-law, Bizet completed his incidental music for Alphonse Daudet's *L'Arlésienne* by the end of the summer. Although the score was warmly received by such musicians as Ernest Reyer and Jules Massenet, Daudet summed up the general reaction when he described the play as "a most dazzling failure, with the most charming music in the world" (Curtiss 1959, 338). Theatre critics and public were hostile to what they perceived as an uneasy alliance between the drama and the music, and the play closed after twenty-one performances. On 10

November 1872, however, three weeks after the closure of the play, Pasdeloup conducted the immensely successful first performance of Bizet's suite from *L'Arlésienne* at the Cirque d'Hiver. Bizet spent the summer of 1873 at 17 rue de Paris, Le Port-Marly (SNCF: Marly-le-Roi). By this time, *Carmen* was already in preparation, and in September 1873, Bizet played parts of the work to the singer Galli-Marié, who was to create the title role. During the summer of 1874, Bizet lived outside Paris, in a villa at Bougival, returning to the city in order to work with singers, especially Galli-Marié, on *Carmen*. By 1 September 1874, the opera was in rehearsal at the Opéra-Comique, but serious preparations did not begin until mid-November: rehearsals were held almost every weekday from then until the end of the year, and Bizet attended all but a few of them. Progress was often hindered, though, by the nonappearance of Galli-Marié and other principals. As a relief from the theatrical environment, Bizet enrolled in César Franck's organ class at the Conservatoire, although none of his fellow pupils knew his identity until the day before the première of *Carmen*, when he gave tickets to two of them (Camille Benoît and Vincent d'Indy). Though the first night on 3 March 1875 was a critical fiasco for Bizet, later performances proved to be a greater artistic (if not box office) success. By early May, Bizet was complaining of various ailments, including feelings of suffocation, angina, muscular rheumatism, and several painful abscesses. Despite protests from his family, Bizet insisted on leaving for Bougival, and on 28 May he arrived with his wife and son. He died there shortly after midnight on the morning of 3 June 1875. His funeral, held on Saturday 5 June at the Trinité, was attended by four thousand mourners, including the entire company of the Opéra-Comique. Pasdeloup conducted the orchestra, and Gounod delivered the eulogy. Bizet's body was buried temporarily in Montmartre Cemetery and moved soon afterwards to Père-Lachaise.

Adrien Boieldieu (6 December 1775–8 October 1834)

From about 1817 to 1825, Boieldieu lived at 33 rue Taitbout, 9e (F13, Métro: Chaussée-d'Antin). It was here that he composed the work that was to give him his greatest success: *La dame blanche*, first performed at the Opéra-Comique on 10 December 1825. In about 1825 Boieldieu moved to the Hôtel Tuffakine, 10 boulevard Montmartre (on the site of the present passage Jouffroy), 9e (F14, Métro: Richelieu-Drouot), where for some years Rossini and Carafa also had apartments. Boieldieu died here in 1834 and was given a state funeral at les Invalides. He was buried in Père-Lachaise Cemetery.

Nadia Boulanger (18 September 1887–22 October 1979) and Lili Boulanger (21 August 1893–15 March 1918)

The elder Boulangers settled in 1877 at 35 rue de Mauberge, 9e (E14, Métro: Cadet or Poissonnière), and Nadia was born there. In 1893, the family moved to 30 rue La Bruyère, 9e (E13, Métro: Saint-Georges), where Lili was born. From October 1904, these two immensely gifted sisters lived at 36 rue Ballu (now 1 place Lili-Boulanger), 9e (D12, Métro: Place de Clichy). Lili Boulanger was among the most original composers of her generation, and, despite her tragically early death at the age of twenty-four, she produced several works of genius, including the song cycle *Clairières dans le ciel,* three magnificent psalm settings, and the tender, valedictory *Pie Jesu* (dictated to Nadia, as Lili was by now too weak to hold a pen). She was buried in Montmartre Cemetery.

In the house in rue Ballu (figure 1.10) Nadia Boulanger taught generations of composers, among them Aaron Copland, Virgil Thomson, Lennox Berkeley, Igor Markevich, and Jean Françaix. She taught beginning in 1921 at the American School in Fontainebleau, and later at the Ecole Normale de Musique. Nadia spent the war years in America and returned to

1.10 The interior of the Boulanger apartment in the rue Ballu.

Paris in 1946, when she also began to teach a class in accompaniment at the Conservatoire. In 1948 she conducted a celebrated recording of the Fauré Requiem, and in 1950 she became director of the American School. The intersection of the rue Ballu with the rue de Vintimille was renamed place Lili-Boulanger in 1970.

Joseph Canteloube (21 October 1879–4 November 1957)

In 1906 Joseph Canteloube arrived in Paris to study with Vincent d'Indy, with whom he had been corresponding for four years. Canteloube's first Paris address was 23 rue Le Verrier, 6e (M13, Métro: Vavin). In November 1907 he entered the Schola Cantorum, where he attended d'Indy's composition course for the next seven years. He had met Déodat de Séverac on an earlier visit to the city, and the two became friends. Among the others in Canteloube's circle were Roussel, Magnard, and Albéniz, whose acquaintance he had made at the Sunday musical meetings at Blanche Selva's house. By 1911 Canteloube was living at 146 rue de Rennes, 6e (L12, Métro: Saint-Placide), which was to remain his Paris address for the rest of his life. During the early 1920s he made several pioneering music broadcasts on French radio, for which he gave lecture recitals about Scarlatti, Séverac, Weber, and Roussel from the studio in the Eiffel Tower. The first of these (on Scarlatti) was broadcast on 28 January 1924 under difficult circumstances: rain was leaking through the studio roof, and an assistant had to hold an umbrella over Canteloube as he played. In the same year the second set of the *Chants d'Auvergne* was first performed (the first set was given the following year). On 26 June 1933, Canteloube's opera *Vercingétorix* was given its première at the Opéra with Georges Thill in the title role. In an early review, Guy de Lioncourt described the libretto as "exactly what Richard Wagner would have written if the composer of Siegfried had been a French citizen" (Cougniaud-Raginel 1988, 87). *Vercingétorix* is perhaps Canteloube's most eloquent musical homage to the Auvergne. It was among the earliest works to include parts for the recently invented electronic instrument, the Ondes Martenot. Canteloube calls for four Ondes; according to his own account of the work (printed in *Le Matin* on 20 June 1933), these instruments play "at all the mystical moments in the score." Canteloube's interest in folk music was all-important to him: as well as composing the sets of songs from the Auvergne, he made arrangements of music from a number of other French regions—Alsace, Languedoc, Touraine, and the Basque country. In 1944–45 he gave a series of recitals with the singer Geneviève Rex entitled "La musique à travers les provinces de France," and these were followed by many similar concerts in Paris and elsewhere.

Alfredo Casella (25 July 1883–5 March 1947)

Casella first visited Paris with his mother in January 1896, and he returned in the autumn to begin his studies at the Conservatoire. Mother and son stayed first at a hotel described by Casella as "located near the Madeleine in the Cité du Retiro, a dark and narrow street which ends in the Faubourg-Saint-Honoré. The hotel, which was closed a number of years ago, was a modest place kept by an old Madame Durand, who was kind and attentive to my mother" (Casella 1955, 37). Shortly afterwards, Casella and his mother moved to an apartment on the fifth floor at 15 boulevard Péreire, 17e (C9, Métro: Wagram), overlooking the Batignolles rail terminal. Casella later recalled that "the noise of six hundred daily trains was frightful; however, in compensation, we had air, light, and a fine view of the distant hills of Argenteuil" (37–38). At the Conservatoire, his piano teacher was Louis Diémer, in whose class Gabriel Grovlez was a fellow pupil. Among those whom Casella met in his early years in Paris were Pablo de Sarasate and Georges Enesco, still in his teens, as was Casella. In 1898 Casella heard Debussy's *Prélude à l'après-midi d'un faune* for the first time, and met Debussy afterwards. In the winter of 1900, Casella attended the composition classes given by Fauré, and there he first encountered Ravel. The two became great friends, and for a time they were neighbours (Ravel lived at 19 boulevard Péreire in 1901–1905). Casella described one of their frequent meetings in the street: "On my way home one day in January, 1904, I found [Ravel] seated on a bench, attentively reading a manuscript. I came up to him and asked what it was. He said: 'It is a quartet I have just finished. I am rather satisfied with it.' It was the String Quartet in F which has become universally famous" (68).

In 1906 Casella took up a most unusual post for the time: harpsichordist in the early music ensemble run by Henri Casadesus (also the composer of numerous ostensibly baroque pieces performed by the group—Casella described him as a "talented and sympathetic rascal"). In 1909, Casella (with Falla and others) joined Ravel's Société Musicale Indépendante. In 1913 Georges Clemenceau appointed him critic at *L'Homme Libre*, and he also worked as a conductor: Debussy admired his performances of the *Trois nocturnes* and *Ibéria* and the two men were on friendly terms. As Casella's success as a composer grew, he continued to work as a pianist. On 28 January 1915 at the Salle Gaveau, he played in the first performance of Ravel's Piano Trio. In autumn 1915, Casella moved to Rome, where he had been appointed professor of piano at the Liceo di Santa Cecilia, after two decades in Paris.

Emmanuel Chabrier (18 January 1841–13 September 1894)

Chabrier was born at Ambert (Puy-de-Dôme) and educated in Clermont-Ferrand. His family settled in Paris in 1856, at 23 rue Vaneau, 7e (K11, Métro: Vaneau), then at 40 rue Vaneau. While a law student (1860–63), Chabrier went almost every Saturday to Paul Verlaine's house at 26 rue Lecluse, 17e. These visits were affectionately recalled by the poet in his sonnet to Chabrier, published in 1888:

> Chez ma mère charmante et divinement bonne
> Votre génie improvisait au piano.
> Et c'était tout autour comme un brûlant anneau
> De sympathie et d'aise qui rayonne. . . .

[At my charming and saintly mother's house, your genius was improvising at the piano. It was as if a glowing ring of friendship and comfort was radiating around us.]

After taking a law degree, Chabrier entered the civil service in October 1863 but continued his musical studies privately and cultivated a large circle of poets, artists, and musicians. In 1863–64 he collaborated with Verlaine on two operettas: *Fisch-ton-kan* and *Vaucochard et fils Ier,* written for private performance. During the Franco-Prussian War, the siege of Paris, and the Commune, Chabrier was obliged, as a government servant, to follow Thiers's government, to Tours, Bordeaux, and Versailles. His first great musical success was the première of *L'étoile* at the Bouffes-Parisiens on 28 November 1877. A little more than a year later, *Une éducation manquée* was given its first performance (1 May 1879).

When Chabrier resigned from the civil service in November 1880, he was living with his wife in an apartment at 23 rue Mosnier (rue de Berne after 1884), 8e (E11, Métro: Europe). Regular visitors at Chabrier's lively musical evenings included his near-neighbour Edouard Manet (and his pianist wife Suzanne, to whom Chabrier had earlier dedicated the *Impromptu* for piano in 1873), along with such fellow composers as Chausson, Duparc, d'Indy, Messager, and Saint-Saëns. In 1881, his first year of full-time composition, Chabrier wrote the *Dix pièces pittoresques* for piano. In 1882, Chabrier and his wife travelled to Spain, an experience which was to have a profound effect on his music, notably in *España*, which he had originally written for piano but orchestrated at the suggestion of the conductor Lamoureux. When it was first performed on 4 November 1883, the audience immediately called for an encore, and Chabrier became an instant celebrity. The same year, he wrote the delightful *Trois valses romantiques* for two pianos, a work that was later to captivate the student Ravel: with Ricardo Viñes, he played them to the composer in February 1893. In 1885 Chabrier completed the opera *Gwendoline*, one of his more overtly Wagnerian scores. It was given a successful première at the Théâtre de la Monnaie in Brussels on 10 April 1886 but not produced at the Paris Opéra until 1893 (by which time Chabrier was too ill to appreciate the occasion).

Chabrier's last Paris address was 13 avenue Trudaine, 9e (D14, Métro: Anvers), where he composed *Le roi malgré lui* (première at the Opéra-Comique on 18 May 1887), the *Joyeuse marche* (1888), and the exquisite *Ode à la musique* (1890), a house-warming present for his friend Jules Griset and almost the last piece he completed before illness prevented further work. Chabrier was buried in Montparnasse Cemetery.

Chabrier was a close friend of several great artists, especially Manet. Both lived on the rue Mosnier for a time, and Chabrier was also acquainted with Monet, Renoir, and Cézanne. His important collection of Impressionist paintings included works by Monet, three Renoirs, a Cézanne, and a magnificent group of Manets, including the artist's last masterpiece, *A Bar at the Folies-Bergère* (1881–82, Courtauld Institute Galleries, London), which Chabrier acquired in 1884 and which hung over the piano in his home at avenue Trudaine.

Gustave Charpentier (25 June 1860–18 February 1956)

During Charpentier's childhood in Tourcoing, he worked in a spinning mill, but an annual scholarship from the people of Tourcoing enabled Charpentier to enter the Paris Conservatoire in 1881. Never fond of institutions, he preferred to enjoy the delights of Montmartre. When he joined Massenet's composition class in 1885, he made excellent progress and won the Prix de Rome in 1887. While in Rome he began work on his masterpiece *Louise*. He completed the opera in Paris, to his own libretto, and it was a resounding success at its première at the Opéra-Comique on 2 February 1900. In many ways it is the finest (and certainly the most human) operatic evocation of life in Montmartre. In 1912 Charpentier was elected to the Institut de France following Massenet's death, and the next year he produced *Julien, ou la vie du poète*, an ambitious sequel to *Louise*. This too was a success at its première (Opéra-Comique, 4 June 1913). He lived another forty-three years, but he completed no more operatic projects, though he started several (including a further sequel to *Louise* that was about the heroine's daughter Marie). Though he supervised a film version of *Louise* in 1936, Charpentier became increasingly reclusive. His address for more than sixty years was 66 boulevard de Rochechouart, 18e (D14, Métro: Anvers). He was buried in Père-Lachaise Cemetery.

Marc-Antoine Charpentier (circa 1643–24 February 1704)

Charpentier was born in Paris but studied in Rome with Carissimi. On returning to his native city at the end of the 1660s, he was given an apartment by Marie de Guise in her magnificent Paris residence. As the person who had effective control of the entire house of Lorraine from 1675, the highly cultured Mlle de Guise lived in considerable splendour at the Hôtel de Clisson, 58 rue des Archives (formerly rue du Chaume), 3e (H16, Métro: Rambuteau). After remaining here for almost twenty years, Charpentier left in about 1687. He was treated as a guest of the family, paid a salary, given board and lodging, and provided with the necessary peace and quiet to work productively. Charpentier wrote several important pieces for family occasions (including a number for funerals) and other works for institutions in which the de Guise family took a particular interest, such as the boys' school known as the Hôtel de l'Enfant-Jésus, for which Charpentier wrote some Christmas pieces. He also collaborated with Molière, following the latter's dispute with the quarrelsome Lully.

By the mid-1680s, Charpentier was able to call upon a considerable number of musicians attached to the de Guise household, including eleven singers and a highly proficient instrumental ensemble. Perhaps the most remarkable of these was the theoretician Etienne Loulié, inventor of a musical chronometer (forerunner of the metronome), a "sonometer" for tuning the harpsichord, and a device for ruling stave lines. The household was an intensely musical one, where a number of concerts were performed every week, as well as music for Masses and for other liturgical purposes. Charpentier left the de Guise household in about 1687, shortly before the death of Marie de Guise on 3 March 1688. She had wanted to secure for him an important official post and did so at the very end of her life: for the next ten years Charpentier worked for the Jesuits, as master of music at Saint-Louis (now Saint-Paul–Saint-Louis), rue Saint-Antoine, 4e, and at the Jesuit College, 123 rue Saint-Jacques.

In 1692, Charpentier was living on the rue Dauphine. As well as writing sacred music, including the famous Messe de Minuit (probably for performance at the Jesuit church of Saint-Louis for midnight Mass on Christmas 1694), Charpentier also composed music for the Jesuits' numerous theatrical ventures, including ballets. For these occasions the Jesuit College welcomed large audiences and drew on the expertise of the best choreographers and stage designers. Charpentier's only major theatrical venture elsewhere during these years was the opera Médée, first performed at the Académie Royale (Opéra) on 4 December 1693 and published by Ballard the following year, with a dedication to Louis XIV.

In June 1698, Charpentier was appointed as choirmaster at the Sainte-Chapelle, one of the most illustrious musical posts in Paris, in a building that had been described three centuries earlier as "one of the most beautiful abodes in paradise."

Charpentier had lodgings in the choir schoolhouse on the rue de Jérusalem (on the site of the present quai des Orfèvres). On several occasions Charpentier was rebuked for his outspoken remarks and his occasional inattention to official duties, but this in an institution that was notably quarrelsome, and Charpentier was fortunate enough never to have had any misconduct officially recorded. His best-known work from this period is the Te Deum, first performed in 1702. Charpentier died at about 7 A.M. on Sunday, 24 February 1704.

Ernest Chausson (20 January 1855–10 June 1899)

Ernest Chausson grew up in a prosperous home. He then studied law (he was sworn in as a barrister on 8 May 1877), but he never went into practice. During his adolescent and student years, Chausson frequented the salon of Madame de Rayssac at 19 rue Servandoni, 6e (Métro: Saint-Sulpice), where he met such artists as Henri Fantin-Latour and Odilon Redon (who also played the violin on these occasions). Chausson later studied composition with Franck (1880–83) and joined Massenet's instrumentation class at the Conservatoire. Chausson produced his first mature works in the early 1880s, including the tone poem *Viviane*, written in summer 1882 and dedicated to his fiancée, Jeanne Escudier.

1.11 Chausson's villa at 22 boulevard de Courcelles.

The couple were married on 20 June 1883 at the church of Saint-Augustin, and spent their honeymoon in Bayreuth. The Chaussons lived in a magnificent house at 22 boulevard de Courcelles, 17e (E10, Métro: Villiers), where the composer's parents had lived since 1875 (figure 1.11). Chausson held a noted salon here, attended by musicians—Franck, Fauré, Chabrier, Debussy, Dukas, Albéniz, Cortot, and Ysaÿe among them—and artists and writers such as Manet, Redon, Degas, Renoir, Rodin, Gide, and Mallarmé.

It was in the comfortable environment of the boulevard de Courcelles that Chausson composed the finest works in his relatively small output: the *Poème de l'amour et de la mer* (1882–90, revised in 1893), the symphony (1889–90), the Concerto for Violin, Piano, and String Quartet (1889–91), the *Poème* for violin (1896), the piano quartet (1897), many fine songs, and the opera *Le roi Arthus* (1886–95), first performed in Brussels in 1903, four years after the composer's premature death in a cycling accident. One of Chausson's more unusual ventures was the music he composed for the Petit Théâtre de la Galerie Vivienne, a puppet theatre which enjoyed great success from 1888 until its closure in 1892. For this theatre Chausson composed delightful scores for puppet productions of Shakespeare's *The Tempest* and for Maurice Bouchor's *La légende de Sainte-Cécile* (dedicated to Raymond Bonheur, to whom Debussy was to dedicate the *Prélude à l'après-midi d'un faune*). Chausson's funeral was held at the church of Saint-François-de-Sales on 15 June 1899. He was buried in Père-Lachaise Cemetery.

Like his friend Chabrier, Chausson was on excellent terms with many leading artists. His collection included paintings by Corot, Degas, Delacroix, Gauguin, Manet, Renoir, Redon, and many others.

Luigi Cherubini (14 September 1760–15 March 1842)

Towards the end of his life, Cherubini's address in Paris was 25 rue du Faubourg-Poissonnière, 9e (F15, Métro: Bonne-Nouvelle). In 1822 he was appointed director of the Conservatoire, a position he took very seriously, with the result that he composed relatively little during the last twenty years of his life. In 1841 he was the first musician to become a commander of the Légion d'Honneur, and the following year he was given a state funeral at which his own D minor Requiem was performed. He was buried in Père-Lachaise Cemetery.

Frédéric Chopin (?1 March 1810–17 October 1849)

Chopin arrived in Paris in mid-September 1831 and found lodgings at 27 boulevard Poissonnière, 2e (F14, Métro: Rue Montmartre), a fifth-floor room which he described in a letter to his friend Alfons Kumelski: "You wouldn't believe what a delightful lodging I have—a little room, beautifully furnished with mahogany, and a little balcony over the boulevard from which I can see from Montmartre to the Panthéon and the whole length of the fashionable quarter; many persons envy me my view, but none my stairs" (Chopin 1931, 152).

Chopin gave his first Parisian concert, originally announced for 15 January 1832, on 26 February at the Salle Pleyel (then in rue Cadet). Both Mendelssohn and Liszt attended the concert, and Chopin and Liszt subsequently became friends. During 1832 also, Chopin met Berlioz. During the early months of 1833 Chopin lived at 4 cité Bergère, 9e (F14, Métro: Rue Montmartre), and his concert engagements included an appearance at the benefit for Harriet Smithson organised by Berlioz at the Salle Favart (the other performers included Liszt and Rubini). By 20 June 1833, Chopin was living at 5 rue de la Chaussée-d'Antin, 9e (F13, Métro: Opéra), in the apartment owned by Dr. Hermann Franck. (This was the building in which Mozart had stayed in July 1778). Chopin did not give concerts with anything like the regularity of such pianists as Liszt or Kalkbrenner, but on 26 April 1835 he enjoyed an immense popular success with his performance of the Polonaise op. 22 at a Conservatoire concert. Late in 1836, while living at 23 rue Laffitte, Liszt introduced Chopin to George Sand (see entry for Liszt).

In October 1839, Chopin's friend Julian Fontana found an apartment for him at 5 rue Tronchet, 8e (F12, Métro: Madeleine), and another for George Sand at 16 rue Jean-Baptiste-Pigalle, 9e (E13, Métro: Trinité). Chopin moved to his new address, behind the Madeleine, on 10 October 1839. On 26 April 1841 at the Salle Pleyel (rue de Rochechouart), he made one of his rare concert appearances to play the Polonaise op. 40, the F major Ballade, and the C-sharp minor Scherzo. On 9 October 1841, Chopin wrote to Fontana, from Sand's country house at Nohant, that he was moving to Sand's Paris address: "About the moving, Mr. Pelletan of the rue Pigalle has been formally notified today by Mme Sand.... Have my letters sent to 16 rue Pigalle, and impress that very earnestly on the porter" (Chopin 1931, 248). In July 1842, Chopin found a more spacious apartment at 9 place d'Orléans (now square d'Orléans), 9e (E13, Métro: Trinité), and Sand installed herself at no. 5 in the same square; leases were signed on 5 August 1842. Built around a private courtyard, this elegant group of relatively secluded houses and apartments was located just off rue Taitbout. There was a carriage entrance on the rue Saint-Lazare. The place d'Orléans remained Chopin's Paris address for seven years, until the summer of 1849 (though relations with Sand were severed in July 1847). On 16 February 1848, Chopin gave his first Paris concert in several years, once again at the Salle Pleyel. The programme included the Cello Sonata (with Auguste Franchomme) and two of Chopin's last and greatest piano works: the Berceuse and the Barcarolle.

1.12 The house at 12 place Vendôme, where Chopin died.

The 1848 revolution started the following week, and Chopin spent much of the rest of the year in England and Scotland. Chopin spent from June to August 1849 at 74 rue de Chaillot, 16e (G8, Métro: Iéna), where his visitors included Jenny Lind. By mid-September, already gravely ill, he had moved into an apartment at 12 place Vendôme, 1er (G12, Métro: Opéra), where he died at 2 A.M. on 17 October (figure 1.12). Chopin's funeral at the Madeleine on 30 October 1849 was attended by about three thousand mourners, and included a performance of Mozart's Requiem with Pauline Viardot and Luigi Lablache among the soloists. Chopin was buried at Père-Lachaise Cemetery. In a ceremony there on the first anniversary of Chopin's death, Auguste Clésinger's monument was unveiled, as Polish earth was sprinkled on the grave.

Aaron Copland (14 November 1900–2 December 1990)

Copland spent the summer of 1921 at the American School in Fontainebleau. In October 1921 he began his studies in Paris with Nadia Boulanger. His addresses in Paris were 207 boulevard Raspail, 14e (M12, Métro: Raspail), in 1921, villa d'Alésia, 14e (P11, Métro: Alésia), in 1922, and 66 boulevard Pasteur, 15e (M10, Métro: Pasteur), from October 1923 until June 1924, when Copland returned to the United States. Throughout his stay in Paris, Copland shared rooms with Harold Clurman, and his compositions from this time included the piano piece *Le chat et la souris* (published by Durand in 1921) and the ballet *Grohg*.

Couperin Family

Louis Couperin (1626–29 August 1661) was appointed to the post of organist at Saint-Gervais on 9 April 1653. He was the first of the Couperin dynasty to settle in Paris, where he was encouraged by Chambonnières. He lived in the organist's house next to the church with his brothers Charles and François (uncle of the famous François "le Grand"). This house was in a street known as the rue du Montceau-Saint-Gervais, then rue du Pourtour-Saint-Gervais, now 2–4 rue François-Miron, 4e (J15, Métro: Hôtel-de-Ville). The house standing on this site today (the first building to the left of the church porch) was built in the 1730s.

Following Louis's death, his brother Charles Couperin (9 April 1638 until sometime before 26 February 1679) was appointed organist of Saint-Gervais on Christmas Day of 1661 and the following year married Marie Guérin in the church. Their son, François Couperin ("le Grand," 10 November 1668–11 September 1733), was only ten years old when his father died, but the church authorities at Saint-Gervais decided that he should inherit the post on his eighteenth birthday. In the interim, the organist's duties were performed by the distinguished composer Michel-Richard Delalande, for whom François sometimes deputised. In fact, he became organist earlier than planned: a document dated 1 November 1685 decreed that François should be paid three hundred livres per year for undertaking the post; he was just short of his seventeenth birthday. After his father's death, François Couperin continued to live in the organist's house attached to Saint-Gervais, with his widowed mother (who died in 1690). Couperin married Marie-Anne Ansault on 26 April 1689. In January 1693 he was appointed as one of the organists at the Royal Chapel in Versailles and the following year became harpsichord tutor to the dauphin. In 1697 Couperin and his wife moved into a larger apartment on the rue Saint-François (now rue Debelleyme), 3e, keeping only a pied-à-terre in the Saint-Gervais house. From this period on, he enjoyed great success as a harpsichordist at the court of Louis XIV. The death of the king in 1715 did not have any significant effect on Couperin's musical activities, and in 1713 he began the systematic publication of his music with the *Premier Livre* of harpsichord pieces, issued from his new address on the rue Saint-Honoré, between the Palais Royal and the rue des Bons-Enfants. In 1716 he moved to the rue des Fourreurs (now rue des Halles), 1er, and, in 1717, to the rue de Poitou in the Marais, 3e (Métro: Saint-Sébastien-Froissart), from which he published the *Second Livre* of harpsichord pieces. His last move was in 1724, to a spacious apartment on the rue Neuve-des-Bons-Enfants. This building is still standing, on the corner of rue Radziwill and rue des Petits-Champs, 1er (G13, Métro: Palais Royal). It was here that Couperin died, but it is not known where he or his wife is buried.

François Couperin's health was already poor by the early 1720s, so he arranged for his cousin Nicolas Couperin (20 December 1680–25 July 1748) to become his assistant at Saint-Gervais from December 1723. Nicolas lived in the organist's house, moving into the new building (still standing) when it was put up in 1732–34. On 12 December 1733, he was formally appointed François's successor. Nicolas was the first member of the Couperin family to be buried beneath the organ in the church.

Armand-Louis Couperin (25 February 1727–2 February 1789) inherited the post of organist from his father, Nicolas, in 1748 and in 1752 married Elisabeth-Antoinette Blanchet, a fine musician and the daughter of one of France's greatest harpsichord makers. Three of their children became musicians: Pierre-Louis (15 March 1755–10 October 1789), Gervais-François (22 May 1759–11 March 1826), and Antoinette-Victoire (circa 1760–1812). Armand-Louis accumulated a bewildering assortment of posts and, with his children, operated something akin to a family corporation to cover the numerous responsibilities involved. In addition to his work at Saint-Gervais, he was organist at Saint-Barthélemy (until 1772), Saint-Jean-en-Grève, the convent of the Carmes-Billettes, Notre-Dame-de-Paris (from 1755), the Sainte-Chapelle (from 1760), Sainte-Marguerite, and the Royal Chapel (from 1770). His wife was organist at the abbey of Montmartre.

Armand-Louis was killed in a traffic accident while returning from vespers at the Sainte-Chapelle to Saint-Gervais, where his son Pierre-Louis had already started the service. Pierre-Louis succeeded his father in several posts, but never recovered from the shock of the latter's death and died a few months later. He was followed at Saint-Gervais (and in other posts) by his brother Gervais-François, who took over the responsibilities immediately. In 1790, the title page of his *Complainte béarnoise* described Gervais-François as "organiste du Roi en sa Ste Chapelle de Paris, de St Gervais, de St Jean, de Ste Marguerite, et des Carmes Billettes." He also took over from his father at Notre-Dame.

In 1791, Gervais-François and his mother, Elisabeth-Antoinette, moved to a small apartment in the Palais de Justice, next to the Sainte-Chapelle. His marriage in September 1792 to Hélène-Narcisse Frey necessitated a change in domestic arrangements. His mother moved to Versailles, where, having become organist at Saint-Louis, she remained active until her death at the age of eighty-seven. Gervais-François survived the secularising zeal of the Revolution and played on one occasion (6 November 1799) for a dinner in Saint-Sulpice (redesignated as a Temple to Victory) at which Napoléon was the guest of honour. Once the churches reopened, Gervais-François Couperin took up his old posts in those which had not been destroyed. After his death in 1826, his daughter Céleste-Thérèse Couperin (1793–14 February 1860) filled in for a few months at Saint-Gervais, then moved to Saint-Jean–Saint-François until 1830, when she was obliged to resign following complaints from parishioners about the poor quality of her playing. She was the last musician in this extraordinary musical dynasty.

Claude Debussy (22 August 1862–25 March 1918)

Debussy was born at 38 rue au Pain, Saint-Germain-en-Laye (RER: Saint-Germain-en-Laye), where his parents had moved after their marriage in November 1861 (*see* Maison Debussy under "Museums and Libraries"). On the ground floor was the china shop which his parents kept from 1862–64 (it is currently the Tourist Information office for Saint-Germain-en-Laye). The business did not flourish, and in autumn 1864 the family moved to a house owned by Madame Manoury (Debussy's maternal grandmother) in Clichy. In May or June 1865 the family moved again, to 11 rue de Vintimille, 9e (D12, Métro: Place de

Clichy). In 1868 Debussy's father, Manuel, took a job working for the Dupont printing works, and the family moved to an apartment on the fourth floor of 69 rue Saint-Honoré, 1er (H14, Métro: Châtelet). In October 1872 Debussy enrolled at the Conservatoire and joined the piano class of Antoine-François Marmontel and the solfège class of Albert Lavignac. Marmontel wrote of Debussy's potential in his report of an exam on 13 January 1874: "A charming boy. Real artistic temperament. Will become a distinguished musician. A great future."

In September 1875 the family moved, with Madame Manoury, to 13 rue Clapeyron, 8e (D11, Métro: Rome). Following the completion of his studies with Marmontel and his earliest compositions (a piano trio, and songs to texts by Alfred de Musset, all dating from 1879), Debussy was recommended by Marmontel to Nadejda von Meck as a suitable pianist for her resident piano trio. In August 1880 Debussy went to work for this remarkable woman in Interlaken, in Arcachon (where he played Tchaikovsky's Fourth Symphony in a piano duet arrangement with von Meck, the work's dedicatee), and in Florence. Here he presented Mme von Meck with his 1879 trio and began work on a symphony. In November 1880, Debussy was engaged as accompanist to the singing teacher Mme Moreau-Sainti on the rue Royale, where he met Marie-Blanche Vasnier. From this time he stayed regularly at the Vasnier house, 28 rue de Constantinople, 8e (E11, Métro: Villiers). During 1881 he studied composition with Ernest Guiraud at the Conservatoire and spent the summer in the service of von Meck, this time in Moscow. The following year his first published composition appeared: "Nuit d'étoiles," setting a poem by Théodore de Banville. Again he spent some of the summer in Russia and composed several more songs. In December he succeeded Paul Vidal as accompanist of the choral society La Concordia which was conducted by Widor. Here he met Gounod, who reacted sympathetically to the young composer. In 1883, Debussy came in second in the Prix de Rome competition; the following year he won it, with L'enfant prodigue. He arrived at the Villa Medici in Rome in February 1885, and in November that year he met Liszt, who encouraged him to listen to the music of Palestrina and Lassus.

Returning from Rome in March 1887, Debussy moved back in with his parents at 27 rue de Berlin (now rue de Liège), 8e (E12, Métro: Liège). In 1888 he travelled to Bayreuth, where he met, among others, Gabriel Fauré and Robert Godet. At the 1889 Exposition universelle, in the

1.13 A general view of the 1889 Exposition universelle site.

shadow of the new Eiffel Tower, Debussy, with his friends Robert Godet
and Paul Dukas, went to hear the performers of exotic folk music from
Spain, China, Java, and elsewhere (figure 1.13). This experience was to
have a profound influence; he was impressed in particular by the Javanese
Village on the esplanade des Invalides, which included dancers and a
gamelan orchestra: music which was to open up new musical horizons to
Debussy. Also as part of the exposition, Rimsky-Korsakov conducted
two concerts of Russian music in the Trocadéro which were a revelation
for Debussy.

In July 1893, at the same time as he completed the String Quartet,
Debussy moved into an apartment on the fifth floor of 10 rue Gustave-
Doré, 17e (D9, Métro: Wagram). On 22 December 1895, at the Salle d'Har-
court, 40 rue de Rochechouart, the *Prélude à l'après-midi d'un faune* was
given its first performance, conducted by Gustave Doret in the presence of
Stéphane Mallarmé and Pierre Louÿs. It was also at this time that he met
Yvonne Lerolle (see "Envoi") and was briefly engaged to Thérèse Roger.

By 15 January 1899, Debussy was living at 58 rue Cardinet (figure
1.14), 17e (D9, Métro: Malesherbes), and on 19 October that year he married Rosalie (Lilly) Texier. Louis Laloy visited Debussy in the "little
apartment on the fifth floor" in 1902 and described it as follows: "His study
was on the right of the dining room; the table in front of the window, an
upright piano in Brazilian rosewood further away from the door. A little

1.14 Debussy's
apartment at 58
rue Cardinet in
1997.

later, the firm of Pleyel, who were always generous towards artists,
offered him a fine instrument in mahogany, which he showed me and
played to me delightedly. The visitor's armchair was on the left and almost
opposite his. It was there that he sat me down" (Nichols 1992, 190).

At the apartment on the rue Cardinet, Debussy finished the *Trois nocturnes* and *Pelléas et Mélisande*, and composed *L'isle joyeuse* and the *Estampes*. In February 1904 he accompanied Mary Garden in a recording of the
Ariettes oubliées and an extract from *Pelléas*. That July, Debussy left Lilly,
and in September he moved to 10 avenue Alphand, 16e (F6, Métro: Argentine). On 10 February 1905, Ricardo Viñes gave the first public performance of *L'isle joyeuse* and *Masques* at the Salle Aeolian, 32 avenue de
l'Opéra. The next month Debussy finished *La mer*. This was a turbulent
time in Debussy's domestic life: in 1904 he had begun a passionate affair
with Emma Bardac, whose divorce from Sigismond Bardac was finalised
in May 1905. Debussy in turn divorced Lilly in August, and in October
1905, with Emma Bardac, Debussy moved to 80 avenue du Bois de
Boulogne (now avenue Foch), 16e, at no. 24 (figure 1.15) in the private
square surrounded by villas (F6, Métro: Porte Dauphine). This was the
month in which *La mer* was given its first performances: at the Lamoureux
concerts, conducted by Chevillard (15 October 1905), and the following
day at Jean Marnold's house, when Ravel and Viñes performed Debussy's

1.15 Debussy in the garden of his house at 80 avenue du Bois de Boulogne.

1.16 Debussy and Stravinsky at 80 avenue du Bois de Boulogne in 1910. The photographer was Satie.

piano duet version. Two weeks later (30 October 1905), Emma gave birth to their daughter Claude-Emma ("Chouchou"). Debussy remained at 80 avenue du Bois de Boulogne for the rest of his life. In 1910 Debussy was photographed at home with Stravinsky by Erik Satie (figure 1.16). The villa was described by Pasteur Valléry-Radot: "[Debussy] lived off the avenue du Bois de Boulogne, at the end of a long drive lined with villas and enveloped in trees. You came to a gate, then up several steps, and found yourself in a rather dark hallway. Then you went into a room full of light, which seemed to be invaded by trees from a small garden. The atmosphere was peaceful, everything struck a uniformly sober note, even though the furniture was of different styles. At the far end of the room, a large work-table; to the right, a tiny piano in black wood; a Buddha; several Japanese drawings on the walls; roses" (Nichols 1992, 203).

His stepson (and pupil) Raoul Bardac described some of the ornaments in Debussy's study: "Debussy was devoted to various objects, silent but faithful companions, which decorated his work table: very simple pens made of reeds and always of the same make, special blotters, a pot for tobacco, a cigarette box, the toad Arkel [named after the character in *Pelléas et Mélisande*], a model of a sleeping Chinaman and so on" (Nichols 1992, 196).

Following Debussy's death on 25 March 1918, he was temporarily buried at Père-Lachaise Cemetery, but the following year he reached his final resting place in Passy Cemetery, where, as he had wished, he was "among the trees and the birds."

Léo Delibes (21 February 1836–16 January 1891)

At the time of his greatest theatrical successes, Delibes lived at 220 rue de Rivoli (figure 1.17), 1er (G12, Métro: Tuileries). At the Conservatoire he studied composition with Adam and the organ with Benoist, and sang as a choirboy at the Madeleine (and occasionally at the Opéra, including in the première of Meyerbeer's *Le prophète* in 1849). At the age of seventeen, Delibes became organist of Saint-Pierre-de-Chaillot. After a number of early works written for Offenbach's Bouffes-Parisiens and elsewhere, he worked as chorus master at the Opéra-Comique and, beginning in 1864, at the Opéra (Salle Le Peletier). Two years later, his ballet

1.17 The rue de Rivoli in Delibes's time. Photograph by Adolphe Braun, 1855. The house in which Delibes lived (no. 220) is on the left, near the top of the photograph.

La source (co-written with Léon Minkus) was a considerable success and did much to reestablish the status of ballet as an independent entity at the Opéra (rather than as a divertissement in operas). It was also the subject of a fine early ballet painting by Degas: *Portrait of Mlle Eugénie Fiocre at the Ballet "La source"* (circa 1866–68, Brooklyn Museum, New York), which suggests that the cast may have included a real horse as well as dancers. Act 2, scene 1, from *La source* was included in the programme for the opening gala at the new Opéra Garnier on 5 January 1875.

Coppélia, one of the most celebrated of all classical ballets, was first performed on 2 May 1870 at the Opéra (Salle Le Peletier). The star of the evening was Giuseppina Bozzacchi (1853–70) as Swanilda; she danced the part eighteen times before dying of fever on 23 November 1870 (her seventeenth birthday), during the siege of Paris. Delibes's greatest and most ambitious ballet, *Sylvia*, was first performed at the Opéra (Palais Garnier) on 14 June 1876 with a cast that included Rita Sangalli in the title role and Louis Mérante (the work's choreographer) as the shepherd Aminta. Delibes was also a prolific opera composer, and perhaps his crowning achievement was *Lakmé*, set in an exotic (Indian) location, first performed at the Opéra-Comique on 14 April 1883. He died at the age of fifty-four and was buried in Montmartre Cemetery.

Frederick Delius (29 January 1862–10 June 1934)

In May 1888 Delius arrived in Paris, where he stayed in the luxurious apartment of his uncle, Theodor Delius, at 43 rue Cambon, 1er (G12, Métro: Madeleine). The younger Delius described the city as "ten times more beautiful than London." He met Messager, and probably Fauré, at this time. After a trip to Bradford and a holiday in Brittany, Delius returned to the rue Cambon in October 1888 but moved a few weeks later to Ville d'Avray (SNCF: Sèvres–Ville d'Avray). Here he rented the Chalet des Lilas à la Chaumière, a cottage on the banks of a small lake. (The artist Corot had his family home here and often painted the village and its lakes.) Delius stayed at Ville d'Avray until June 1889, meanwhile revising the *Florida Suite*, and spent the summer in Norway with Grieg. In September, he was back in Paris to visit the 1889 Exposition universelle.

By October 1889, Delius had moved to 8 boulevard de la Mairie, Croissy-sur-Seine (RER: Chatou-Croissy). Croissy was famous for the floating restaurant La Grenouillère (immortalised in paintings by Monet and Renoir), before it burnt down in 1889. Delius stayed until the following June, when he left for Leipzig, Jersey, and Saint-Malo. Delius spent winter to summer 1891 back at Croissy.

On his return to Paris in autumn 1891, Delius settled at 33 rue du Couédic (formerly rue Ducouëdic), 14e (P12, Métro: Mouton-Duvernet). Here he finished the opera *Irmelin* and over the next few years made some remarkable friends, including the artists Edvard Munch, Alfons Mucha, and Odilon Redon, and the dramatist August Strindberg. In about 1894 Delius met Paul Gauguin, who had a studio at 6 rue Vercingétorix (Métro: Montparnasse). Musical friends included Florent Schmitt and Maurice Ravel, both of whom made piano reductions of his operas (Ravel arranged *Margot la Rouge*). It was at a dinner party in Paris in 1895 that Delius met his future wife, Jelka Rosen. The same year, he finished *The Magic Fountain* and started work on *Koanga*. This was given a remarkable private performance at the home of Adela Maddison, 157 rue de la Pompe, 16e (Métro: Victor-Hugo), in March 1899, described in a letter to Jelka: "Gabriel Fauré and a few of the best young French musicians played my opera [*Koanga*] at Mrs. Maddison's this afternoon. Prince and Princess de Polignac and a few other musical people were there. And I think I may say they were quite enthusiastic" (Carley 1983, 149). Jelka Rosen described Delius's apartment on the rue du Couédic in her "Memories of Frederick Delius": "We went to his dear little flat in rue Ducouëdic on Montrouge. It was a small old house. But he had persuaded the old propriétaire to knock two small rooms into one, and that made a delightful two-windowed sitting room with a grand piano, a red carpet and a square table. Next to it a small bedroom with a very big bed, and a tiny kitchen" (409–10). In 1895 Delius was told that he had contracted syphilis. It was to leave him an invalid in later years.

In 1899, Delius finished *Paris: The Song of a Great City*. By this time he had settled with Jelka in the house she had bought at Grez-sur-Loing (the village lies between Fontainebleau and Nemours, just off Route N7). Jelka had discovered the house, which had belonged to the marquis de Carzeaux, while she was on a painting trip to Grez in 1897. It is situated

1.18 Delius at the piano in his house at Grez-sur-Loing. Gauguin's *Nevermore* is hanging behind the piano.

next door to the twelfth-century church, and has a large garden leading down to the river. The couple married in 1903, and at Grez Delius wrote his greatest works (figure 1.18). Many friends and colleagues came to visit the composer here, including Grainger, Beecham, and Elgar. Delius was an enthusiastic collector. In 1898 he bought Gauguin's *Nevermore* (Courtauld Institute Galleries, London) from the artist, and he also owned fine works by his friend Munch, and by Rodin, whom Jelka knew well.

Gaetano Donizetti (29 November 1797–8 April 1848)

Donizetti made a trip to Paris in January 1835, his first journey outside Italy. He attended the première of Bellini's *I puritani* at the Théâtre Italien on 24 January 1835 and began rehearsing *Marino Faliero* for its première in the same theatre on 12 March 1835. The cast included four of the great singers who had appeared in *I puritani:* Giulia Grisi, Rubini, Tamburini, and Lablache. Donizetti left for Naples on 20 or 21 March 1835 and, on returning to Paris on 21 October 1838, took lodgings at 5 rue de Louvois, 2e (G13, Métro: Quatre-Septembre), where Adolphe Adam was also living at the time. Adam was one of many musicians who were impressed by Donizetti's kindness. Adam later recalled Donizetti's generous nature: "In 1838, we lived in the same house, rue de Louvois. We often visited one another there; he worked without a piano and wrote without stopping.... I put on my opera *Le brasseur de Preston* at the Opéra-Comique. A spectator seated in the orchestra drew attention to himself by his enthusiasm and his frantic applause; it was Donizetti, and when I saw him on arriving home that evening, I found him happier over my success than I was, and I felt more honoured by his friendship and approbation than by the happy outcome of my opera" (Weinstock 1964, 139).

The first French performance of *Roberto Devereux* was given at the Théâtre Italien on 27 December 1838 (Donizetti composed a new sinfonia for the occasion). He spent much of the next two years in Paris. Important premières of his operas written especially for Parisian theatres during that period include *La fille du régiment* at the Opéra-Comique on 11 February 1840 and *La favorite* at the Opéra on 2 December 1840. Donizetti was in Paris again on 2 March 1841, staying near the Théâtre Italien at the Hôtel Manchester, 1 rue de Gramont, 2e (G13, Métro: Quatre-

Septembre), which was to be his usual Paris address until illness and insanity overcame him. Donizetti left in August 1841 but returned in autumn 1842 after a year spent mostly in Vienna. Soon afterwards came the huge success of Donizetti's comic masterpiece *Don Pasquale*. The première was at the Théâtre Italien on 3 January 1843. After spending another season in Vienna, Donizetti came back to Paris in July 1843, staying first at 19 rue d'Antin, 2e (G13, Métro: Opéra), then at the Hôtel Manchester. *Dom Sébastien*, to a libretto by Scribe, was given its first performance on 11 November 1843 at the Opéra; this was his last opera written especially for a Parisian audience, though *Maria di Rohan* (first given in Vienna on 15 June 1843) was revised by the composer for its Paris première on 14 November. Donizetti left in December 1843. He did not return to Paris until August 1845, and his friends were shocked by the change in his appearance. On 16 August Adolphe Adam wrote to his friend Spiker that Donizetti "has been in Paris for about a fortnight and is in an alarming mental state. He has never been mentally strong and the nervous ailment from which he is suffering gives him a dazed air, almost cretinous" (Adam 1996, 169). Partial paralysis and insanity had taken their toll on the composer, and on 25 December 1845 Adam reported bleakly on his condition: "Poor Donizetti is becoming an imbecile: during the last six months his affliction has made dreadful progress; it is a softening of the brain which affects his intellectual faculties. The cause has been attributed to too much work and too many women. He is now a man entirely lost to the art of music. He may perhaps vegetate for a few years, but his soul is no longer alive." The stricken Donizetti was taken from Paris to Dr. Jean Mitivié's clinic at Ivry-sur-Seine on about 1 February 1846. On 23 June 1847, he was moved from the sanatorium to an address just off the Champs-Elysées, 6 avenue Chateaubriand (now rue Arsène-Houssaye), 8e (F8, Métro: Charles de Gaulle–Etoile). His nephew Andrea attempted to take the dying composer back to Bergamo, but the police placed guards at the house on 26 August to prevent any such move. The reasons for this police action remain uncertain. Eventually, at noon on 19 September 1847, Donizetti, paralysed and insane, left Paris with his nephew. He died in Bergamo on 8 April 1848.

Paul Dukas (1 October 1865–17 May 1935)

Dukas was born at 10 rue Coquillère, 1er (H14, Métro: Les Halles). He began attending Théodore Dubois's harmony classes at the Conservatoire in 1881, the year from which his earliest surviving compositions date. During his time in Dubois's class, Dukas also acquired an excellent knowledge of orchestration, not only by attending numerous concerts, but also by playing timpani in the Conservatoire orchestra. In 1885 he was admitted to Guiraud's composition class and first met Debussy. It was the beginning of a friendship which was to last until Debussy's death. Dukas visited Bayreuth in 1886, and in 1888 he was awarded second prize in the Prix de Rome competition, for his cantata *Velléda* (the first-prize winner was Camille Erlanger). Dukas did his military service in 1889–90.

His first major composition after his return to Parisian musical life was the overture *Polyeucte*, completed on 6 October 1891 and first performed at the Lamoureux concerts on 23 January 1892. The same year, he became music critic for the *Revue indépendante*. In 1893, Dukas moved to 9 rue des Petits-Hôtels, 10e (E15, Métro: Poissonnière); it was also in 1893 that Debussy dedicated *La damoiselle élue* to him. Over the next few years Dukas wrote several of his most important works: the Symphony in C (first performed 3 January 1897), *L'apprenti sorcier* (first performed on 18 May 1897), and the Piano Sonata (dedicated to Saint-Saëns and first performed on 10 May 1901).

In 1900 Dukas began composing the opera *Ariane et Barbe-Bleue*, which was to occupy him for the next eight years. In 1905 he moved to 41 rue Washington, 8e (F9, Métro: George V), where he finished *Ariane*. In 1907 Dukas established a lasting friendship with Manuel de Falla (who had just arrived in Paris), and introduced Falla to his older compatriot Isaac Albéniz. In April 1909, succeeding Paul Taffanel, Dukas was appointed professor of orchestration at the Conservatoire. In 1910 he moved to 20 rue de l'Assomption, 16e (J4, Métro: Ranelagh), in the quieter district of Passy. In 1912 he completed the "poème dansé" *La Péri*. This magical ballet score is the last of Dukas's last major works to have survived, as most of the music he wrote after this date was destroyed in terrible bouts of self-criticism.

In 1915, Dukas moved to 38 rue Singer, 16e (J5, Métro: La Muette), and the following year he married Suzanne Pereyra. Their daughter,

Adrienne, was born in 1919. Fauré dedicated his Second Piano Quintet to Dukas in 1921. In 1923 Dukas became an officer of the Légion d'Honneur, and in 1928 he was appointed professor of composition at the Conservatoire, where his pupils included Messiaen, Duruflé, Alain, Rodrigo, and Langlais. By 1929 Dukas was living at 84 rue de Ranelagh, 16e (J4, Métro: Ranelagh). He was made a member of the Institut de France in 1934. He died the following year and was buried in Père-Lachaise Cemetery. The Dukas memorial issue of *Revue Musicale*, issued in May–June 1936, contains works by nine of his friends and pupils, among them Falla, Pierné, Rodrigo, and Messiaen.

Henri Duparc (21 January 1848–12 February 1933)

Duparc was born in Paris and attended the Collège de Vaugirard, where César Franck worked as music teacher. During his school years, Duparc's earliest composition, *Six rêveries* for piano, was privately printed for the young composer as a birthday gift from his grandmother. In about 1868 Duparc met the MacSwiney family, who lived at 7 avenue de Villars, 7e (K10, Métro: Saint-François-Xavier), where d'Indy had an apartment from 1863 until his death in 1931 (figure 1.19).

1.19 D'Indy and Duparc both lived here, at 7 avenue de Villars, near les Invalides.

An apartment on the fifth floor became Duparc's home after he married Ellie MacSwiney on 9 November 1871 at the Eglise des Missions étrangères, on the rue du Bac (the couple were unable to marry in their local church of Saint-François-Xavier, as it was under repair at the time). During the siege of Paris (1870) Duparc served in the 18th battalion of guards, stationed at Bagnolet, and during this difficult time he composed "L'invitation au voyage," first performed at a Société Nationale concert on 9 March 1872. His other most famous songs were written in the 1880s: "Phidylé" (dedicated to Chausson) appeared in about 1882, and "La vie antérieure" was completed in 1884 (though he first worked on it ten years earlier). In 1888 Franck honoured Duparc, his former pupil, with the dedication of the D minor Symphony; the younger composer was devastated by his teacher's death two years later. Already showing signs of mental instability, in the early 1890s Duparc began to suffer from violent fits of despair, during which he destroyed a number of works (including

1.20 Duparc's apartment at 6 place Saint-François-Xavier (now place du Président-Mithouard).

the draft of an almost complete opera, *Roussalka*). In 1897, Duparc moved to a new address nearby (figure 1.20), at 6 place Saint-François-Xavier (now place du Président-Mithouard), 7e (K10, Métro: Saint-François-Xavier). The Duparcs suffered a series of discouragements: her mother died in 1905, and his eyesight was deteriorating. Having little wish to remain in the city, Duparc and his wife left for good the following year to live in virtual seclusion.

Marcel Dupré (3 May 1886–30 May 1971)

Dupré was born in Rouen but came to Paris in 1902 to study at the Conservatoire. His teachers included Louis Diémer for piano, Alexandre Guilmant for organ, and Widor for fugue. It was Widor who gave Dupré his first job, as his assistant at Saint-Sulpice in 1906. In October 1916, Vierne went to Switzerland to receive treatment for his eyes, and Dupré

1.21 Marcel Dupré outside his house at 40 boulevard Anatole-France, Meudon.

substituted for him as organist at Notre-Dame. Vierne was away for five years, and during that time Dupré acquired a reputation as a brilliant improviser as well as a gifted composer. In 1925 he bought a handsome villa (figure 1.21) at 40 boulevard Anatole-France, Meudon (SNCF: Meudon-Montparnasse).

A few weeks later he discovered that the organ belonging to his teacher Guilmant (whose house, until his death in 1911, was also in Meudon) was for sale. He acquired this magnificent Cavaillé-Coll instrument and installed it in the newly built private concert hall in his house. Originally the organ had three manuals, but Dupré expanded them to four. In 1926 Dupré was appointed professor of organ at the Paris Conservatoire, where his pupils included Messiaen, Langlais, and Jehan Alain. Following Widor's retirement at the end of 1933, Dupré was appointed organist at Saint-Sulpice, a post he held until his death. Among early visitors to the organ gallery was the ageing Glazunov, who had settled in Paris in 1932 and went regularly to Mass at Saint-Sulpice until his final illness and death in 1936. In 1937 Dupré played for the wedding of the duke of Windsor and Wallis Simpson at the Château de Candé. As well as teaching at the Conservatoire and elsewhere, and working at Saint-Sulpice, Dupré toured extensively in America, Britain, and elsewhere. After becoming director of the Conservatoire in 1954, he retired two years later when he reached his seventieth birthday. As Widor's assistant and then as organist, he played at Saint-Sulpice for sixty-five years. On 30 May 1971 (the Feast of Pentecost), Dupré played for two Masses there in the morning, then returned home to Meudon, where he died later the same day. His funeral was held in Saint-Sulpice on 3 June 1971.

Maurice Duruflé (11 January 1902–16 June 1986)

Born in Louviers (Normandy), Duruflé arrived in Paris in 1919. There he was introduced to Charles Tournemire by Maurice Emmanuel. In 1920 Duruflé entered the Conservatoire, where his teachers included Gigout for the organ and Dukas for composition. During his years of study he often substituted for Tournemire at Sainte-Clotilde, and from 1927 he served as a deputy for Vierne at Notre-Dame-de-Paris. In 1930 Duruflé was appointed at Saint-Etienne-du-Mont, and lived for many years at 6 place du Panthéon, 5e (L14, Métro: Cardinal-Lemoine), in the accommodation provided for the organist. Here he wrote all his mature music, notably the Requiem, given its first performance under Roger Désormière for a broadcast on 2 November 1947. Duruflé conducted the work himself for the 1958 recording made in Saint-Etienne-du-Mont.

Duruflé was in demand as an organist as well as composer. His repertoire included many works by Bach (of which he recorded several). He was the soloist in the first performance of Poulenc's Organ Concerto, conducted by Nadia Boulanger, at a private concert at the home of the princesse de Polignac (the dedicatee) on 16 December 1938. The public première of the work, conducted by Désormière and again featuring Duruflé as soloist, was given on 21 June 1939 at the Salle Gaveau. In May 1975, Duruflé was involved in a serious motor accident, and he never fully recovered his health. From this time on, his wife Marie-Madeleine continued alone as organist of Saint-Etienne-du-Mont. Duruflé died, after many years of poor health, at a clinic in Louveciennes.

Georges Enesco (19 August 1881–4 May 1955)

Born in Romania, Enesco joined Massenet's class at the Conservatoire in January 1895, when he was thirteen (he would later speak of Massenet with great affection). Enesco's early Paris works include a violin sonata dedicated to Eva Rolland, his landlady's daughter. It was played by Rolland and Enesco at a concert in June 1897 consisting entirely of music by the fifteen-year-old composer (Massenet was present). Enesco also studied with Fauré, whom he described as "inspiring—and we adored him." Enesco left the Conservatoire in 1899, having been awarded a first prize for violin, for which he was given an instrument by Bernadel. During the 1914–18 war, Enesco lived in Romania, where he met and fell in love with Marie Cantacuzino, whom he was later to marry. He returned to Paris after the war and soon embarked on the opera *Oedipe*, generally considered to be his masterpiece. From the 1920s, Enesco lived at 26 rue de Clichy, 9e (E12, Métro: Trinité). When he returned to Paris after World War II, he continued to live at this address, but in his final years he had to give up his spacious third-floor apartment and move into a cramped two-room basement, where he was often visited by his pupil and friend Yehudi Menuhin. Enesco was buried in Père-Lachaise Cemetery.

Gabriel Fauré (12 May 1845–4 November 1924)

Fauré, who was born in Pamiers (Arriège), became a pupil at the Ecole Niedermeyer, in October 1854, when he was nine. The students lived in the school at 10 rue Neuve-Fontaine-Saint-Georges (now rue Fromentin), 9e (D13, Métro: Blanche or Pigalle). His piano teacher beginning in spring 1861 was Camille Saint-Saëns, who was to become a lifelong friend. The regimen at the school was strict; pupils were allowed out only on Sundays to visit their "correspondant," an adult acting in loco parentis. From 1861 on, Fauré's "correspondante" was Saint-Saëns's mother. That year he composed his first song, "Le papillon et la fleur" (setting a poem by Victor Hugo).

Fauré left the Ecole Niedermeyer on 28 July 1865 and in January 1866 took up his first post, as organist of Saint-Sauveur in Rennes. His first publishing contract (with Choudens) was signed in 1869, and two songs were published the same year. Early in 1870 he left Rennes and became organist, briefly, at Notre-Dame-de-Clignancourt (place Jules-Joffrin, 18e). Fauré was excited to be back in Paris, but soon the Franco-Prussian War plunged the city into chaos. Fauré enlisted in the National Guard on 16 August 1870 and was discharged on 19 March 1871, whereupon he immediately became organist at Saint-Honoré d'Eylau (place Victor-Hugo, 16e). It was a very brief appointment: during the Commune, Fauré, using a forged passport, fled the city and made his way on foot to Rambouillet, fifty kilometres to the southwest of Paris. The Ecole Niedermeyer moved to Switzerland, and Fauré was invited to spend the summer at Cours-sous-Lausanne teaching composition. The school returned to Paris in October 1871, and Fauré took up a post as assistant organist to Widor at Saint-Sulpice, for a monthly salary of eighty francs. This remarkable pair would amuse themselves with improvisation contests during Mass, Widor, the titulaire, on the large organ and Fauré on the choir organ. In 1873, Fauré was living at 19 rue Taranne (now 167 boulevard Saint-Germain), 6e (Métro: Saint-Germain-des-Prés). In January 1874 Fauré left (being replaced by André Messager, his friend and fellow pupil at the Ecole Niedermeyer) so that he could deputise for Saint-Saëns at the Madeleine. During the early 1870s Fauré gradually became better known, and he attended some of the best Parisian salons, notably that of Pauline Viardot, to which he was first invited in 1872.

In July 1874 Fauré moved to 7 rue de Parme, 9e, just off the rue d'Amsterdam (D12, Métro: Liège or Place de Clichy). It was at this time that Fauré wrote his earliest instrumental masterpieces, completing the First Violin Sonata in 1876 and starting work on the First Piano Quartet. In April 1877 he was appointed maître de chapelle at the Madeleine and moved same month into an apartment at 13 rue Mosnier (rue de Berne since 1884), 8e (E11, Métro: Europe). He shared this apartment with André

Messager until his marriage. In July 1877 his traumatic engagement to Marianne Viardot (Pauline's youngest daughter) was announced, but it was broken off in October, to Fauré's immense distress. In January of the following year, two of his most famous songs received their first performances: "Après un rêve" (6 January) and "Au bord de l'eau" (19 January). Over the next few years, Fauré travelled extensively, particularly in Germany, where he immersed himself in Wagner's music and became friendly with Liszt in Weimar. In December 1879, Choudens published the first collection of *Vingt mélodies* (later taken over by Hamelle). Fauré's work was receiving regular performances in Paris, and on 14 February 1880 the composer gave the premières of the First Piano Quartet and the Berceuse for violin and piano at a Société Nationale concert. In 1882 he travelled to London with Messager to hear Wagner's *Ring* performed by artists from Bayreuth, and on 9 December Saint-Saëns gave the premières of Fauré's First Impromptu and First Barcarolle.

1.22 Fauré's lodgings at 93 avenue Niel.

1.23 Fauré's apartment at 154 boulevard Malesherbes.

On 27 March 1883, Fauré married Marie Fremiet (daughter of the distinguished sculptor Emmanuel Fremiet). At about the same time he moved to 93 avenue Niel, 17e (D8, Métro: Péreire), where he wrote songs such as "Aurore," "Fleur jetée," and "Les roses d'Ispahan," as well as the Second Piano Quartet (figure 1.22). In October 1886 the family moved to 154 boulevard Malesherbes, 17e (D9, Métro: Malesherbes), where they were to live until April 1911 (figure 1.23). It was while living here that he wrote many of his most famous pieces, including the Requiem (first version 1888, revised version by 1894, final version 1900), the Pavane and "Clair de lune" (his first Verlaine setting), both composed during summer 1887 in Le Vésinet), the songs "Au cimetière" (November 1888) and "En prière" (1889 or 1890), and the song cycles *La bonne chanson*

(1892–94) and *La chanson d'Eve* (1906–10). Here too Fauré wrote many of his mature piano works, including several of the nocturnes and barcarolles, the suite *Dolly* (1894–97), and the Theme and Variations op. 73 (1895). His duties at the Madeleine included playing the organ for Gounod's funeral on 27 October 1893 (he improvised on a theme from Gounod's *Rédemption*) and again for his friend Verlaine's funeral on 10 January 1896. He was also busy after October 1896 as a composition teacher at the Conservatoire, having succeeded Massenet. Fauré's most celebrated pupil was Ravel (from January 1898). In March 1898, Fauré made one of his regular visits to London and received a commission from Mrs. Patrick Campbell to

1.24 Fauré's apartment at 32 rue des Vignes.

1.25 and 1.26 Interior views of Fauré's apartment at 32 rue des Vignes.

write incidental music for *Pelléas et Mélisande*. He returned to conduct the first performances in June. (Later, in 1902, he attended several rehearsals for Debussy's *Pelléas* at the Opéra-Comique.) On 15 June 1905, a month after his sixtieth birthday, Fauré was named as director of the Conservatoire, a post he held for fifteen years; he retired in 1920.

Fauré's last move, in April 1911, was to 32 rue des Vignes (figures 1.24, 1.25, and 1.26), 16e (J5, Métro: La Muette), where his first major project was the opera *Pénélope*, completed on 12 January 1913. (At the time Fauré was in Monte Carlo, where the première was given on 4 March 1913.) At the end of 1913, Fauré recorded five piano rolls for the Welte Mignon company in Paris. During these years Fauré wrote his restrained and beautiful late works: song cycles such as *Mirages* (1919) and *L'horizon chimérique* (1921), as well as chamber works, including the Second Violin Sonata (1916–17), the two cello sonatas (1917 and 1921), the Second Piano Quintet (1919–21), and the Piano Trio (1922–23). He died at 32 rue des Vignes, having completed the String Quartet (which he had started in secret during summer 1923) only a few weeks earlier. Following a state funeral at the Madeleine (figure 2.2), Fauré was buried in Passy Cemetery.

César Franck (10 December 1822–8 November 1890)

Franck, born in Liège (Belgium), began his musical studies there, and by the time he was twelve years old, he had won a first prize for piano. In May 1835 the Franck family moved to Paris, settling at 22 rue de Montholon, 9e (E14, Métro: Cadet). Franck's father urged his son to take up a career as a piano virtuoso and arranged a Paris debut for him, which passed largely unnoticed. He took private lessons in harmony with Reicha (who had taught Berlioz, Liszt, and Gounod) until his father was able to obtain French nationalisation papers, which enabled Franck to enter the Conservatoire in October 1837. He won a first prize for piano the following year, and one for counterpoint in 1840. His father, always an irascible and difficult man, withdrew Franck from the Conservatoire in April 1842, preventing his son from entering the Prix de Rome competition, as he felt that Franck should be devoting his efforts to playing the piano rather than to composition.

While his family returned to Belgium, Franck remained in Paris. Liszt, Chopin, Donizetti, Meyerbeer, Thomas, Halévy, and Auber subscribed to the first edition of his three trios op. 1 in 1843. The same year, he first met Liszt, who became Franck's friend and champion. The Franck family returned to Paris permanently by 1845 and settled at 15 rue La Bruyère, 9e (E13, Métro: Saint-Georges). César's father was greatly disappointed by Franck's declining interest in playing the piano and by the poor public reaction to Franck's oratorio *Ruth*, first performed in 1846. To earn a living, Franck took private pupils, taught at several institutions, and accepted an appointment as assistant organist at Notre-Dame-de-Lorette (18 bis rue de Châteaudun, 9e, Métro: Notre-Dame-de-Lorette), the church with the first Parisian organ (built in 1838) by Cavaillé-Coll, for whom Franck was later to become an "artistic representative." Franck spent a great deal of time at the home of his fiancée, Félicité Desmousseaux, on the rue Blanche and indeed took an apartment himself at 45 rue Blanche, 9e (E12, Métro: Trinité or Blanche).

It was inevitable that Franck's father would oppose his son's marriage to a woman from a theatrical family; nevertheless, both his parents were present at the wedding at Notre-Dame-de-Lorette on 22 February 1848. The wedding took place under decidedly difficult circumstances during the 1848 revolution: the bridal party were able to reach the church only by clambering over a barricade with the help of some of the insurgents stationed there. The couple moved into a new apartment at 69 rue Blanche, 9e (E12, Métro: Blanche). Abbé Dancel, who had been a priest at Notre-Dame-de-Lorette (and who officiated at the Francks' wedding) took up a new appointment at Saint-Jean–Saint-François, in the Marais, and he soon recruited Franck as organist. In 1853 Franck took up his new post at Saint-Jean–Saint-François, 6 rue Charlot, 3e (Métro: Saint-Sébastien-Froissart). The church had a fine organ (1844) by Cavaillé-Coll, about which Franck was most enthusiastic: "My new organ? It's an orchestra!" (Davies 1970, 73).

In 1858 Franck was appointed organist at the large new church of Sainte-Clotilde (23 bis rue Las-Cases, 7e, Métro: Solférino), where he was to be *titulaire* until his death (*see* Sainte-Clotilde under "Churches"). After living in apartments on the rue de Rennes (1863) and boulevard Montparnasse (1863–65), he moved in 1865 to the address which was to be his home for the rest of his life, 95 boulevard Saint-Michel, 5e (L13–L14, RER: Luxembourg). Franck and his family occupied the whole ground floor of the building, which was demolished in the 1920s (figure 1.27). Among his part-time teaching posts was one at the Jesuit College (in

rue de Vaugirard), where in the 1860s his pupils included Henri Duparc, who became a devoted disciple. In 1872 Franck succeeded Benoist as organ professor at the Conservatoire. He was unpopular with his colleagues, not least because his classes were often unofficial composition seminars. D'Indy joined this class in October 1872. Later pupils included Chausson, Pierné, Tournemire, Dukas, Ropartz, Vierne, Lekeu, and Augusta Holmès (with whom Franck fell in love). Franck's best-known works come from the last years of his life: the Piano Quintet (1878–79), the *Prélude, Choral et Fugue* for piano (1884), Symphonic Variations (1885), violin sonata (1886), symphony (1886–88), and *Trois chorals* for organ (1890). Among those who attended his funeral at Sainte-Clotilde on 10 November 1890 were Fauré, Lalo, Widor, and Delibes. Chabrier delivered the oration at the graveside in Montrouge Cemetery: "Farewell, Master, and take our thanks.... In you, we salute one of the greatest artists of the century, and also an incomparable teacher whose wonderful work has produced a whole generation of forceful musicians, believers, and thinkers. ... We salute, also, the upright and just man, so humane, so distinguished, whose counsels were sure, as his words were kind" (D'Indy 1910, 59–60). Later, Franck's remains were transferred to Montparnasse Cemetery.

George Gershwin (26 September 1898–11 July 1937)

Gershwin first visited Paris in 1925, and he was there again in 1926 to stay for a week with his friends Mabel and Robert Schirmer (a member of the music publishing family). On 11 April Gershwin inscribed a photograph to them, including a quotation from the opening of *An American in Paris*, a work which was at that stage no more than an idea. During this visit he also met George Antheil, who later recalled an amusing moment over dinner: "It seemed a most opportune time to ask him a question which had long been troubling me—why his famous *Rhapsody in Blue* was not published by the firm of his closest friend. 'Oh,' replied George (to Mabel's and Bob's intense embarrassment), 'I offered it to Schirmers' as soon as it was finished, but they turned it down. They said it was not commercially feasible.' And he grinned" (Antheil 1945, 179).

Gershwin came back to Paris (with his brother Ira) for an extended stay on 25 March 1928, and they lived at the Hôtel Majestic, 19 avenue Kléber, 16e (F7, Métro: Kléber). Gershwin began serious work on *An American in Paris*, but there was much else to occupy him, including a private performance of Schubert and Schoenberg by the Kolisch Quartet in his hotel room on 27 March and, on 31 March, an enthusiastically received performance of *Rhapsody in Blue*. Among those Gershwin met during this 1928 visit were Diaghilev, Ibert, Honegger, Nadia Boulanger, Tansman, and Prokofiev (Gershwin went to see him on 8 April). On 6 April Gershwin and his brother took an afternoon walk from their hotel down the avenue Kléber to the Trocadéro, then across the river to the Eiffel Tower. They took the lift to the top and were thrilled by the view. Once they had come back down to the second stage, they walked the rest of the way. According to Ira's diary: "It was 26 flights down to the first landing and 12 down from there—38 in all and boy how my legs trembled when we finally got to the street" (Kimball and Simon 1973, 94). Apart from a brief trip to Berlin and Vienna (22 April–6 May), Gershwin remained in Paris until early June, working mostly on *An American in Paris*.

When the young duo-pianists Mario Braggiotti and Jacques Fray presented themselves to the composer, they were surprised to see, on top of the piano, a collection of taxi horns (Gershwin had been on several shopping expeditions down the nearby avenue de la Grande Armée to acquire them). Braggiotti later recalled what followed: "'Oh,' he said, 'you're looking at those horns. Well, in the opening section of *An American in Paris* I would like to get the traffic sound of the place de la Concorde during the rush-hour, and I'd like to see if it works. I've written the first two pages of the opening. Jacques, you take this horn—this is in A flat. Mario, you take this—it's in F sharp. Now, I'll sit down and play, and when I go this way with my head, you go "quack, quack, quack" like that in the rhythm.' So we took the horns, and for the first time we heard the opening bars of *An American in Paris*—a lanky American walking down the Champs-Elysées. He captured the atmosphere, the feeling, the movement, the rhythm so perfectly. Well, when we came to the horn parts, he nodded and we came in. That was the first and last time that I ever played French taxi horns accompanied by such an illustrious composer" (Kimball and Simon 1973, 95).

On 30 May, Gershwin went to a musical party at Samuel Dushkin's house (160 rue de l'Université, 7e). Dushkin played Bach, Horowitz played his *Carmen* transcription, and Dushkin and Gershwin played the latter's *Short Story* and *Blue Interlude*. Gershwin, who was back in New York on 18 June, finished the piano score of *An American in Paris* by August, and the orchestral score on 18 November. The première took place at Carnegie Hall a little more than three weeks later, on 13 December 1928.

Charles Gounod (17 June 1818–18 October 1893)

Gounod was born at 11 place Saint-André-des-Arts, 6e (J14, Métro: Saint-Michel), a house since demolished to make way for the rue Danton. After the death of Gounod's father (an artist) in 1823, the family moved to 20 rue des Grands-Augustins, 6e (J14, Métro: Saint-Michel). In October 1829, Gounod entered the Lycée Saint-Louis, and in the early 1830s, he took private lessons in composition from Reicha. He entered the Conservatoire in 1836, where his teachers included Halévy (counterpoint), Le Sueur (composition), and Zimmermann (piano). By 1839 he was living in a ground-floor apartment at 8 rue de l'Eperon, 6e (K14, Métro: Odéon). This was the year in which he won the Prix de Rome. He left Paris on 5 December 1839. In Rome, he was on excellent terms with Ingres, who was director of the Villa Medici. Gounod met Fanny Mendelssohn, who introduced him to the music of Bach and Beethoven. The music of Palestrina that he heard in the Sistine Chapel made a deep and lasting impression. In 1842, Gounod left Rome for Vienna, where he had two Masses performed, then continued to Berlin and Leipzig, where Felix Mendelssohn played organ music by Bach for him.

On Gounod's return to Paris in May 1843 he moved to the rue Vaneau, 7e, to live with his mother. (Shortly after Gounod's arrival, the young Karl Marx took up residence at 38 rue Vaneau, where he stayed from November 1843 to February 1845). In November 1843 Gounod was appointed organist at the Eglise des Missions étrangères (at the corner of the rue du Bac and the rue de Babylone), where his enthusiasm for Palestrina found little favour with the congregation but where he was to remain for five years. In October 1847, he was granted permission by the archbishop of Paris to attend courses at Saint-Sulpice with a view to becoming a priest, though he was soon to abandon his theological studies. If the reminiscences of Pierre-Auguste Renoir (as reported by Ambroise Vollard) are to be believed, Gounod may have taught music in the early 1850s at a school run by the Frères des Ecoles chrétiennes, where Renoir was a pupil (the young artist was a promising musician). Pauline Viardot, whom Gounod had previously met in Rome, urged him to write an opera, and offered to sing the title role. The result was *Sapho*, first performed at the Opéra (Salle Le Peletier) on 16 April 1851. It was a failure which nevertheless attracted some positive reviews, including one by Berlioz.

In April 1852, Gounod married Anna Zimmermann at a church in Auteuil. She was one of the four daughters of Pierre Zimmermann, Gounod's distinguished piano teacher at the Conservatoire. The same year, Gounod was appointed director of the Orphéon de la Ville de Paris, a large choral society for children and amateurs, which he conducted for the next eight years. On 10 April 1853, Pasdeloup conducted the first performance of the *Méditation sur le 1er prélude de S. Bach*, better known as Gounod's Ave Maria (though the version with this text did not appear until 1859), originally composed as a sophisticated joke, but soon to become a best-seller. Much more significant for Gounod was the first performance of his *Messe solennelle de Sainte-Cécile*, given on St. Cecilia's Day (22 November) 1855 at Saint-Eustache. In 1853 Gounod's father-in-law died, and Gounod inherited the Zimmermann family country house at Montretout in Saint-Cloud, now 3 rue Gounod (SNCF: Saint-Cloud). He was subsequently to spend much of his time here, especially during the summer months.

In October 1857, Berlioz wrote that "poor Gounod has gone mad.

He's now in Dr. Blanche's clinic." Prone throughout his life to bouts of mental instability, Gounod was treated by the famous Dr. Emile Blanche, and lived for a couple of weeks at the clinic in Passy (17 rue d'Ankara, 16e) where Gérard de Nerval had been a patient in 1853–54, and where Guy de Maupassant was to spend the last eighteen months of his life in 1892–93 (figure 1.28). Two years later, *Faust* was given its première at the Théâtre Lyrique on 19 March 1859 and ran for more than fifty performances during its first year. Berlioz and Meyerbeer were among the composers who admired the work from the start. Originally *Faust* had spoken dialogue, but Gounod substituted sung recitatives in 1860 and added a ballet in 1869 so that the work could be performed at the Opéra. Following the first London production in June 1863, Gounod suffered another breakdown and returned to Dr. Blanche's care in Passy. The première of *Mireille* on 19 March the following year (Théâtre Lyrique) was coolly received by the Parisian public.

In 1867, the year in which *Roméo et Juliette* had its very successful première (Théâtre Lyrique, 27 April), Gounod was living in a ground-floor apartment at 17 rue de La Rochefoucauld, 9e (E13, Métro: Trinité), a building in which the composer Halévy had lived in the 1840s, and in which the artists Jean-François Millet and Alexandre

1.28 Dr. Emile Blanche's clinic in the rue d'Ankara, where Charles Gounod, Gérard de Nerval, and Guy de Maupassant all received treatment.

Cabanel had apartments in 1864. The outbreak of the Franco-Prussian War caused Gounod to flee Paris with his family, moving first to Varengeville-sur-Mer (near Dieppe), then to London. His popularity in the English capital was immense, and his admirers were highly placed: *Faust* was said to have been Queen Victoria's favourite opera. In May 1871, Gounod's wife returned to Paris, but by then her errant husband was already pursuing an ill-fated romance with Georgina Weldon, with whom he lived at Tavistock House in Bloomsbury beginning in November 1871. Gounod returned briefly to Paris 1873 for the première of his incidental music to *Jeanne d'Arc* (Théâtre de la Gaîté, 8 November 1873). Martin Cooper has observed (in his *New Grove* article on Gounod) that "the work was a failure, and it is recorded that, with the composer's notorious English mistress sitting three boxes away from his wife, the most popular number was 'Rentrez, Anglais.'" Back in London, Gounod's health was giving increasing cause for concern, and he finally escaped from the clutches of Mrs. Weldon in June 1874 by returning to Paris in the company of Dr. Blanche.

In 1879, Gounod moved to his last Paris address, a handsome second-floor apartment at 20 place Malesherbes (now place du Général-Catroux), 17e (D10, Métro: Malesherbes), which included a magnificent salon organ by Cavaillé-Coll, one of the very few instruments of this kind built by Cavaillé-Coll himself. (It was removed from the building in 1937 to the

1.29 Gounod playing his salon organ at 20 place Malesherbes (*L'Illustration*, 28 October 1893).

Institut des Jeunes Aveugles in Bordeaux but the instrument still survives in something approaching its original state.) This imposing building had been designed by Gounod's brother-in-law. The composer's study in his apartment has been described in detail by James Harding (1973, 204): "Gounod's workroom, high-ceilinged and lit through stained-glass windows, had oak panels and churchlike vaulting. A platform at the end of the room supported an organ. (The bellows were pumped in the basement by a hydraulic machine.) A medallion of Christ's head was prominently fixed to the instrument. The writing table, which contained a movable keyboard to be pulled out when needed, stood directly beneath the window. Scenes from the Passion were carved on a wooden Renaissance mantelpiece embellished with a bronze medallion of Joan of Arc. A Pleyel grand piano filled the centre of the room. One of the walls had book-cases crammed with religious and philosophical works and scores. The rest of the furniture included a pair of divans draped in Persian rugs, small tables and chairs" (figure 1.29).

During his last years, Gounod spent as much time as possible at his country house in Saint-Cloud. With Saint-Saëns, he inaugurated the Cavaillé-Coll organ at the new church on 21 October 1877, and he played here regularly for the rest of his life. Gounod died in Saint-Cloud on 18 October 1893. His state funeral took place at the Madeleine ten days later, with Fauré playing the organ (and improvising on a theme from Gounod's *Rédemption*). Gounod was buried in Auteuil Cemetery.

André Grétry (8 February 1741–24 September 1813)

After spending his early years in Liège and Rome, Grétry arrived in Paris in autumn 1767. For twelve years he lived at a house on the rue Traversière (later rue Molière), 1er, in which Voltaire had also lived. It was here that he composed his first big Parisian success, *Zémire et Azor* (1771). This house was destroyed when the avenue de l'Opéra was opened in 1867. In 1780 Grétry was living in a fourth-floor apartment at 52 rue de Richelieu, 2e (G13, Métro: Quatre-Septembre), and by 1787 he was at 21 rue Poissonnière, 2e (G15, Métro: Bonne-Nouvelle). At this time he had to endure the deaths from tuberculosis of three of his children, and a string of unsuccessful operas. Under the protection of Marie-Antoinette, he was appointed to several official posts, including those of royal censor and director of the queen's private music. His operas *Pierre le Grand* (1790) and *Guillaume Tell* (1791) had some success, but the Revolution had damaging consequences for his livelihood. He was elected to the Institut de France in 1795, however, and he lived to see some of his works successfully revived after 1805. His last address in Paris was probably 4 rue de la Chaussée-d'Antin, 9e (F13, Métro: Opéra). Grétry was buried in Père-Lachaise Cemetery.

Reynaldo Hahn (9 August 1874–28 January 1947)

Hahn, born in Caracas, Venezuela, moved with his family to Paris in 1878. They settled in a luxurious apartment at 6 rue du Cirque, 8e (G10–F10, Métro: Champs-Elysées–Clemenceau), close to the Elysée Palace. There Hahn composed his *Chansons grises*, a group of Verlaine settings, published in 1893 when Hahn was only eighteen years old. The family remained at 6 rue du Cirque until the death of his father in 1897. At this time, the young composer became a close friend of Marcel Proust and of Sarah Bernhardt. Hahn and his mother moved in 1897 to 9 rue Alfred-de-Vigny, 8e (E9, Métro: Courcelles), close to the parc Monceau. At this address, he wrote his first successful theatrical works, including *La Carmélite* (1902). Hahn also began a successful career as a conductor, specialising in Mozart; he conducted *Don Giovanni* at the Salzburg Festival in 1906 with Lilli Lehmann and Maggie Teyte in the cast. Following the death of Hahn's mother in 1912, he saw active service in World War I. Hahn then moved to 7 rue Greffulhe, 8e (F12, Métro: Madeleine), north of the place de la Madeleine, his address for the rest of his life. His most famous operetta, *Ciboulette*, was a triumphant success at its first performance (Théâtre des Variétés, 7 April 1923). In 1925 he wrote the musical comedy *Mozart* in collaboration with Sacha Guitry. In 1933 Hahn became chief music critic for the Paris newspaper *Le Figaro*, and after the harrowing war years, some of which Hahn spent in hiding (he was partly Jewish), he was appointed director of the Opéra in 1945. He died at 7 rue Greffulhe on 28 January 1947, and his funeral was held at the Madeleine on 3 February. Désiré-Emile Inghelbrecht conducted Fauré's Requiem with performers from the Opéra. Hahn was buried in Père-Lachaise Cemetery in the family grave.

Ferdinand Hérold (28 January 1791–19 January 1833)

Hérold was born at 10 rue Hérold (formerly part of the rue d'Argout), 1er (G14, Métro: Palais Royal or Sentier). He entered the Conservatoire in 1806, where his teachers included Kreutzer for violin and Méhul for composition. Hérold won the Prix de Rome in 1812 and after his stay in Rome returned to a post as *maestro di cembalo* at the Théâtre Italien. Though his health was poor (by 1821 he was already suffering from tuberculosis), he was sent by the Théâtre Italien to Italy to look for new talent. He returned with Giuditta Pasta, destined to become one of the greatest singers of her age, and the score of Rossini's *Mosè*. In November 1826, Hérold become principal voice coach at the Opéra. Two years later, his ballet *La fille mal gardée* received its première there (17 November 1828). Hérold's opera *Zampa* was first performed on 3 May 1831, and the following year his last opera, *Le pré aux clercs*, triumphed at its first performance, but by then Hérold was too ill to take a curtain call. At the height of his success, Hérold lived at 3 boulevard des Italiens, 2e (F13, Métro: Richelieu-Drouot). He was buried in Père-Lachaise Cemetery.

Arthur Honegger (10 March 1892–27 November 1955)

Honegger enrolled at the Conservatoire in autumn 1911, commuting, for the first two years, from his hometown of Le Havre. In September 1913 he moved to rue Say (in the 9e), but was mobilised in 1914. On returning to Paris, he settled on 18 October 1916 at 21 rue Duperré, 9e (D13, Métro: Pigalle), an apartment in which Olivier Métra, the prolific composer of waltzes and other salon pieces, had once lived (a fact which amused Honegger greatly). He remained here until the end of November 1931. It was while at this address that Honegger composed the two works which have remained his most popular: *Le roi David* and *Pacific 231*. *Le roi David* had an immense success at its first performance on 13 June 1921. Another notable performance of it took place on 25 August 1923 in the small church at Annecy-le-Vieux, in a concert with Fauré's Requiem. A charming memento of this occasion is a photograph of the aged Fauré and youthful Honegger side by side. Despite the international acclaim which greeted *Le roi David*, Honegger never earned royalties from it: he had sold the work outright to the Lausanne publisher Foetisch for 420 francs.

In November 1931, he moved to 1 square Emmanuel-Chabrier, 17e (D10, Métro: Villiers), where he lived until March 1936. Here he composed much of *Jeanne d'Arc au bûcher* (first performed in 1938). On 7 March 1936 Honegger moved to 71 boulevard de Clichy, 9e (D13, Métro: Blanche), where he lived for the rest of his life, and where he wrote late masterpieces such as the *Symphonie liturgique* (1945–46) and *Une cantate de Noël* (1953). Honegger was buried in Saint-Vincent Cemetery. James Harding has written an evocative description of Honegger's apartment: "His studio in the boulevard de Clichy was stacked with books. Besides all his published scores there were studies of his music and articles about him. Thousands of volumes on psychology, philosophy and literature in general bore witness to his eclecticism. Each was meticulously numbered and arranged.... There were also shelves full of the detective novels he liked to read in bed. He lived with his wife Andrée Vaurabourg and his daughter on the third floor.... Photographs of composers whom his fellow members of the Six would never have allowed into their homes— d'Indy, Fauré, Ravel—decorated the walls. Under a bust of Debussy, another of his renegade preferences, hung an enormous collection of pipes. Honegger was an inveterate smoker. He composed in permanent blue haze" (Harding 1972, 122).

Vincent d'Indy (27 March 1851–2 December 1931)

D'Indy spent his early childhood at 97 rue du Bac, 7e (J11, Métro: Rue du Bac), brought up by his grandmother, Countess Rézia d'Indy, an austere disciplinarian. In 1863, he moved to 7 avenue de Villars, 7e (K10, Métro: Saint-François-Xavier), his Paris address for sixty-eight years, until his death in 1931 (figure 1.19). This was also the building in which Henri Duparc had an apartment for a number of years, and in 1869 the two of them travelled to Munich to hear *Tristan und Isolde* and *Das Rheingold*. During the Franco-Prussian War, d'Indy served in the National Guard, and in 1871 he was one of the earliest members of the Société Nationale. The following year, Duparc encouraged d'Indy to show his music to Franck. The master's verdict was harsh. Having earlier taken private lessons from Lavignac (harmony) and Marmontel (piano), d'Indy enrolled at the Conservatoire to study with Franck. In 1873, on a trip to Germany, he met Liszt in Weimar and saw Wagner at Bayreuth. Three years later he went back for the first performance of the *Ring* cycle. The *Symphonie sur un chant montagnard français* (or *Symphonie cévenole*), perhaps his best-known work, was completed in 1886, and the opera *Fervaal* in 1895. In 1896, d'Indy, with Alexandre Guilmant and Charles Bordes, founded the Schola Cantorum. This remarkable institution flourished under d'Indy's administration after moving to larger premises in 1900 (*see* Schola Cantorum under "Institutions"). D'Indy's teaching methods were exhaustive: the four-volume *Cours de composition musicale* gives some indication of his approach, and the course he taught could last up to seven years. D'Indy was a complex and paradoxical character. He could be seen as an inflexible aristocrat (with an obsessive interest with French military history) whose teaching was oppressively thorough, but those who studied with him included such original minds as Roussel, Satie, and Varèse. D'Indy's admiration for Franck knew no bounds, and his book about his great teacher is an exercise in hagiography. Yet d'Indy had other sides to his personality. Even detractors were sometimes won over by his charm, he was extremely well read, and he was one of the first musicians to rediscover the genius of Monteverdi. He maintained an interest in new music and, surprisingly, admired some aspects of Debussy's music. During World War I his own compositions reached a low point with the Third Symphony (regrettably subtitled "De bello gallico"). Subsequently, he became a savage critic of Ravel, Stravinsky, and Les Six (with the exception of Honegger). Robert Orledge (in his *New Grove* article on d'Indy) has described d'Indy's life as "a strange conflict between reason and feeling, between strict moral Roman Catholicism and the pagan sensuality of nature and legend from which he derived so much of his musical inspiration. As a man he either fascinates or irritates in the extreme, and it is his least attractive qualities that have received the most publicity." D'Indy was buried in Montparnasse Cemetery.

André Jolivet (8 August 1905–20 December 1974)

In 1937, Jolivet was living at 28 rue du Four, 6e (K13, Métro: Mabillon). His last Paris address was at 59 rue de Varenne, 7e (J11, Métro: Varenne), and it was there that he died. His earliest music was influenced by Varèse, with whom Jolivet studied for several years. Jolivet's piano work *Mana* was greatly admired by Messiaen (who wrote a preface to the score, first published in 1946). These two composers, together with Yves Baudrier and Daniel-Lesur, founded the group La jeune France, which gave its inaugural concert on 3 June 1936. As director of music at the Comédie-Française (1943–59), Jolivet composed and conducted a large amount of incidental music. For the concert hall, Jolivet wrote a number of concertos, including works for Ondes Martenot, piano, harp, trumpet, percussion, cello, and violin. He was buried in Montmartre Cemetery.

Charles Koechlin (27 November 1867–31 December 1950)

Koechlin was born in Paris. In 1874 he entered the Ecole Monge, later to become the Lycée Carnot. By 1879, the family were living on the rue Rembrandt, in the 8e. In 1883 Koechlin moved to 14 rue Pierre Charron, 8e (Métro: George V), and began to attend concerts regularly, usually with his older sister Elisabeth. In 1887 he entered the Ecole Polytechnique but, after falling ill with tuberculosis, went to Algeria for a long convalescence. On his return in 1889 he determined to become a composer. He began to attend classes at the Conservatoire the following year and began studying with Massenet in 1892. In 1894 he moved to 1 place d'Iéna, 16e (Métro: Iéna). Koechlin studied fugue with André Gédalge and joined Fauré's class in 1896. Teacher and pupil immediately struck up a friendship. In May 1898 Koechlin orchestrated Fauré's incidental music for *Pelléas et Mélisande* and travelled with him to London for the first performances in June. By 1900, Koechlin was beginning to have his music performed; in April Jane Bathori devoted an evening to his songs. In March 1902, Koechlin moved to 10 avenue des Tilleuls, villa Montmorency, 16e (K3, Métro: Jasmin). There he met Suzanne Pierrard, with whom he played tennis and music. They married in April the following year and had a honeymoon in Italy. The couple moved to a house on the rue de l'Yvette, 16e, in the autumn. In October 1909, Koechlin moved to 30 villa Molitor, 16e (Métro: Chardon-Lagache), his Paris address until 1930. In December 1912, Koechlin orchestrated Debussy's *Khamma* at the request of the composer. The following year Koechlin attended the Paris première of Fauré's *Pénélope* and the first performance of *Le sacre du printemps*. In 1914 he met Milhaud, and the two became friends. During 1917 Koechlin and his family moved from Paris to Valmondois, a village about fifty kilometres north of Paris where La Fontaine had written some of his fables. Here Koechlin rented a house with a large garden which he enjoyed cultivating. On 28 September 1918, Koechlin sailed for New York as part of a delegation to promote French culture, and he was there when he learned of the armistice. He returned on 12 January 1919 and was reunited with his family at Le Canadel. By the end of March he was back in Valmondois, from which he travelled regularly to Paris. In 1922 he gave lessons to Poulenc, Tailleferre, and Sauguet, and the family moved to Méry-sur-Oise. On 27 September 1925, Koechlin returned to his Paris address (30 villa Molitor) and the following year wrote his book on Fauré. In January 1930 he moved to Boulogne-sur-Seine, though he returned to Paris in June the following year (square Henri-Delormel, 14e). Koechlin moved to 26 rue des Boulangers, 5e (Métro: Cardinal-Lemoine), his last Paris address, on 17 July 1934.

Koechlin first became interested in films during 1933, and they soon became a passionate enthusiasm: in 1934 he went to the cinema more than sixty times, and he was a devoted movie-goer for the rest of his life. This was reflected in a series of works from the 1930s which took their inspiration directly from films. In 1933 he composed the *Seven Stars' Symphony*, with movements depicting Douglas Fairbanks, Lilian Harvey, Greta Garbo (her movement featured the Ondes Martenot), Clara Bow, Marlene Dietrich, Emil Jannings, and Charlie Chaplin (first performed in Paris on 14 December 1944, conducted by Manuel Rosenthal). The following year he began a series of pieces for Lilian Harvey, and in 1937 he composed his *Danses pour Ginger* [Rogers] and the charming *Epitaphe de Jean Harlow* for flute, alto saxophone, and piano. *Les eaux vives* was one of several new compositions written for the Fêtes de la Lumière at the 1937 exposition (others were by Honegger, Milhaud, and Messiaen). In 1939 Koechlin composed two of his finest pieces based on Kipling, *Les Bandar-Log* and *La loi de la jungle*, as well as *Vers le soleil*, a set of seven pieces for Ondes Martenot, an instrument which Koechlin used in many of his works. On 19 December 1946 a complete performance was given in Brussels, with Franz André conducting, of Koechlin's music for Kipling's *Jungle Book*, followed by the Paris première under Roger Désormière at the Théâtre des Champs-Elysées on 14 April 1948. Koechlin continued to compose until the end of his life. He died, aged eighty-three, at Le Canadel (in the Var), in the house he had designed himself in 1913, and which was to remain a favourite retreat for the rest of his life.

Charles Lamoureux (28 September 1834–21 December 1899)

One of the most important French conductors at the end of the nineteenth century, Lamoureux had several addresses in Paris, including 7 avenue Frochot, 9e (D13, Métro: Pigalle), and 64 rue Saint-Lazare, 9e (E13, Métro: Trinité). Born in Bordeaux, he studied the violin at the Paris Conservatoire. In 1860 he founded the Séances Populaires de Musique de Chambre, initially with Edouard Colonne as second violin. The programmes included, in addition to established classics, some of the earliest French performances of chamber music by Brahms (including, in 1869–70, one of the piano quartets, the String Sextet op. 18, and the Piano Quintet). From the early 1870s Lamoureux began to organise and conduct orchestral concerts. In 1881 the Société des Nouveaux Concerts (the Concerts Lamoureux) initiated a weekly series, and Lamoureux began his tireless and often controversial advocacy of Wagner, which culminated in a complete performance of *Tristan und Isolde* on 28 October 1899, less than two months before the conductor's death. He was buried in Montmartre Cemetery.

Guillaume Lekeu (20 January 1870–21 January 1894)

Lekeu moved to Paris with his family in June 1888 and lived at 83 rue d'Assas, 6e (L13, Métro: Notre-Dame-des-Champs). In September 1889 he was introduced to César Franck and took twenty lessons in all (at the master's nearby apartment in boulevard Saint-Michel) between autumn 1889 and Franck's death in November 1890. Lekeu was devastated by Franck's death but continued his studies with d'Indy. In 1892 he completed his most famous work, the Violin Sonata, commissioned by Ysaÿe. Following his family's move to Angers, Lekeu was staying with them (at 19 rue Lenepveu) when he contracted typhoid fever, from which he died the day after his twenty-fourth birthday.

Franz Liszt (22 October 1811–31 July 1886)

After Liszt and his family arrived in Paris on 11 December 1823, they lodged at the Hôtel d'Angleterre, 10 rue du Mail, 2e (G14, Métro: Sentier), opposite the premises of the Erard piano firm (figure 1.30). The purpose of the visit was to enrol Liszt as a pupil at the Conservatoire, but

1.30 The building at 13 rue du Mail, where the Erard piano firm had its premises. Liszt stayed at the hotel opposite on his first visit to Paris. In 1878 he stayed with Madame Camille Erard at no. 13.

1.31 The rue de Montholon, where Liszt lived in the late 1820s and early 1830s.

when Liszt and his father presented themselves to the director, Cherubini, he informed them that it was only possible for French nationals to study there. Instead, Liszt took private lessons from Ferdinando Paer. He gave his first public concert in Paris at the Théâtre Italien on 7 March 1824, an occasion greeted with wonderment by one critic: "I am convinced that the soul and spirit of Mozart have passed into the body of young Liszt.... His little arms can scarcely stretch to both ends of the keyboard, his little feet scarcely reach the pedals, and yet this child is beyond compare; he is the finest pianist in Europe." In August 1825, Liszt moved a few yards east, to the Hôtel de Strasbourg, at 22 rue Neuve-Saint-Eustache (now part of the rue Aboukir), 2e (G14, Métro: Sentier). His opera *Don Sanche* was performed on 17 October 1825 at the Opéra with Adolphe Nourrit in the title role and Rodolphe Kreutzer conducting. Towards the end of 1826, Liszt began to take composition lessons from Anton Reicha, whose pupils also included Berlioz, Gounod, and Franck. Liszt later recalled that "studies in counterpoint and fugue with Reicha took up all my time during 1827 and 1828." His father Adam died at Boulogne of typhoid fever on 28 August 1827. In October, Liszt and his mother moved to 38 rue Coquenard (renamed rue Lamartine in 1848), 9e (E14, Métro: Cadet), then to 7 rue de Montholon (figure 1.31), 9e (F14–F15, Métro: Cadet or Poissonnière); the nearby church of Saint-Vincent-de-Paul now stands in place Franz-Liszt. He also began to give private piano lessons. For much of the time, Liszt remained in seclusion, giving few concerts and seldom venturing out of the house. The press, hearing rumours about his mental collapse, leapt to its own conclusions:

on 23 October 1828 *Le Corsaire* published an entirely fictitious obituary notice with the headline "Death of the Young Liszt." From the late 1820s onwards, Liszt met a number of important writers—Balzac, de Musset, Gautier, Hugo, Dumas père, and Heine—and the artist Delacroix.

On 4 December 1830 (the day before the première of the *Symphonie fantastique*), Liszt visited Berlioz, and the two became friends, though Berlioz always remained ambivalent about Liszt's music. Other composers whom he met in the early 1830s were Meyerbeer, Alkan, Mendelssohn, Chopin, and Paganini. By January 1832, Liszt was living at 61 rue de Provence, 9e (F13, Métro: Chaussée-d'Antin), and much of his limited concert activity consisted of accompanying eminent performers such as Maria Malibran and playing at private occasions such as a soirée at the Austrian Embassy, where his fellow performers included Rossini, Chopin, Giulia Grisi, Rubini, and Tamburini. In 1833 he returned to giving public concerts, including the Bach Triple Concerto with Herz and Chopin (3 April). It was also in 1833 that he first met Marie d'Agoult, the love of his life, with whom he spent the next decade. In 1834 Liszt gave concerts with Hiller, Chopin, and Berlioz, and he continued to meet Marie d'Agoult in secret. In June 1835, he eloped to Switzerland with the pregnant Marie and after a time settled in Geneva. They returned on 16 October 1836 and lived at the Hôtel de France, 23 rue Laffitte, 9e (F13, Métro: Le Peletier). In the salon that they shared with George Sand, Chopin and Sand met for the first time: Liszt introduced them. The building, in which two of the most celebrated musical love-affairs of the nineteenth century were pursued, is now demolished. In spring 1837, Liszt gave a concert with Thalberg, played some of Chopin's Etudes op. 25 (unpublished at the time), and shared a concert with Alkan and the fourteen-year-old César Franck. In May Liszt and Marie d'Agoult stayed with George Sand at Nohant on their way to Italy. The couple settled in Como, and their daughter Cosima (later to become Hans von Bülow's, then Wagner's, wife) was born there on 24 December 1837.

For the next decade, Liszt roamed Europe as a virtuoso pianist. In April 1840 he came to Paris to see Marie d'Agoult and his children and gave a successful concert at the Salle Erard on 20 April. It was not a long stay: on 6 May 1840 he crossed the Channel for a visit to London which included a performance on 25 May at Buckingham Palace for Queen Victoria's twenty-first birthday. Marie d'Agoult and the children moved in about 1840 to 10 rue des Mathurins, 9e (Métro: Saint-Augustin). Back in

1.32 *Galop chromatique*, anonymous watercolour dated 18 April 1843, depicting a concert at the Conservatoire. It shows Liszt at the piano with Habeneck conducting and the singer Luigi Lablache.

the city from March 1841 to early May, Liszt played, among other concerts, Beethoven's *Emperor* Concerto, conducted by Berlioz (25 April). Wagner was in the audience. The next day, 26 April, Liszt attended a concert given by Chopin at the Salle Pleyel and reviewed it. His next Paris appearance was a short visit in June 1842: a charity concert in Neuilly and a recital at the Salon Obrist Thorn.

Two sensational concerts at the Théâtre Italien on 16 and 25 April 1844 were followed by others: on 4 May Liszt played the Weber *Konzertstück* (conducted by Berlioz), and he appeared again on 11 May and 28 May. On 15 June he played in Versailles, but he was back in Paris by 23 June to play at the Conservatoire (figure 1.32). This was to be his last public appearance in Paris as a pianist. The 1844 visit also had a darker side: after several lonely years in Paris, Marie d'Agoult decided that the time had come to break with Liszt. It was a stormy time, and Liszt was given custody of their three children, whom he wisely placed in the care of his mother, Anna. By the end of June 1844 he was back on tour.

In October 1845 Liszt returned for a holiday with his mother and children, and on 13 January 1846, he was the pianist in a private performance of his *Festival Cantata in Honour of Beethoven*, at the home of his friend Jules Janin (30 rue de Vaugirard, 6e). In 1846, the *Revue Indépendante* published Marie d'Agoult's *Nélida*, a bitter satire on her relationship with Liszt, and their letters descended into quarrelsome accusation and recrimination. In 1848 Liszt settled in Weimar.

Liszt visited Paris in April 1861, staying at 31 rue Saint-Guillaume, 7e (J12, Métro: Rue du Bac), at the home of his daughter Blandine, her husband Emile Ollivier (a distinguished politician), and Liszt's mother (Blandine died at the age of twenty-six on 9 September 1862, following the birth of her son Daniel). Liszt renewed his friendships with Berlioz, Pauline Viardot, Rossini, Gounod, and Halévy, at whose house he heard and admired Bizet's piano playing. He also went to dine with the emperor Napoléon III at the Tuileries palace and was raised to the rank of commander of the Légion d'Honneur. On 26 May Wagner arrived in Paris and saw Liszt, their first meeting since 1856. Before his departure for Brussels on 8 June, Liszt saw Marie d'Agoult for the first time since 1840. According to her diaries, the meetings were awkward, but there was still a bond of affection between them. After they had said their farewells on 8 June, she wrote: "Ineffable charm! It is still he, and he alone, who makes me feel the divine mystery of life. With his departure I feel the emptiness around me and I shed tears."

In early October 1864, Liszt was in Paris with Cosima for a reunion with his mother. He saw Marie d'Agoult at a dinner on 6 October, and the two met again on 12 October, before Liszt's departure with Cosima to visit Blandine's grave at Saint-Tropez.

On 6 February 1866 Liszt's mother died in Paris at Emile Ollivier's house, and on 4 March Liszt arrived to stay with his son-in-law. On 8 March he played at the salon of Princess Pauline Metternich to an audience of about fifteen people. In addition to solos, he performed two movements from the "Gran" Mass in a piano duet arrangement, with

Saint-Saëns as his partner. On 15 March, Liszt conducted a performance of "Gran" Mass at Saint-Eustache (reviewed unfavourably by his old friend Berlioz). Liszt went to hear César Franck playing at Sainte-Clotilde and, according to d'Indy, was "lost in amazement and evoking the name of J. S. Bach in an inevitable comparison." On 5 May he appeared at one of Rossini's private concerts, playing his arrangements for two pianos of *Les préludes* and *Tasso* with Francis Planté, and on 11 May Liszt and Saint-Saëns performed the "Dante" Symphony on two pianos in a soirée at the home of the artist Gustave Doré. Liszt also had a long meeting with Gounod. On 22 May 1866, he returned to Rome.

Marie d'Agoult died in Paris on 5 March 1876 (she was buried in Père-Lachaise Cemetery). Liszt visited Paris 9–18 June 1878, as the Hungarian member of an international jury adjudicating musical instruments at the Exposition universelle. At the first meeting Eduard Hanslick (representing Austria) proposed Liszt as honorary president, and he was elected by acclamation. During this visit, Liszt stayed with Mme Camille Erard at 13 rue du Mail, 2e (G14, Métro: Sentier).

Liszt made two more visits to Paris in the final months of his life. On the first, from 20 March to 3 April 1886, he stayed at the Hôtel de Calais, 5 rue des Capucines, 1er (G12, Métro: Madeleine). He attended two performances of the "Gran" Mass conducted by Edouard Colonne at Saint-Eustache on 25 March and 2 April, and a dinner was held in Liszt's honour at the Hostellerie du Lyon d'Or on 31 March at which Saint-Saëns and Louis Diémer played *Les préludes* on two pianos; the evening ended with an "Epilogue au piano" performed by Liszt himself. It was during this stay that Nadar took his celebrated portrait photographs of the composer. After a visit to England and a week in Antwerp, Liszt returned near the end of April as the guest of his friends Mihály and Cécile von Munkácsy at 53 avenue de Villiers, 17e (D9, Métro: Malesherbes). Liszt went with Gounod to the performance of *Saint Elisabeth* at the Trocadéro on 8 May and he heard a private performance of Saint-Saëns's *Le carnaval des animaux* at Pauline Viardot's house (50 rue de Douai). A few days later he caught a heavy cold and was confined to bed for his last four days in the city. He returned to Weimar on 17 May, where he spent the last few weeks of his life.

Jean-Baptiste Lully (28 November 1632–22 March 1687)

Born in Florence, Lully arrived in Paris in 1646. By 1652 he had attracted the attention of Louis XIV, and on 23 February 1653, Lully danced in the same ballet as the young king. From this time, he was responsible for the instrumental music in court ballets, and by 1656 he was conductor of the "Petits Violons." When he was given French citizenship in 1661, he changed his name from Lulli to Lully (and taking the opportunity to invent an aristocratic lineage, styled himself Jean-Baptiste de Lully). In July 1662 he was appointed master of music to the royal family and married Madeleine Lambert at Saint-Eustache. Louis XIV was among the witnesses (later he had to rebuke Lully for overtly homosexual behaviour at court). In 1664 Lully began to write music for Molière's plays. This uneasy partnership, which Lully used shamelessly to his own advantage, lasted until 1670, when *Le bourgeois gentilhomme* was first performed at Chambord. In 1672, Lully purchased the royal privilege for the performance of opera, which granted him the right to establish the Académie Royale de Musique, the company which became known as the Opéra. This privilege gave Lully the power to veto any other performances of entirely sung stage works. He reduced to two the number of singers allowed to appear in any production not put on by the Opéra (and reduced the allowable size of the orchestra to six players), thus ensuring a near stranglehold on the production of opera. Following Molière's death, Lully was able to move the Opéra from a converted tennis court to the theatre in the Palais Royal. Lully's megalomania made him a number of committed enemies (including La Fontaine, who described him as "lewd and evil-minded"). Such was his desire for control of the French lyric stage, that he went so far as to ban (in 1677) the use of music in puppet theatres. In 1681, Lully purchased (and delighted in using) the title *secrétaire du roi*, with the full approval of the king.

At the height of his fame, Lully was immensely wealthy. He owned four houses near the Palais Royal: 10 rue des Moulins, 1er (G13, Métro: Pyramides); 43 rue Sainte-Anne, 1er (G13, Métro: Pyramides); the Hôtel Lully at 45 rue des Petits-Champs and 47 rue Sainte-Anne, 1er (G13, Métro: Pyramides), built for Lully by Daniel Gittard in 1671, thanks in part to a generous loan from Molière; and the house next door, at 47 rue des Petits-Champs, completed in 1682. He let this last property to tenants at an annual rent of sixteen hundred livres.

In 1683, Lully moved to a mansion surrounded by gardens, on the site of 28 rue Boissy-d'Anglas, 8e (G11, Métro: Madeleine). He died there from blood poisoning, caused by striking his foot with the pointed cane which he used for beating time. Lully was buried in the church of the Petits-Pères, now Notre-Dame-des-Victoires.

Bohuslav Martinů (8 December 1890–28 August 1959)

Martinů arrived in Paris in October 1923. He soon sought out Albert Roussel, who became not only Martinů's teacher but also a warmly supportive friend. After brief stays in hotels, Martinů stayed in the homes of friends, including Jan Masaryk's apartment on the rue Jasmin, before settling at 11a rue Delambre, 14e (M12, Métro: Vavin). He was living here in 1926 when he first met, and fell in love with, Charlotte Quennehen. Here he composed two early operas, *The Soldier and the Dancer* and his "film-opera" *The Three Wishes*, as well as *La bagarre*, the orchestral work with which Koussevitzky successfully introduced his music to America (the première was in Boston on 18 November 1927). In spring 1929, he moved with Charlotte to 12 rue Mandar, 2e (G14, Métro: Sentier), near les Halles, where they remained for almost four years. On 21 March 1931, the couple were married in Paris. The following year Martinů won the Elizabeth Sprague Coolidge Prize for his String Sextet, and he was able buy a Pleyel piano with the thousand dollars in prize money. A private performance of the sextet was given for Mrs. Coolidge at the Hôtel Majestic (19 avenue Kléber, 16e); the enthusiastic Roussel was in the audience. In about 1933 the Martinůs moved to the rue de Vanves, then to avenue du Parc Montsouris, about which Charlotte recalls the trials of living in a seventh-floor apartment with no elevator. In about 1938, they moved again, to 24 rue des Marronniers, 16e (J5, Métro: La Muette). Several of Martinů's most important works figure among the music from his later Paris years, notably *Julietta* (composed between May 1936 and January 1937). On 10 June 1940 the Martinůs fled occupied Paris. Charles Münch helped them find sanctuary in Rançon. Once American visas had been arranged, Paul Sacher paid for the sea crossing, and the couple sailed from Lisbon for New York at the end of March 1941. After twelve years in America, Martinů and his wife returned to Paris in May 1953, staying at an apartment in the avenue Mozart, in the 16e, which the publisher Pierre Heugel found for them. In September 1953 they settled in Nice and, a few years later, in Switzerland.

Jules Massenet (12 May 1842–13 August 1912)

Though not born in Paris, Massenet was living in the city by the time of the February uprising in 1848. At that time the Massenet family resided on the rue de Beaune, 7e (H12–J12, Métro: Rue du Bac). The house number is unknown, but it may have been no. 1. Massenet began his studies at the Conservatoire in autumn 1852. During the year 1855–56, he lived with his elder sister Julie and her husband, the painter Pierre-Paul Cavaillé, in their apartment on the corner of the rue Condorcet and the rue de Rochechouart, 9e (E14, Métro: Cadet). From summer 1856 until autumn 1857, Massenet lived at Chambéry, and he returned to Paris for the start of the new academic year at the Conservatoire in autumn 1857. In 1858 he gave a concert in Tournai, started to take a few private piano pupils, and worked as a timpanist at the Théâtre Lyrique. At the Conservatoire, he won a first prize for piano in July 1859. He moved to a place of his own by autumn 1861, the attic of 5 rue Ménilmontant (renamed rue Oberkampf in 1864), 11e (H17, Métro: Filles-du-Calvaire). At the Conservatoire, he joined Ambroise Thomas's composition class. After two earlier unsuccessful attempts, Massenet won the Prix de Rome in August 1863 and left for the Villa Medici in Rome on 26 December. He remained there until December 1865.

Back in Paris, Massenet found an apartment at 14 rue Taitbout, 9e (F13, Métro: Chaussée-d'Antin), and he spent a good deal of time at the family home of Louise Constance de Gressy (also known as Ninon), nearby at 51 rue Laffitte, 9e (F13, Métro: Le Peletier). The couple were married on 8 October 1866, and, after a short honeymoon, they settled in the apartment at 51 rue Laffitte. Massenet was now beginning to make his way as a composer, having written a one-act opera for the Opéra-Comique entitled *La grand' tante*, and his First Suite for orchestra, performed by Pasdeloup on 24 March 1867. The events of the Franco-Prussian War, the siege of Paris, and the seventy-two days of the Commune affected Massenet in much the same way as it did many of his colleagues. He joined the National Guard and later recalled 1870 as "a dismal date for my poor country—the Prussian cannons, answering those of Mont Valérien, often lugubriously punctuated the fragments that I tried to write down during the short moments of rest that guard duty, marching around Paris, and military exercises on the ramparts, left us" (Irvine 1994, 58). Like many others, Massenet fled Paris during the Commune, to live at Bayonne, near Biarritz. By December 1871, Massenet and his wife were living at 38 rue Malesherbes. In 1879 this road was renamed rue du Général-Foy, and the house was renumbered in 1892 as 46 rue du Général-Foy, 8e (E10, Métro: Villiers). The confusion of renaming and renumbering notwithstanding, this remained Massenet's Paris address for more than thirty years, from 1871 until autumn 1903. Here he composed his oratorio *Marie-Magdeleine* (first performed on Good Friday 1873, with Pauline Viardot as Méryem and Edouard Colonne as conductor), and *Le roi de Lahore*, the first of his works to be performed at the Opéra, on 22 April 1877. The following year he was appointed professor of composition at the Conservatoire, and on 30 November 1878 he was elected a member of the Académie des Beaux-Arts at the Institut de France, in a closely fought battle with Saint-Saëns. Massenet composed all his most famous operas while living at 46 rue du Général-Foy, among them *Manon* (Opéra-Comique, 19 January 1884), *Le Cid* (Opéra, 30 November 1885), *Esclarmonde* (Opéra-Comique, 15 May 1889), *Werther* (Vienna Hofoper, 16 February 1892, also given at the Opéra-Comique the following year), *Thaïs* (Opéra, 16 March 1894), and *Cendrillon* (Opéra-Comique, 24 May 1899). In 1899 Massenet bought a large country house at Egreville (Seine-et-Marne), soon known as the Château Massenet, and the address to which Massenet and his wife would move in the summer months. In November 1903, the couple changed their Paris residence, to an apartment overlooking the Jardin du Luxembourg at 48 rue de Vaugirard, 6e (K13, Métro: Odéon). Here Massenet worked on his last operas, including *Chérubin* (Monte Carlo, 14 February 1905) and *Don Quichotte* (Monte Carlo, 19 February 1910). Massenet died in his apartment on the rue de Vaugirard on 13 August 1912. Four days later he was buried in the little churchyard of Saint-Martin, Egreville, in a small ceremony attended by a few friends, including his former pupils Reynaldo Hahn and Gustave Charpentier, his widow, and his only daughter, Juliette. She lived until 1935, while the redoubtable Mme Massenet died in 1938, in her ninety-seventh year.

Felix Mendelssohn (3 February 1809–4 November 1847)

As part of an extended tour of Europe, Mendelssohn spent November 1831 to April 1832 in Paris. During these months he stayed at 5 rue Le Peletier, 9e (F13, Métro: Richelieu-Drouot), just opposite the old Opéra. He saw Meyerbeer's *Robert le Diable* there and found it exaggerated and vulgar. Among the composer-pianists that Mendelssohn met were Chopin (whose Paris debut he attended on 26 February 1832) and Kalkbrenner. Some aspects of Parisian musical life astonished Mendelssohn, not least the performance of the Scherzo from his Octet given as part of a Mass in memory of Beethoven at Saint-Vincent-de-Paul on 26 March 1832: "A Requiem during which they played the Scherzo! No, it's impossible to imagine anything more outrageous than to have the priest at the altar and my Scherzo cheering up the vaults of the church" (Bailbé 1987, 33). There were at least three other performances of the Octet given during Mendelssohn's visit, including one at Pierre Baillot's class in the Conservatoire, which drew the warmest praise from its young composer. Baillot also included one of Mendelssohn's string quartets in his chamber concerts. Among Mendelssohn's orchestral music, the overture to *A Midsummer Night's Dream* was coolly received by French critics and described in the *Revue Musicale* (25 February 1832) as "monotonous and lacking in life." But his appearances as a pianist were generally greeted with more enthusiasm: he performed Beethoven's Fourth Piano Concerto in March 1832 when his playing delighted the critic of the *Revue Musicale* (24 March 1832): "Mendelssohn showed such delicacy of talent, refinement of execution, and a dignified sensibility which deserves the highest praise" (34).

André Messager (30 December 1853–24 February 1929)

Messager came to Paris in 1869 from his home town of Montluçon (Allier) to study at the Ecole Niedermeyer. Among his teachers were Saint-Saëns and Fauré, both of whom were to remain friends. In 1877 Messager moved into an apartment, which he shared with Fauré, at 13 rue Mosnier (now rue de Berne), 8e (E11, Métro: Europe or Rome). He had several appointments as an organist, including a spell as Widor's assistant at Saint-Sulpice in 1874, organist of Saint-Paul–Saint-Louis in 1881, and maître de chapelle at Sainte-Marie-des-Batignolles in 1882–84. In 1886 his ballet *Les deux pigeons* was produced at the Opéra, and in 1898 the Bouffes-Parisiens produced what has remained his most famous stage work, the operetta *Véronique*. He was also active as a conductor. By 1902, he was living at 174 boulevard Malesherbes, 17e (D9, Métro: Wagram). This was the year in which he conducted the première of Debussy's *Pelléas et Mélisande* (Opéra-Comique, 30 April 1902), and moved to 6 avenue Matignon, 8e (G10, Métro: Franklin D. Roosevelt). Among Messager's other Paris addresses were 157 boulevard Haussmann, 8e (F9, Métro: Saint-Philippe-du-Roule), and 103 rue Jouffroy-d'Abbans, 17e (D8–D9, Métro: Courcelles). Messager was buried in Passy Cemetery.

Olivier Messiaen (10 December 1908–28 April 1992)

Messiaen's father was appointed to a post at the Lycée Charlemagne in 1919 and the family moved from Nantes that year to 65 rue Rambuteau, 4e (H15, Métro: Rambuteau). This was Messiaen's home as a student and the place where he wrote some of his first published works, such as the *Diptyque*, *Trois mélodies*, and *La mort du nombre* (others were written at an aunt's country house in Fuligny-par-Ville-sur-Terre, in the Aube). He was still living at 65 rue Rambuteau during his final years at the Conservatoire (during which he made two unsuccessful attempts at the Prix de Rome in 1930 and 1931), and at the time of his appointment as titulaire at the Trinité in September 1931, a post he secured thanks to the active support of his

1.33 Messiaen had an apartment here at 77 rue des Plantes, from 1932 to 1938.

1.34 Messiaen's last Paris address at 230 rue Marcadet.

teacher Marcel Dupré and of Charles Tournemire. Following his marriage to Claire Delbos on 22 June 1932, Messiaen moved by the end of the year to 77 rue des Plantes (figure 1.33), 14e (P11–R11, Métro: Alésia), on a corner of place de la Porte de Chatillon. Here he composed part of *L'Ascension*, the motet *O sacrum convivium!* and the orchestral version of the *Poèmes pour Mi* (other works were composed during summer holidays at Petichet in the Isère, and at Grenoble).

His son Pascal was born on 14 July 1937, and Messiaen moved early in 1938 to 13 villa du Danube, 19e (D21, Métro: Danube). Following military service, imprisonment in Silesia (where he composed the *Quatuor pour la fin du Temps*), and demobilisation, he returned to occupied Paris in 1941. Here he wrote several of his most important works, among them *Visions de l'Amen* (1943), *Trois petites liturgies de la Présence Divine* (1943–44), *Vingt regards sur l'Enfant-Jésus* (1944), and, later, the *Turangalîla-Symphonie* (1946–48). The aftereffects of an operation left his wife incapacitated (she died in 1959), and Messiaen brought up their son single-handedly at 13 villa du Danube. He took on increasingly important teaching positions at the Conservatoire, as well as working at the Trinité and composing. In 1962 Messiaen married the pianist Yvonne Loriod (who was also the dedicatee of most of his piano works from *Visions de l'Amen* onwards). From 1962 on, they lived at 230 rue Marcadet (figure 1.34), 18e (B12, Métro: Guy Môquet), Messiaen's Paris home for the rest of his life, and the address at which he spent many years completing his opera *Saint François d'Assise*, first performed at the Opéra on 28 November 1983. Messiaen was buried at Petichet (Isère), overlooking the Lac de Laffrey and the mountain of Grand Serre.

Giacomo Meyerbeer (5 September 1791–2 May 1864)

Meyerbeer spent many years in Paris, the city where he had several of his greatest operatic triumphs. Among the works first performed in Paris were *Robert le Diable* (21 November 1831), *Les Huguenots* (29 February 1836), *Le prophète* (16 April 1849), and *L'étoile du Nord* (16 February 1854), all with librettos by Eugène Scribe. The house in which Meyerbeer died was at 2 rond-point des Champs-Elysées, 8e (G10, Métro: Franklin D. Roosevelt). At the time of his death, he had been at work on revisions to *L'Africaine*, which was in rehearsal at the Opéra. The work was finished by François-Joseph Fétis and given its première on 28 April 1865 before an audience that included the emperor and empress: an appropriately spectacular posthumous tribute to the composer.

Darius Milhaud (4 September 1892–22 June 1974)

Milhaud first came to Paris from Aix-en-Provence in 1909 and took an apartment at 2 boulevard des Italiens, 9e (F13, Métro: Richelieu-Drouot). In 1912 he moved to 5 rue Gaillard, now rue Paul-Escudier (figure 1.35), 9e (E12, Métro: Blanche), within easy reach of the Conservatoire (newly relocated on the rue de Madrid), where his teachers included Dukas and Widor. This was Milhaud's Paris address for more than a decade (though he spent 1916–18 as Paul Claudel's secretary in Brazil), and it was here that he composed his earliest successes, notably *L'homme et son désir* (1918), *Le boeuf sur le toit* (1919), *Saudades do Brasil* (1920–21), and *La création du monde* (1923). He moved in the mid-1920s to 10 boulevard de Clichy, 9e (D13, Métro: Pigalle), which was to remain his Paris address for the rest of his life (figure 1.36). While living there, Milhaud composed his grandest and most ambitious opera, *Christophe Colomb* (1928), written in collaboration with Paul Claudel, as well as the highly original trilogy of chamber operas ("Opéras-minutes," each lasting only a few minutes, composed in 1927) and his celebrated two-piano piece *Scaramouche*

1.35 Milhaud in his apartment at 5 rue Gaillard (now rue Paul Escudier) in 1920.

1.36 Milhaud's apartment at 10 boulevard de Clichy.

(1937). As a Jew, Milhaud was forced to flee Paris before World War II, during which he taught at Mills College in Oakland, California. One performance of *Scaramouche* known to have taken place in occupied Paris was given at the Ecole Normale de Musique on 1 June 1943. On this occasion the performers outwitted the authorities by listing both the work and its composer as anagrams in the programme: "Mous-Arechac" by the

Egyptian-sounding "Hamid-al-Usurid." On returning to Paris, Milhaud became professor of composition at the Conservatoire in 1947 and combined this post with teaching appointments in America. Despite serious illness throughout his life, Milhaud was an astonishingly prolific composer: his last work is designated op. 441.

Wolfgang Amadeus Mozart (27 January 1756–5 December 1791)

Mozart, with his parents and sister, arrived in Paris for the first time on the afternoon of 18 November 1763. They lived throughout the winter in the Hôtel Beauvais (figure 1.37), rue Saint-Antoine, now 68 rue François-Miron, 4e (J16, Métro: Saint-Paul). During this stay Mozart wrote his first keyboard sonatas and early in 1764 his first printed works (the Sonatas K6 and K7) were published in Paris. The title page of his *Sonates pour le clavecin... oeuvre première* describes the composer as "J. G. Wolfgang Mozart de Salzbourg, agé de sept ans." It was during this visit that Carmontelle (pseudonym for Louis Carrogis) drew his famous portrait of Mozart, Nannerl, and their father, in several different versions (there are examples in the Musée Carnavalet, the British Museum, and Castle Howard). In mid-April 1764, the Mozarts left for London, where they lived for more than a year. After a few months in Holland, the family returned to Paris on 10 May 1766 and stayed until 9 July. They stayed at

1.37 The Hôtel de Beauvais, now 68 rue François-Miron, where Mozart stayed in 1763–64. Engraving by Marot (1619–79).

the house of a M. Bire, on the rue Traversière (now 8 rue Molière), 1er (G13, Métro: Pyramides). On this occasion the prolific Carmontelle produced a drawing of Wolfgang and Leopold alone.

Mozart next visited Paris on 23 March 1778, accompanied by his mother. They stayed on the rue du Bourg-l'Abbé, 3e (H15, Métro: Etienne-Marcel), and at the Hôtel des Quatre Fils Aymon (now 10 rue du Sentier), 2e (G14, Métro: Sentier). Joseph Legros, director of the Concert Spirituel, commissioned the "Paris" Symphony (K297/300a). It was first performed at the Salle des Suisses in the Tuileries on 18 June 1778. Other works composed during this stay were the ballet *Les petits riens*, first performed at the Opéra on 11 June 1778, and the Concerto for Flute and Harp, written for the flute-playing duc de Guines and his daughter.

On 3 July 1778, tragedy struck: Maria Anna, Mozart's mother, died at the age of fifty-seven. Her funeral took place at Saint-Eustache the following day (according to the parish registers), and the occasion is commemorated by a plaque in the south aisle. She was buried at one of the cemeteries in the parish, probably that of the Saints-Innocents, on the site of les Halles. By 9 July 1778, Mozart had left his apartment on the rue du Sentier and wrote to his father that he was staying with Mme d'Epinay and Baron von Grimm in "a pretty little room with a very pleasant view" (Anderson 1938, vol. 2, 831) at 5 rue de la Chaussée-d'Antin, now between the rue Halévy and the rue Meyerbeer, 9e (F13, Métro: Opéra). As an adult, Mozart did not enjoy the success (or find the commissions) he had hoped for in Paris, and he left the city at the end of September 1778, never to return. The Hôtel Beauvais is the only one of Mozart's Parisian addresses still standing.

Jacques Offenbach (20 June 1819–5 October 1880)

Offenbach arrived in Paris from his hometown of Cologne in November 1833, and his earliest address (the lodgings he shared with his brother) was at 23 rue des Martyrs, 9e (Métro: Notre-Dame-de-Lorette). He had come to study at the Conservatoire and later made a considerable name for himself as a cello virtuoso. At the time of his marriage in 1844, Offenbach moved to a small apartment in the passage Saulnier (now rue Saulnier), 9e (E14, Métro: Cadet). In 1855 he began the hugely successful series of productions at the Théâtre des Bouffes-Parisiens, and in 1858

Offenbach and his family moved to a spacious apartment on the fourth floor of 11 rue Laffitte, 9e (F13, Métro: Richelieu-Drouot), his Paris home for almost twenty years. Here Offenbach held regular social gatherings on Friday evenings. Bizet and Delibes, the photographer Nadar, and the artists Degas, Detaille, Doré, and Renoir numbered among the guests. It was here that Offenbach finished *Orphée aux enfers* in autumn 1858. The triumphantly successful première took place at the Bouffes-Parisiens on 21 October 1858, with sets by Doré. By May 1859 it had reached its 150th performance. Later that year when Louis-Napoléon's troops returned victorious from the Battle of Magenta, the soldiers marched to tunes from the opera, and the following year, Offenbach was granted French naturalisation (to celebrate the occasion, the emperor ordered a special performance of *Orphée* at the Opéra-Comique).

In 1859 Offenbach poked fun at one of the heroines of French history in *Geneviève de Brabant*, and in February 1860 produced a Wagner parody *Le musicien de l'avenir* as part of a Carnival season revue (characteristically, Wagner never forgave Offenbach). Later that year, Offenbach composed his only full-length ballet, *Le papillon*, choreographed by Marie Taglioni, one of the greatest ballerinas of the age, by then in retirement. She wished to create a ballet at the Opéra for the young dancer Emma Livry, whom Taglioni thought of as her successor. This delightful ballet was given its première on 26 November 1860, running for forty-two performances, but its success was to be eclipsed by tragedy: in 1862, during the dress-rehearsal for a new production of *La muette de Portici* (one of the few operas in which the title role is not sung), Livry danced too close to a gas lamp and her dress caught fire. Engulfed in flames, she suffered terrible burns from which she died eight months later.

In 1864, Offenbach had his next big operatic success with *La belle Hélène*, the first of his great collaborations with Henri Meilhac and Ludovic Halévy. As usual, he worked at breakneck speed to get the score finished in time. Halévy later recalled Offenbach composing *La belle Hélène*, "orchestrating at the little desk in his study on the rue Laffitte. He wrote, wrote, wrote—with what speed!—then, from time to time, in search of a harmony, he would strike a few chords on the piano with his left hand while his right hand still flew writing across the paper. His children came and went around him, shouting, playing, laughing, singing. Friends and collaborators arrived.... Entirely at ease, Offenbach chatted, talked, joked . . . and his right hand travelled on and on and on" (Harding 1980, 150). The première was on 17 December 1864, at the Théâtre des Variétés, with Hortense Schneider in the title role. More success followed in 1866 with *Barbe-Bleue* and *La vie parisienne*. The Exposition universelle in 1867 brought a huge influx of visitors to Paris, and Offenbach produced *La Grande-Duchesse de Gérolstein*, again with Hortense Schneider in the title role, now demanding (and getting) an astronomical fee of forty-five hundred francs a night. The work began its long and immensely successful run at the Théâtre des Variétés on 12 April. The following year saw the première in the same theatre of *La Périchole* (6 October 1868).

The Franco-Prussian War was an uncomfortable time for the German-born Offenbach, who was accused by his detractors of being unpatriotic. After the ravages of the siege and the Commune, he was uncomfortable with the new Third Republic and never recaptured the popular success of his earlier work until he completed the revised and much expanded version of *Orphée aux enfers*, first given at the Théâtre de la Gaîté-Lyrique on 7 February 1874. The composer himself conducted the hundredth performance of this production, and by the end of the year more than two million francs had been taken at the box office. But Offenbach was not an astute businessman, and in 1875 a mountain of debts obliged him to relinquish the Gaîté-Lyrique, which he had taken over on 1 June 1873. In 1876, Offenbach was persuaded to cross the Atlantic for a series of concerts and a production of *Orphée aux enfers* as part of the American centennial celebrations. The same year, Offenbach moved with his family to an apartment on the third floor of 8 boulevard des Capucines, 9e (F13, Métro: Opéra). It was here that the composer worked on his last great operatic venture, *Les contes d'Hoffmann* (it was given its posthumous première at the Opéra-Comique on 10 February 1881). Offenbach's funeral took place at the Madeleine on 7 November 1880. He was buried in Montmartre Cemetery.

Princesse Edmond de Polignac [Winnaretta Singer]
(8 January 1865–26 November 1943)

The magnificent Polignac residence stands at 43 avenue Georges-Mandel, formerly avenue Henri-Martin (figure 1.38), 16e (H6, Métro: Rue de la Pompe), on the corner of the rue Pasteur-Marc-Boegner (formerly rue

1.38 The Polignac mansion at 43 avenue Georges-Mandel.

Cortambert). This imposing building was one of the most remarkable centres of artistic activity in early twentieth-century Paris. The princesse de Polignac, born Winnaretta Singer, was heiress to the Singer sewing machine fortune. In July 1887 she married Prince Louis de Scey-Montbéliard, but the unhappy marriage was annulled in February 1892. In December 1893, she married the ageing aesthete Prince Edmond de Polignac (who died in 1901).

The list of works dedicated to the princess, many of which she commissioned, is immensely impressive, including Fauré's *Cinq mélodies* op. 58 (the Verlaine settings "Mandoline," "En sourdine," "Green," "A Clymène," and "C'est l'extase") and the incidental music for *Pelléas et Mélisande*, Ravel's *Pavane pour une infante défunte*, Satie's *Socrate*, Stravinsky's *Renard*, Weill's Second Symphony, Falla's *El retablo de Maese Pedro*, and Poulenc's Concerto for Two Pianos and Organ Concerto. In addition, her musical evenings saw many important private performances of early music including, in 1895, possibly the only nineteenth-century performance of Rameau's *Dardanus* and, in the 1930s, Bach cantatas and Monteverdi madrigals conducted by Nadia Boulanger. Among other works to be first performed chez Polignac were Debussy's *En blanc et noir* on 22 January 1916 (played by Walter and Thérèse Rummel) and Stravinsky's *Oedipus rex* on 29 May 1928, with Stravinsky at the piano, on the eve of the official première.

1.40 The princesse de Polignac at her Cavaillé-Coll salon organ.

There were two performing spaces in the house: the larger was the "grand salon," a magnificent mirrored music room with seating for approximately 250 people (figure 1.39). The smaller room, the atelier, had a separate entrance on the rue Cortambert and contained the princess's Cavaillé-Coll organ (now at a seminary in Méréville). It was reserved for the most select musical evenings (figure 1.40).

Marcel Proust recalled his experiences at the early years of the Polignac salon in an article in *Le Figaro* on 6 September 1903: "The musical sessions in the hall [the grand salon] on the rue Cortambert, invariably splendid from the musical point of view, at which one heard both perfectly executed ancient music such as the performances of *Dardanus* and original and enthusiastic interpretations of all the latest songs by Fauré, Fauré's Sonata [for Violin and Piano op. 13], and the dances of Brahms were also, as society columnists like to say, 'supremely elegant.' Often held during the day, these occasions sparkled with the many brilliant points of light that the rays of the sun, shining through the prismatic windows, set up in the studio." At the outbreak of World War II, the princess moved to England. She died there and was buried in the Singer family mausoleum in Torquay.

1.41 Here, at 83 rue de Monceau, Poulenc wrote many of his early works.

1.42 The entrance to 5 rue de Médicis, Poulenc's Paris home from 1936 until his death.

Francis Poulenc (7 January 1899–30 January 1963)

Poulenc was born at 2 place des Saussaies, 8e (F11, Métro: Miromesnil or Saint-Augustin), close to the Elysée Palace. His childhood was a happy one, and the family was prosperous: his father and two brothers ran the chemical firm now known as Rhône-Poulenc. Tragedy struck with the death of his mother in 1915 and of his father two years later. Poulenc subsequently moved in with his elder sister Jeanne and her husband at 83 rue de Monceau (figure 1.41), 8e (E10, Métro: Villiers). Here Poulenc wrote his first successful works, such as the *Mouvements perpétuels*, the Sonata for Piano Four Hands, and the *Rapsodie nègre* (dedicated to Satie), all published by the London firm of J. & W. Chester in 1919. In 1936 Poulenc moved to 5 rue de Médicis (figure 1.42), 6e (K13–K14, Métro: Odéon; RER: Luxembourg). This was a house owned by his uncle Papoum, overlooking the Jardin du Luxembourg. In 1947, Poulenc moved to an apartment on the sixth floor of the same building, which remained his Paris home until his death. He spent a good deal of his time on concert tours with the baritone Pierre Bernac and others and did much of his composing at his country home in Noizay (Touraine), where he had owned a house since 1928. Poulenc died suddenly at his home at 5 rue de Médicis. He was buried in Père-Lachaise Cemetery.

Sergei Prokofiev (27 April 1891–5 March 1953)

Prokofiev was in Paris in 1921 for the first performance of *Chout* by the Ballets Russes, and that summer he moved to the Brittany coast to compose the Third Piano Concerto. According to his *Autobiography*, Prokofiev moved to Paris in October 1923, but until 1930 he lived at various temporary addresses. His Paris compositions of the 1920s included the Second Symphony (1924) and *Le pas d'acier* (1925–26), commissioned by Diaghilev. Another Diaghilev ballet, *L'enfant prodigue*, and the Third Symphony both date from 1928–29; they received their premières within a fortnight of each other in May 1929. In spring 1930, Prokofiev and his family finally settled in an apartment at 5 rue Valentin-Haüy, 15e (L10, Métro: Ségur), just off the place de Breteuil. They lived in five rooms on the third floor of the building, and this was to remain Prokofiev's base for the next six years, though he toured extensively. Here he composed the Fourth Piano Concerto in 1931 (written for left hand only, a commission from Paul Wittgenstein). In 1933 Prokofiev was commissioned by the Belgoskino film studios in Leningrad to write the music for *Lieutenant Kijé*. The suite drawn from this score immediately established itself as one of his most popular works. The last work Prokofiev began in Paris is one of his greatest achievements: the ballet *Romeo and Juliet*. First suggested by the Kirov in 1934, the commission was subsequently taken over by the Bolshoi (which then cancelled the contract). The problem Prokofiev faced with the end of the ballet was succinctly stated by the composer himself: "Living people can dance, the dying cannot." Accordingly, he devised a happy ending (with Romeo arriving before it was too late). This version was completed in summer 1935 and was rejected. Prokofiev undertook substantial revisions immediately, completing the work in 1936 (the first performance took place in Brno two years later). Also in 1935, Prokofiev wrote his Violin Concerto no. 2 for the violinist Robert Soetens. In the spring of 1936, Prokofiev left Paris after deciding to settle permanently in Moscow.

Sergei Rachmaninoff (1 April 1873–28 March 1943)

Rachmaninoff rented several Paris apartments and usually stayed in them during the summer months. His Paris address was at 41 boulevard Haussmann, 9e (F12, Métro: Havre-Caumartin), in 1925, the year in which the publishing house TAIR was established at 22 rue d'Anjou. (The firm was named after Rachmaninoff's daughters TAtiana and IRina.) Four years later, in summer 1929, the Rachmaninoff family rented Le Pavillon, a villa at Clairefontaine-en-Yvelines, about fifty kilometres southwest of Paris. The grounds of Rachmaninoff's villa were adjacent to those of the French president's residence at Rambouillet. Rachmaninoff returned to Clairefontaine each summer for several years, eventually resolving to spend his summers in Switzerland, on the shores of Lake Lucerne, only when his Villa Senar was finally completed.

Jean-Philippe Rameau
(baptised 25 September 1683–12 September 1764)

Rameau, who was born in Dijon, is first known to have lived in Paris in 1706, when he was described on the title page of his first book of harpsichord pieces as organist to the Jesuit Fathers on the rue Saint-Jacques and to the Fathers of Mercy (on the site of 47 rue des Archives, 3e). According to his own recollections, reported in the obituary in the *Mercure de France,* his first address in Paris was on the rue de l'Observance (now rue Antoine-Dubois), 6e, opposite the priory of the Cordeliers (demolished in 1804). The distinguished organist here was Louis Marchand, of whom Rameau was a fervent admirer. The 1706 collection of harpsichord pieces gives his address as vieille rue du Temple, "vis-à-vis les Consignations, chez un Perruquier." He left Paris in 1709 to take up an appointment in Dijon, and he worked subsequently in Lyon and Clermont-Ferrand. (The *Traité d'harmonie,* published by Ballard in 1722, describes him as organist at the cathedral there.) His address after he returned in February 1723 is unknown, but by 1726, when he married Marie-Louise Mangot in the church of Saint-Germain-l'Auxerrois, he was living on the rue des Petits-Champs, 1er, within the parish of Saint-Eustache. In 1727, Daquin beat Rameau in the competition for the appointment of organist at the church of Saint-Paul. In August that year, Rameau's address was "Aux Trois

Rois" on the rue des Deux Boules, and by 1731 he was living on the rue de Richelieu, "près de l'Hôtel de la Paix." In 1732 he was appointed organist of Sainte-Croix-de-la-Bretonnerie in the Marais. This church was demolished in the 1790s, but it stood on the site of the present square Sainte-Croix-de-la-Bretonnerie, 4e. Rameau held the post at Sainte-Croix until 1738. In November 1732, when his daughter Marie-Louise was baptised, his address was on the rue des Chantres (on the site of the present Magasins du Louvre), from which he published *Hippolyte et Aricie* the following year. This was his first stage work, composed when Rameau was almost fifty years old, and it was followed by a succession of operatic works written during the last thirty years of his long life. By the time *Les Indes galantes* was published in 1735–36, he had moved to the Hôtel d'Effiat, 21 rue des Bons-Enfants, later demolished to make way for the rue du Colonel-Driant (opened in 1915). In 1744, he was living on the rue Saint-Thomas-du-Louvre (on the site of the place du Carrousel), and the following year he was living on the rue Saint-Honoré near the Palais Royal. By 1746 Rameau and his family were living in an apartment on the site of 59 rue de Richelieu, 2e (G13, Métro: Quatre-Septembre), the home of the financier Alexandre La Riche de La Poupelinière, where he remained until about 1752 (he appears also to have retained a house on the rue Saint-Honoré, which some publications give as his address). From 1752 he lived on the rue des Bons-Enfants, presumably on the west side of the street, as the inventory of Rameau's belongings states that his apartment had a view of the Palais Royal. That evidence also suggests that the house was situated in the northern part of the rue des Bons-Enfants, which was demolished to make way for the present Banque de France. His neighbours in the building included the young scientist Lavoisier. Rameau died here just before his eighty-first birthday and was buried in the church of Saint-Eustache.

Maurice Ravel (7 March 1875–28 December 1937)

The first home Ravel knew as a child in Paris was at 40 rue des Martyrs, 9e (E14, Métro: Saint-Georges or Pigalle). In 1888 the family were living at 73 rue Jean-Baptiste Pigalle, 9e (D13, Métro: Pigalle), and, by 1899, just around the corner at 7 rue Fromentin, 9e (D13, Métro: Blanche or Pigalle), opposite the Ecole Niedermeyer, where Fauré had been a student. On 28 January 1898, Ravel joined Fauré's composition class at the

1.43 Programme for the Société Nationale concert on 27 May 1899 at which Ravel made his conducting debut with the first performance of his "ouverture de féerie" *Shéhérazade.*

SALLE DU NOUVEAU THÉÂTRE
15, Rue Blanche, 15

SOCIÉTÉ NATIONALE
DE MUSIQUE

278ᵐᵉ CONCERT

AVEC ORCHESTRE ET CHŒURS

Fondée en 1871 SAMEDI 27 MAI 1899, à 9 heures précises

Ouverture des portes à 8 heures 1/2

PROGRAMME

1. SHÉHÉRAZADE, ouverture de féerie .... MAURICE RAVEL
   (1re aud.)
2. CHŒUR DES BATELIERS DU VOLGA .... CHARLES KŒCHLIN
   d'après un thème populaire russe.   *(1re aud.)*
3. PSAUME CXXXVI .... J. GUY ROPARTZ
   (1re aud.)
4. NEVERMORE (PAUL VERLAINE) .... SYLVIO LAZZARI
   M. PIERRE LUPIAC, de l'Opéra-Comique.   *(1re aud.)*
5. LA TÊTE DE KENWARC'H (LECONTE DE LISLE) ...... PIERRE DE BRÉVILLE
   Chant de mort gallois du VIᵐᵉ Siècle.
   M. DARAUX et les Chœurs.

6. HYMNE VÉDIQUE op. 9 [LECONTE DE LISLE] .... ERNEST CHAUSSON
   (1re aud.)
7. LES DJINNS (VICTOR HUGO) .... GABRIEL FAURÉ
8. CATALONIA (suite populaire, n° 1) .... J. ALBENIZ
   (1re aud.)
9. 8ᵐᵉ BÉATITUDE (MAD. COLOMB) .... CÉSAR FRANCK
   « Bienheureux ceux qui souffrent persécution pour la justice,
   parce que le royaume des cieux est à eux. »
   La Vierge Marie. — MADAME BALARD.
   La Voix du Christ. — MONSIEUR DARAUX.
   Satan. — MONSIEUR BALARD.

Le Concert sera dirigé par M. VINCENT d'INDY et les Auteurs

Les personnes désirant faire partie de la SOCIÉTÉ NATIONALE, sont priées d'envoyer leur adhésion à l'AGENCE, 20, RUE DES MARAIS. La cotisation annuelle est de 25 francs, donnant droit à **trois entrées réservées** par Concert.

ORGANISATION & DIRECTION DE CONCERTS, AGENCE : 20, RUE DES MARAIS

Conservatoire (having previously studied privately with André Gédalge), and he was to remain there for several years, in the meantime becoming devoted to Fauré, who likewise took an eager and benevolent interest in his most original pupil's progress. Ravel made his conducting debut at a Société Nationale concert on 27 May 1899, with his "ouverture de féerie" *Shéhérazade* (figure 1.43). His best-known work from these student years was the piano version of the *Pavane pour une infante défunte* (composed for piano in 1899, orchestrated in 1910).

111 | MUSICIANS

In April 1901 the family moved again, in the same locality, to 40 bis rue de Douai, 9e (D12, Métro: Blanche), but by September 1901 they had moved to 19 boulevard Péreire, 17e, at the northern end of the boulevard, northeast of the place de Wagram (C9, Métro: Wagram). Here, in November of that year, Ravel composed *Jeux d'eau*, the first of his works to show a truly innovative exploration of piano sonority. Here, too, he composed the other works of his early maturity: the String Quartet (1902–1903), with its dedication "à mon cher maître Gabriel Fauré," the song-cycle *Shéhérazade* (1903), and *Sonatine*. Throughout the years 1900–1905, Ravel made repeated attempts at the Prix de Rome, but each ended in failure and disappointment (his best result was a third prize in 1901: *see* Prix de Rome under "Institutions and Orchestras"). In April

1.44 Ravel's apartment at 4 avenue Carnot.

1.45 Ravel with Nijinsky at 4 avenue Carnot. Photograph by Alfredo Casella, 1914.

1.46 and 1.47
Interior views of
Ravel's apartment
in Levallois-Perret,
showing the
remarkable decor
by Léon Leyritz.

1905, the Ravel family moved out of the centre of Paris to 16 bis rue Louis-Rouquier (then rue Chevalier) in the northwestern suburb of Levallois-Perret (C6, Métro: Anatole-France), and the composer completed *Miroirs* (1904–1905) and wrote the *Introduction et allegro* (1905), the *Rapsodie espagnole* (1907–1908), the opera *L'heure espagnole* (finished in October 1907), and *Gaspard de la nuit* (May–September 1908).

Ravel's father, Joseph, died on 13 October 1908. Following this family loss, Ravel, his mother, and his brother Edouard moved to a more central location: 4 avenue Carnot, 17e (figures 1.44 and 1.45), where the composer lived until late 1917 (F7–E7, Métro: Charles de Gaulle–Etoile). It was while living at this fashionable address near the Arc de Triomphe (or while at his retreat at Saint-Jean-de-Luz in the Basque country) that he composed several of his greatest works: *Ma mère l'oye* (1908 and 1911), *Daphnis et Chloé* (1909–12), *Valses nobles et sentimentales* (1910), the Piano Trio (finished just before the outbreak of World War I, in 1914), and *Le tombeau de Couperin* (1914 and 1917). For much of the war, Ravel was out of Paris, serving in the French army as a truck driver (he proudly signed his letters "Driver Ravel"). In January 1917 Ravel's mother died, leaving the composer grief-stricken. On receiving a temporary discharge from military service, he stayed with friends at Lyons-la-Forêt (some 140 kilometres northwest of Paris), where he completed *Le tombeau de Couperin*, each movement of which is dedicated to the memory of a friend killed in the war.

Late in 1917, Ravel and his brother moved from avenue Carnot to Saint-Cloud, where they shared a villa with the Bonnets, Edouard's business associates. In 1919–20 Ravel spent several months in the peaceful isolation of Lapras in the Ardèche, five hundred kilometres southeast of Paris, where he composed *La valse*. After a prolonged search, Ravel finally settled in the small town of Montfort-l'Amaury, forty-five kilometres to the west of Paris, where he purchased the villa Le Belvédère, now the Musée Maurice Ravel, located at 5 rue Maurice-Ravel (SNCF: Montfort-l'Amaury-Méré), within easy reach of Paris by train or bus. It was ready for occupancy in May 1921. It is now an impressive museum, containing many of Ravel's possessions, including his Erard piano, his furniture, and his library. These are as they were at the time of his death, beautifully preserved, as is the highly original decor which Ravel chose for the house (*see* Musée Maurice Ravel under "Museums and Libraries"). When in Paris from 1921 onwards, Ravel would often stay at the Hôtel d'Athènes, opposite the Godebski apartment on the rue Saint-Florentin, 1er (G11, Métro: Concorde), or at 16 bis rue Louis-Rouquier, which his brother Edouard had retained. Ravel had this Levallois-Perret apartment redesigned in the latest style by Léon Leyritz in 1930, and contemporary photographs exist of the interior (figures 1.46 and 1.47). Over the next years, Ravel's health declined, and on 17 December 1937, he was admitted for brain surgery at a clinic on the rue Boileau, 16e (L4, Métro: Michel-Ange-Auteuil). He died there on 28 December 1937. Ravel was buried at Levallois-Perret Cemetery, in the same family grave as his parents and, later, his younger brother Edouard, who died in 1960.

Gioachino Rossini (29 February 1792–13 November 1868)

Rossini and his wife Isabella Colbran arrived in Paris for the first time on 9 November 1823. By then, twelve of his operas had been staged by the Théâtre Italien and he was already a celebrity in Paris. During this visit, the Rossinis stayed as guests of the writer Nicola Bagioli at 6 rue Rameau, 2e (G13, Métro: Quatre-Septembre). Perhaps the most dazzling event during their stay was a banquet held in Rossini's honour on 16 November 1823 at the Restaurant du Veau-qui-Tette, place du Châtelet, with more than 150 guests. The organisers of this lavish occasion included Castil-Blaze and Rossini's publisher Pacini, who rented the first-floor banqueting room of the restaurant, one of the most elegant in Paris. Special medallions were struck, bearing the titles of Rossini's operas, and were presented to each of the guests. Among the composers present were Auber, Boieldieu, and Hérold. At the end of the evening, Le Sueur proposed a toast to Rossini, who responded with a toast to French composers and the prosperity of the Conservatoire. Further toasts were drunk to Gluck, Grétry, Mozart, Méhul, Paisiello, and Cimarosa. Between the toasts, the orchestra played a short piece by each of those composers. *La Gazette de France* described the occasion as "a colossal picnic."

On 7 December 1823, Rossini left Paris for an extended visit to London. He returned briefly on 1 August 1824, took rooms at 28 rue Taitbout, 9e (F13, Métro: Chaussée-d'Antin), then travelled to Bologna on 4 September to see friends and visit his parents. He returned with Colbran to Paris a few weeks later, to fulfil his contracts to write new Italian and French operas for Paris. The couple moved into the Hôtel Tuffakine, 10 boulevard Montmartre (on the site of the present passage Jouffroy), 9e (F14, Métro: Richelieu-Drouot). This building, in which Boieldieu and Carafa also lived, was demolished in 1836. Rossini began his new appointment as co-director of the Théâtre Italien, in an uneasy alliance with Ferdinando Paer. Rossini's first opera for Paris was *Il viaggio a Reims*, written to celebrate the coronation of Charles X in June 1825. The première took place on 19 May 1825 in the Salle Louvois. On 8 December 1825 *Semiramide* was given its Paris première (at the Salle Favart), swiftly followed by the first performance in Paris of *Zelmira* (Salle Favart, 14 March 1826). Rossini's first new opera for the Académie Royale de Musique (the Opéra) was *Le siège de Corinthe* (Salle Le Peletier, 9 October 1826), with Adolphe Nourrit in the role of Néoclès. Rossini's reworking of *Mosè* (as *Moïse*) for a Paris audience received its première at the Salle Le Peletier on 26 March 1827, the original playbill describing the work as an "Oratorio en 4 parties." Rossini's last comedy, *Le comte Ory*, had its première at the Salle Le Peletier on 20 August 1828, and that year, too, Rossini worked on the composition of his greatest and last opera, *Guillaume Tell*, much of it in the peace and quiet of the château at Petit-Bourg, which his friend Alexandre Aguado had acquired in 1827. (The former home of the duc d'Antin, this château lies about thirty kilometres south of Paris, on the banks of the Seine). The first performance was at the Opéra (Salle Le Peletier) on 3 August 1829, with a cast including Nourrit as Arnold, Laure Cinti-Damoreau as Mathilde, and Marie Taglioni as the Tyrolean dancer.

After another visit to Bologna, Rossini returned to Paris on 4 September 1830, this time without Isabella Colbran, from whom he was becoming increasingly estranged. Initially, he stayed with his friend Alexandre Aguado at the Hôtel d'Augny, 6 rue Drouot, 9e (F14, Métro: Richelieu-Drouot), then travelled with him to Spain and returned to Paris. The city had changed since Rossini's last visit: Charles X having been deposed in the July uprising and replaced by the less artistically inclined Louis-Philippe, Rossini was left without an official position. He lived in a small apartment under the roof of the Théâtre Italien (Salle Favart, place Boieldieu, 2e) until 1836. Carlo Severini, who had invited Rossini to take rooms above the theatre, was a neighbour. In January 1832, Rossini dined with Honoré de Balzac at the invitation of Olympe Pélissier, whom he had probably first met the previous summer and whom he was later to marry. Rossini's health was unstable throughout the 1830s, and he composed virtually nothing except part of the *Stabat Mater* and the enchanting *Soirées musicales,* first published by Troupenas in 1835, though at the Théâtre Italien he took a lively interest in new operas by Donizetti and Bellini. In 1836 he toured extensively and returned to Italy, where he remained until 1843. In 1837 he was formally separated from Isabella Colbran. The fire which destroyed the Théâtre Italien (Salle Favart) on the night of 14–15 January 1838 was a particular tragedy for Rossini: his friend Severini died while jumping from the blaze.

Rossini's health continued to give cause for concern, and he returned to Paris on 27 May 1843 for medical treatment. He lived with Olympe at 9 place de la Madeleine, 8e (G11–G12, Métro: Madeleine). During this stay, Rossini also sat for the celebrated portrait by Ary Scheffer (now owned by the Paris Conservatoire). The couple remained in Paris until 20 September 1843, when they left for Italy. Isabella Colbran died on 7 October 1845. He married Olympe Pélissier on 16 August 1846. Often suffering from severe manic-depressive illness, Rossini remained in Italy until 1855, when he and Olympe decided to settle in Paris. They arrived in the autumn, settling first at 52 rue Basse-du-Rempart (no longer extant, on the site of the present rue Edouard VII, 9e), then in Passy, in a villa at 24

1.48 The corner of the boulevard des Italiens and the rue de la Chaussée-d'Antin. Lithograph by Wyld, circa 1850. Rossini's apartment was on the second floor of the building on the left.

1.49 The Villa Rossini in Passy. Lithograph by Benoist, Cicéri, and Bayot, after Doussault, 1861.

rue de la Pompe, 16e, now demolished, which they rented from the publisher Jacques-Léopold Heugel. In 1857 a spacious second-floor apartment was found at 2 rue de la Chaussée-d'Antin, 9e (F13, Métro: Opéra), which was to remain Rossini's winter residence until the end of his life (figure 1.48). Situated on the corner of the boulevard des Capucines, this building is still standing, though it has been substantially altered since Rossini's time. In September 1858, the City of Paris sold Rossini a plot of land in Passy, on the edge of the Bois de Boulogne, in avenue Ingres, 16e (J4, Métro: Ranelagh). The foundation stone for the Villa Rossini was laid on 10 March 1859, and the house was ready by spring 1861, after which it served as Rossini's residence each summer (figure 1.49).

During the last ten years of his life Rossini held a remarkable series of musical soirées in his Paris apartment and at his Passy villa. The first of these took place on 18 December 1858 at 2 rue de la Chaussée-d'Antin, and the last on 26 September 1868 in Passy. The performers represented a dazzling array of contemporary talent. Composers who were present and often played their own works included Liszt (for the first public hearing of his *Légendes*), Verdi, Gounod, Anton Rubinstein, and Saint-Saëns. Among the singers who appeared regularly were Christine Nilsson, Giulia Grisi, and Jean-Baptiste Faure. The great dancer Marie Taglioni, though retired, was a frequent guest and once surprised the assembled company by dancing a gavotte and minuet. Other guests at these evenings included Alexandre Dumas père and fils, Gustave Doré, and Baron Haussmann.

Rossini's last major work was the *Petite messe solennelle*, given its first performance on 14 March 1864 at the Hôtel Pillet-Will, 12 rue Moncey, 9e, for the dedication of the new chapel. This magnificent house was completed in November 1863 and inaugurated in March 1864. It was demolished in 1903. A dress rehearsal held the day before the first performance was attended by Meyerbeer, Auber, Thomas, Carafa, and others, each personally invited by Rossini. The manuscript of this work (in the Fondazione Rossini, Pesaro) bears a dedication to the Countess Pillet-Will, and another to God, describing the work as "Alas, the last mortal sin of my old age!" It is signed "G. Rossini, Passy, 1863."

In October 1868, Rossini was due to make his regular move from Passy back to the rue de la Chaussée-d'Antin for the winter, but he was unwell. His health deteriorated severely in early November, and he died on Friday 13 November 1868. Rossini's funeral was held at the Trinité on

21 November 1868, with a vast congregation of about four thousand mourners. He was buried in Père-Lachaise Cemetery. Olympe died ten years later and was buried in the same tomb. On her death, the Villa Rossini reverted to the City of Paris, and the property was sold, then demolished by a subsequent owner. In 1887 Rossini's body was reinterred in the church of Santa Croce, Florence.

Albert Roussel (5 April 1869–23 August 1937)

In 1885 Roussel became a student at the Collège Stanislas, 22 rue Notre-Dame-des-Champs, 6e (L12, Métro: Notre-Dame-des-Champs), but he left in 1887 to enter the Ecole Navale as a cadet. After several years at sea, he resigned his commission in 1894 and settled in Paris at 11 bis rue Viète, 17e (D9, Métro: Wagram), where Alfred Bruneau also had an apartment. Roussel was initially taught by Eugène Gigout, but in 1898 he enrolled at the Schola Cantorum for d'Indy's composition course, which he completed a decade later. From 1902 on, he taught counterpoint at the Schola Cantorum, where his pupils included Satie and Varèse. In autumn 1909 Roussel took his new wife on a tour of India, sailing from Marseille on 22 September aboard *Ville de la Ciotat*. They arrived in Bombay on 6 October and returned in mid-November via Ceylon, Indochina, Singapore, and Cambodia. For many years (1910–29), Roussel's Paris address was 157 avenue de Wagram, 17e (D9, Métro: Wagram). He was living here at the time of the première of his ballet *Le festin de l'araignée* (Théâtre des

1.50 The interior of Roussel's apartment at 2 square Gabriel Fauré.

Arts, 3 April 1913, conducted by Gabriel Grovlez). Roussel began work on *Padmâvatî* before the outbreak of World War I, during which he served as a driver. (According to an autobiographical note written in February 1916, he was a lorry driver in the 10th Army; by August 1917 he was based in Paris.) He completed *Padmâvatî* in 1918, but had to wait another five years for its première at the Opéra, on 1 June 1923. In 1920, Roussel bought Vasterival, a house at Sainte-Marguerite-sur-Mer, near Varengeville-sur-Mer. From this time on, he spent as much time as possible there and did much of his composing in the peace and quiet of Vasterival, while keeping a base in the capital. From April 1929 his Paris address (figure 1.50) was at 2 square Gabriel Fauré, 17e (D10, Métro: Villiers). During the next few years Roussel experienced the height of his fame, both in Paris and abroad. In 1930, he travelled to Boston for the première of the Third Symphony, conducted by Serge Koussevitzky (24 October 1930). In Paris on 22 May 1931, the ballet *Bacchus et Ariane*, with choreography by Lifar and sets by de Chirico, was first performed at the Opéra (Philippe Gaubert conducted). A few months later, on 28 November 1931, Albert Wolff gave the first Paris performance of the Third Symphony at the Concerts Lamoureux. In February 1934, Roussel caught pneumonia, but after a period of convalescence he was able to work again, completing the Fourth Symphony by the end of the year. The work was conducted at its première by Albert Wolff at a concert at the Opéra-Comique on 19 October 1935. Roussel spent the winter of 1936–37 in Nice (at 79 bis rue de France), and despite continued ill-health he chaired the French jury for the 1937 ISCM Festival. Roussel died at the Villa Mousse-des-Bois in Royan (Charente) and was buried in the cemetery at Varengeville-sur-Mer.

Camille Saint-Saëns (9 October 1835–16 December 1921)

Saint-Saëns was born at 3 rue du Jardinet, 6e (K14, Métro: Odéon). He was a remarkable child prodigy, both as a pianist and as a composer (his earliest surviving manuscript is dated 22 March 1839, when he was not yet four years old). At the Salle Pleyel on 6 May 1846 he gave a concert including Mozart's Piano Concerto K450 (for which he wrote new cadenzas) and Beethoven's Piano Concerto no. 3—he was nine years of age. Shortly afterwards he enrolled at the Conservatoire, where he was taught composition by Halévy. In the 1852 competition for the Prix de Rome, he reached the second round but did not win any prize. This was an eventful year for the sixteen-year-old Saint-Saëns: he met Liszt (the two became friends), and his *Ode à Sainte-Cécile* was awarded a prize by a jury which included Adam, Gounod, and Halévy. In 1853, he was appointed organist at the church of Saint-Merry. At about the same time, he began to attend Pauline Viardot's salon at 50 rue de Douai, and Rossini's musical soirées on the rue de la Chaussée-d'Antin and the Villa Rossini in Passy. In December 1857 he was appointed organist at the Madeleine, with a salary of three thousand francs, and moved from the rue du Jardinet to a fourth-floor apartment at 168 rue du Faubourg-Saint-Honoré, 8e (F9, Métro: Saint-Philippe-du-Roule or Ternes), his address until 1876. In 1858, the publisher Girod paid Saint-Saëns five hundred francs for six duos for piano and harmonium, and the composer bought a telescope with the proceeds; astronomy was to remain a hobby with him for the rest of his life. At the Madeleine, his playing was admired by many musical visitors to the city, and Liszt declared him to be the greatest organist in the world.

He taught at the Ecole Niedermeyer (where his favourite pupil was Fauré; the two became lifelong friends) and assumed its directorship for 1861–65. In 1864, Saint-Saëns entered the competition for the Prix de Rome a second time and, as before, failed to win a prize. In 1867 he had greater success with a cantata to celebrate the Exposition universelle. The jury included Auber, Félicien David, Verdi, and Berlioz, who wrote to a friend: "I have had the pleasure of seeing the prize being given, unanimously, to the cantata of my young friend Camille Saint-Saëns, one of the greatest musicians of our age." Later that year, Saint-Saëns began work on *Samson et Dalila*, but it was to be another ten years before it was completed. In 1868 he composed his Piano Concerto no. 2 in G minor under unusual circum-stances: Anton Rubinstein wanted to make his Paris debut as a conductor, and, since the Salle Pleyel was not available for a few weeks, Saint-Saëns had time to compose a new work for the occasion. The concert was given on 13 May 1868 with Saint-Saëns as soloist and Rubinstein conducting; Saint-Saëns had not spent sufficient time learning his own music, and, apart from the scherzo, the performance was not a success.

At the start of the Franco-Prussian War, Saint-Saëns became a soldier in the 4th battalion of the National Guard (he subsequently became increas-ingly hostile to German music). As an expression of nationalist fervour, he became vice president of the Société Nationale de Musique at its inaugural meeting on 25 February 1871. During the Commune, Saint-Saëns left Paris and gave several successful concerts in London. When the first concert of the Société Nationale took place in the Salle Pleyel on 17 November 1871, Saint-Saëns was among the performers. The same year, he composed the earliest French symphonic poem, *Le rouet d'Omphale*, first performed in its orchestral version at the Société Nationale on 9 January 1872; a year later, Auguste Tolbècque gave the first performance of the Cello Concerto no. 1 at the Société des Concerts du Conservatoire (19 January 1873).

On 24 January 1875, Colonne gave the première of *Danse macabre*, a work which the critic Adolphe Jullien considered to have "everything but a musical idea, good or bad. It can be defined in only two ways: as an aberration or as a hoax" (Bonnerot 1922, 73). The verdict of the public was very different, and the work is also worthy of interest as the first substantial orchestral piece with a part for xylophone. On 3 February same year, Saint-Saëns married Marie-Laure Truffot. Four days later (7 February), Colonne conducted a second performance of *Danse macabre*, and the work was so successful that it received an encore.

In 1876 Saint-Saëns travelled to Bayreuth for the first production of Wagner's *Ring*, which he reviewed for the periodical *Le Bon Sens*. The next year he found a new apartment on the fourth floor at 14 rue Monsieur-le-Prince, 6e (K13, Métro: Odéon), where he remained until 1889, and he gave up his post as organist at the Madeleine. These were years when tragedy mingled with triumph. On 2 December 1877, Liszt arranged the première of *Samson et Dalila* in Weimar, though the work was not given at the Opéra for another fifteen years. On 22 May 1878, Saint-Saëns conducted the first performance of his Requiem in Saint-Sulpice (Widor played the organ). Less than a week later, on 28 May, his two-year-old son André was killed in a terrible accident: hearing the playful shouting of his friends on the floor below, he leant too far out of the apartment window and fell to the ground. Saint-Saëns's wife took their seven-month-old son Jean-François to Reims to recover from this tragedy. There, six weeks after the death of André, Jean-François died of pneumonia. After this, Saint-Saëns's marriage was never happy. In 1881 the couple separated (Marie-Laure Saint-Saëns died in 1950, at the age of ninety-five).

In January 1886, Saint-Saëns was given an unfriendly reception by an audience in Berlin, where news of his anti-German views had preceded him. He took to the Austrian countryside, where he composed *Le car-naval des animaux* for a private Shrove Tuesday concert at the home of the cellist Charles Lebouc, given on 9 March 1886 with Saint-Saëns and Louis Diémer as the pianists. Liszt made his last visit to Paris in May that year. He had heard about *Le carnaval des animaux* and requested a performance. This took place at Pauline Viardot's house in May 1886, once again with Saint-Saëns and Diémer as the pianists. Saint-Saëns's Third Symphony (the "Organ" Symphony) was given its triumphant première at the Royal Albert Hall in London (19 May 1886) and later dedicated to Liszt's memory. The death of Saint-Saëns's mother in December 1888 was another devastating blow. This, coming after the death of his children and the collapse of his marriage, left him a broken man. He abandoned the apartment on the rue Monsieur-le-Prince, sent most of his belongings to his cousin Léon in Dieppe, and left for the Canary Islands.

1.51 The concert given at the Salle Pleyel on 2 June 1896 to celebrate the fiftieth anniversary of Saint-Saëns's debut at the Salle Pleyel. The violinist is Sarasate and the conductor Paul Taffanel. Saint-Saëns is at the piano.

He returned briefly in May, and the Musée Saint-Saëns opened in Dieppe in July. By December 1890, the restless composer was on board a ship to Ceylon. Later he visited Cairo and Alexandria, where he composed *Africa*, for piano and orchestra. No longer relishing life in Paris, he went in 1892 to Point Pescade near Algiers. The Paris première of *Samson et Dalila* at the Opéra on 23 November 1892 was a spectacular success, which did much to raise his flagging spirits, but in October 1893, grief-stricken by the death of Gounod, Saint-Saëns left Paris for another stay in the Canary Islands. In 1895 Saint-Saëns set out for Saigon; by January 1896, he was back in Cairo. In May and June 1896 he returned to Paris for a concert to celebrate fifty years of his artistic career (figure 1.51). The programme included the premières of the Fifth Piano Concerto and the Second Violin Sonata (played by Sarasate and the composer). The concert was successful, but still Saint-Saëns felt the need to travel relentlessly: he was in the Canaries during the winter of 1897–98 and went to Argentina in 1899.

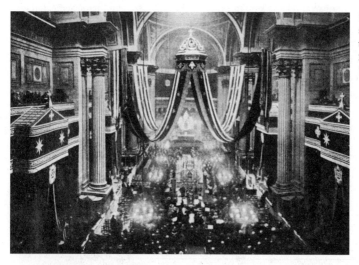

1.52 Saint-Saëns's state funeral at the Madeleine on 24 December 1921.

His Paris address from 1904 to 1910 was 17 rue de Longchamp, 16e (G7, Métro: Iéna). Here he composed one of the earliest film scores, the music for *L'assassinat du duc de Guise*, first shown on 16 November 1908 in the Salle Visions d'Art (Saint-Saëns was in Las Palmas in the Canary Islands at the time and remained there until March 1909). In spring 1910, Saint-Saëns played a complete cycle of the Mozart piano concertos in London. On returning to Paris, he moved to 83 bis rue de Courcelles, 17e (E9, Métro: Courcelles). Considered a reactionary by most younger composers, he was savagely critical of Debussy, though they both appeared at the inaugural concert of the Théâtre des Champs-Elysées on 2 April 1913. A few weeks later he was apparently horrified by the première of *Le sacre du printemps* in the same theatre. He continued to tour ceaselessly, travelling to America in 1915, then to Brazil, Argentina, and Uruguay. He died at the

Hôtel de l'Oasis in Algiers; after a memorial service in the cathedral there, his body was brought back to Paris for a state funeral at the Madeleine on Saturday, 24 December 1921 (figure 1.52). Widor gave the funeral address, declaring: "The man is no more, but his spirit hovers over the world, alive and glorious, and will continue to hover as long as we have orchestras and instruments." Saint-Saëns was buried in Montparnasse Cemetery.

Erik Satie (17 May 1866–1 July 1925)

Satie's family moved from Honfleur (Normandy) to Paris in 1870, living first at 3 cité Odiot, 8e (F9, Métro: George V). Two years later his mother died, and Satie, with his brother Conrad, returned to live with their grandparents in Honfleur. Satie began music lessons there in 1874 with M. Vinot, a pupil of Niedermeyer. In the summer of 1878, Satie's grandmother drowned, and the boy rejoined his father in Paris. On 8 November 1879 Satie entered the preparatory piano class of Emile Descombes at the Conservatoire. Two months later, in January 1880, his first exam reports described him as "gifted but lazy." In 1881 the family moved to a fifth-floor apartment at 70 rue de Turbigo, 3e (G16, Métro: Arts et Métiers or Temple). Satie, who had consistently failed to impress at the Conservatoire, was dismissed by the director, Ambroise Thomas, in June 1882. That was also the year Satie's father, Alfred, established himself as a publisher of salon music (publications were issued from 70 rue de Turbigo in 1882–83, from 26 boulevard Magenta in 1883–86, and from 66 boulevard Magenta between 1886 and 1894, which appears to have been the firm's last year of operation). In 1883 the family moved to 6 rue de Marseille (near the Canal Saint-Martin), 10e (F17, Métro: Jacques-Bonsergent). Satie was admitted as an auditor to Antoine Tardou's harmony classes at the Conservatoire.

In 1884 Satie wrote his first composition, an Allegro for piano, and he heard César Franck playing the organ at Sainte-Clotilde. The following year he was accepted into the piano class of Georges Mathias at the Conservatoire and wrote two waltzes. Satie's last move with his family was in 1886 to 66 boulevard Magenta, 10e (F16, Métro: Gare de l'Est). He was beginning to develop an interest in mysticism and Gothic art: he composed *Ogives* for piano. At the end of 1886 he volunteered for military service, from which he was released in November 1887. That year he completed the *Trois sarabandes*, which were admired by Debussy. Satie's

TROIS MÉLODIES

1. Les Anges   3!
2. Les Fleurs   3!
3. Sylvie   4!

Poésie de
J.P. CONTAMINE de LATOUR
Musique de

ERIK SATIE

OP: 20.

Paris, **ALFRED SATIE**, Éditeur, 66, Boulevard Magenta.

earliest songs were published in 1887 by his father, with endearingly fictitious opus numbers (figure 1.53).

In late 1887 Satie left the family home and moved to 50 rue Condorcet, 9e (E14, Métro: Anvers or Pigalle). He played regularly at the Chat Noir cabaret in Montmartre. In April 1888 Satie completed and copied out the *Trois gymnopédies,* and nos. 1 and 3 were published by Satie's father at 66 boulevard Magenta (in August and November respectively). In 1889, Satie visited the Exposition universelle (and its greatest novelty, the Eiffel Tower) and heard the exotic music, including the gamelan, which so profoundly influenced Debussy; Satie was inspired by the experience to write a *Gnossienne* (now known as no. 5) on 8 July.

1.54 Satie's Mont-
martre address in
the 1890s—6 rue
Cortot.

Forced to find less expensive accommodation (and wanting to escape his creditors), Satie moved in spring 1890 to 6 rue Cortot, 18e (C14, Métro: Lamarck-Caulaincourt), where he remained until the autumn of 1898 (figure 1.54). In 1890 he met Joséphin (Sâr) Péladan, the self-appointed leader of the Ordre de la Rose-Croix Catholique du Temple du Graal, for which Satie became the official composer in 1891–92. He left the Chat Noir in 1891 after a quarrel with the owner and became a pianist at the Auberge du Clou. It was at this time that his friendship with Debussy began to develop, and on 27 October 1892 Debussy inscribed a copy of his *Cinq poèmes de Baudelaire* to "Erik Satie, a gentle medieval musician lost in this century." In December 1892 Satie challenged the director of the Opéra (Eugène Bertrand) to a duel in an unsuccessful attempt to compel him to perform Satie's "Ballet Chrétien" *Uspud*. The following year Satie had a passionate six-month relationship—his only known affair—with the artist Suzanne Valadon; he also met Ravel for the first time, at the Café de la Nouvelle Athènes. His music that year included the *Danses gothiques* and the extraordinary *Vexations*, a short piano piece with the following instruction from the composer: "In order to play this motif 840 times, it would be as well to prepare beforehand, in the deepest silence, with serious immobility." In October 1893 he founded the Eglise Métropolitaine d'Art de Jésus Conducteur. The finest product of this mystical organization, of which Satie was the only member,

1.55 Satie's house
in the rue Cauchy,
Arcueil, photo-
graphed in the
early twentieth
century.

1.56 The staircase
to Satie's room at
34 rue Cauchy,
Arcueil, photo-
graphed by Con-
stantin Brancusi
in 1928.

was the *Messe des pauvres*. Satie had lived in a second-floor room at 6 rue
Cortot, but on 25 July 1896 he moved to a tiny ground-floor room in the
same house, which he described as his *placard* (cupboard). A room in the
house (though not one of those in which Satie lived) is now the Musée
Erik Satie, "Le placard d'Erik Satie" (*see* Musée Erik Satie under "Museums and Libraries").

Satie's final move was to the southern suburb of Arcueil (RER:
Arcueil-Cachan), where he rented a room on the second floor of the Maison des Quatre Cheminées, 22 (now 34) rue Cauchy, from October 1898
until his death in 1925 (figure 1.55). During his twenty-seven years at this
address none of his friends saw the inside of the apartment. Brancusi's
evocative photograph of the staircase was perhaps the closest any of
them came during Satie's lifetime (figure 1.56). In 1899 Satie was a witness at Debussy's marriage to Lilly Texier. His works from the first years
of the century included the *Trois morceaux en forme de poire* for piano duet
(1903). Against the advice of Debussy, Satie enrolled in 1905 as a student
at the Schola Cantorum, taking lessons in counterpoint from Albert
Roussel and attending part of d'Indy's composition course. On 16 January 1911 Ravel performed some of Satie's pieces at a concert of the
Société Musicale Indépendante, and his earlier music began to be redis-
covered by a new generation. *Parade* was first performed in 1917 by the

Ballets Russes, with sets by Picasso, and other works from Satie's last years include *Socrate* and the ballets *Mercure* and *Relâche*. At the scandalous première of *Relâche* at the Théâtre des Champs-Elysées, Satie made his last stage appearance in the conductor Roger Désormière's car. Satie died in the Hôpital Saint-Joseph, rue Pierre Larousse, 14e (P10, Métro: Plaisance), on 1 July 1925. The funeral took place in the little church at Arcueil on 6 July and the remarkable turnout of mourners included Auric, Cocteau, Honegger, Milhaud, Poulenc, Roussel, Tailleferre, and Viñes. Satie was buried in Arcueil Cemetery.

Alexander Scriabin (6 January 1872–27 April 1915)

Scriabin first arrived in Paris in January 1896 with his publisher Belaieff. By 9 February he was staying at 18 rue de Chateaubriand, 8e (F8, Métro: George V). Here he wrote some piano preludes and the Second Sonata, and gave several recitals, including a concert in the Salle Erard on 5 May 1896 which featured the first performance of the Second Sonata, the *Sonate-fantaisie*. After a few weeks in Rome, Scriabin returned to Paris; by 20 June he had a new address at 31 rue Vaneau, 7e (J11, Métro: Saint-François-Xavier). In September, Scriabin was back in Russia.

By the time of his next journey to Paris in October 1897, he was a married to Vera Ivanovna Isakovich. The couple settled at 5 rue de la Néva, 8e (E8, Métro: Ternes). Scriabin's constant money problems (most of his letters to Belaieff from Paris are pleas for funds) were temporarily relieved by his winning the Glinka Prize in November 1897 (for the First Sonata). On 31 January 1898 Scriabin and his wife gave a recital of his music at the Salle Erard. During the spring, Scriabin was hard at work on the Third Sonata and his wife was pregnant with their first child. The couple left Paris by train on 22 April. Their daughter Rimma was born in Moscow on 15 July, and the Third Sonata was completed a month later.

He next visited the city two years later, in June 1900, for the Exposition universelle. He stayed at the Hôtel du Longchamp, near the Trocadéro, and gave a recital on 10 July which included the first performance of a movement from the Third Sonata. He was back in Russia by August.

When Scriabin returned to Paris in November 1904, it was without Vera, from whom he was now estranged, but he was accompanied by his new love, Tatyana Schloezer. Scriabin settled once again at 5 rue de la

Néva, but when Tatyana went to stay with relatives in Brussels, he spent a couple of weeks at an expensive hotel at 16 rue Lord Byron, 8e (F8, Métro: Charles de Gaulle–Etoile), until she returned. Scriabin's main purpose on this visit was to arrange some performances of *The Divine Poem*. The impresario Gabriel Astruc suggested to Scriabin that the best option would be to secure Nikisch as conductor. A date for the first performance was arranged for 29 May 1905, at the Théâtre du Châtelet. Nikisch rehearsed the Lamoureux orchestra on three consecutive days (24–26 May); the reviews of the première were mixed. Scriabin was elated, until he learned from Astruc that all the money from the concert had been spent. With characteristic impulsiveness, Scriabin at once challenged Astruc to a duel, a challenge that was withdrawn as soon as the misunderstanding had been sorted out. In June 1905 Scriabin's first daughter, Rimma, died in Geneva. Shortly afterwards Scriabin finally broke with Vera and moved from Paris with the now pregnant Tatyana to Bogliasco, on the Italian Riviera. Scriabin travelled to America at the end of 1906 but returned to Paris in April 1907, this time renting a ground-floor apartment at 24 rue de la Tour, 16e (H6, Métro: Passy). The following month the celebrated concerts of Russian music from Glinka to Scriabin promoted by Diaghilev were given, a series in which Josef Hofmann played Scriabin's Third Sonata on 23 May. Nikisch was hoping to give the première of *The Poem of Ecstasy* on 30 May, but because the new work was not ready in time, he performed the Second Symphony instead; however, *The Poem of Ecstasy*, Scriabin's most famous orchestral work, was completed in Paris the following month and revised before the end of the year. By mid-July, the Scriabins had moved to Switzerland, and in the autumn Scriabin decided to settle in Lausanne. In 1910 he moved back to Russia for good, thereafter travelling abroad only for concert tours (his last visit to Paris was a brief stopover in April 1914, after a series of London concerts).

Déodat de Séverac (20 July 1872–24 March 1921)

Déodat de Séverac began his musical studies at the Toulouse Conservatoire. He enrolled as a student at the Schola Cantorum in Paris during autumn 1896 and took an apartment in the Latin Quarter at 5 rue Michelet, 6e (L13, Métro: Vavin). His teachers included d'Indy for composition, Guilmant for organ, André Pirro for music history, and Charles Bordes for medieval and Renaissance music; Séverac visited the abbey at Solesmes with Bordes in July 1897. In October 1900, the Schola Cantorum moved from the rue Stanislaus to 269 rue Saint-Jacques, 5e, and by December Séverac was living at 9 rue Serpente, 6e (K14, Métro: Cluny-Sorbonne). Around this time he met Ricardo Viñes and the artist Odilon Redon (he first encountered Debussy in January 1899). In 1902, Séverac became a member of the informal group of composers and writers known as the Apaches and developed his friendship with Ravel and the Godebski family. In January 1903, Séverac moved to 17 rue Brey, 17e (Métro: Charles de Gaulle–Etoile), near his friend Viñes, who lived in the (parallel) rue Troyon at the time. In April 1905, Séverac moved into lodgings at 32 rue Denfert-Rochereau (now rue Henri-Barbusse), 5e (M13, RER: Luxembourg), where he remained until February 1906. From then until 1910, Séverac lived at 116 rue d'Assas, 6e (M13, RER: Port Royal) near Joseph Canteloube, one of Séverac's closest friends, then living on the rue Le Verrier. Early in 1910, Séverac settled in Céret (Pyrénées-Orientales), where he was to live for much of the rest of his life. His only daughter was born in January 1913, and he married Henriette Tardieu the following May. He served as an auxiliary during World War I. Demobilised in 1919, he was made a chevalier of la Légion d'Honneur the following year at the request of the town of Céret. Early in 1921, Séverac's health declined rapidly, and, having fallen into a coma on 22 March, he died two days later.

Igor Stravinsky (17 June 1882–6 April 1971)

Stravinsky was a frequent visitor to Paris from the time of the *Firebird* première in June 1910. On this occasion he visited Debussy at 80 avenue du Bois de Boulogne. Satie photographed the two of them in Debussy's study (figure 1.16). Stravinsky was back in Paris for the first performance of *Petrushka* at the Théâtre du Châtelet on 13 June 1911. In May 1912 he attended the first performance of Nijinsky's ballet *L'après-midi d'un faune* at the Théâtre du Châtelet, and was there on 8 June for the première of *Daphnis et Chloé*, sitting in a box with Maurice Ravel, Florent Schmitt, and Maurice Delage. The following day, he made a short journey out of the city to the home of Louis Laloy at 17 bis rue des Capucins, Bellevue, near

Meudon, on the southwestern fringes of Paris (SNCF: Bellevue). The purpose of the visit was to play through the piano duet version of *Le sacre du
printemps* with Debussy (by that date only Part 1 of the work was written).
Laloy later recalled this historic occasion: "Debussy agreed to play the
bass. Stravinsky asked if he could remove his collar. His sight was not
improved by his glasses, and, pointing his nose to the keyboard, and sometimes humming a part that had been omitted from the arrangement, he led
into a welter of sound the supple, agile hands of his friend. Debussy followed without a hitch and seemed to make light of the difficulty. When
they had finished, there was no question of embracing, nor even of com-
pliments. We were dumbfounded, overwhelmed by this hurricane which
had come from the depths of the ages, and which had taken life by the
roots" (Laloy 1928, 213).

   On 13 May 1913 Stravinsky arrived in Paris for the final rehearsals of
Le sacre du printemps. Debussy and Ravel were both present at the dress
rehearsal on 28 May. The première, at the Théâtre des Champs-Elysées,
took place the next evening (Stravinsky had a ticket for seat 111). During
this epoch-making visit, Stravinsky stayed at the Hôtel Splendide, 1 bis
avenue Carnot, 17e (F7, Métro: Charles de Gaulle–Etoile), opposite
Ravel's apartment at no. 4. After eating oysters on 3 June 1913, Stravinsky
and his wife fell ill with typhus and were confined for more than a month
to the Villa Borghese sanatorium at 29 boulevard Victor-Hugo, Neuilly-
sur-Seine (Métro: Louise-Michel or Les Sablons). There they received
letters from Debussy, Ravel, and Satie, and a visit from Puccini. The
Stravinskys were discharged on about 8 July.

   For the next two decades, Stravinsky's wife and family lived in
Clarens, Morges, Biarritz, and, from October 1924 until 1931, in Nice.
Stravinsky spent much of the time touring and also in Paris, returning to
his family whenever possible. During the 1920s he had use of a studio in
Pleyel's premises at 22–24 rue de Rochechouart, 9e (E14, Métro: Cadet),
which also served as a small but remarkable apartment described in an
unsigned article in *Gringoire*, 27 October 1937: "He had only one room, and
an alcove containing a single piece of Henri II furniture.... Piles of plates
are spread on the small table where he eats, and pyjamas of all colours are
hanging on the wall. The room contains a sofa-bed covered with rough
cloth and a small piano at which Stravinsky... dreams and works, smoking
long cigarettes one after the other to the very end. On the walls are the per-

cussion instruments of the orchestra: bass drums, side drum, triangle, xylophone, Chinese bells, chimes" (Stravinsky and Craft 1979, 213).

During the 1920s, Stravinsky also spent a good deal of time at the apartment of Vera Sudeikina, at 82 rue des Petits-Champs, 2e (G13, Métro: Pyramides or Opéra). He met her, through Diaghilev, on 19 February 1921 (they married on 9 March 1940, after the death of Stravinsky's first wife, Catherine). It was also in Paris that Stravinsky developed an enthusiasm for motor cars. He received a driving licence in Paris on 12 December 1925 and soon bought a car (a Hotchkiss). In 1927, having purchased a Citroën, he got a parking ticket on its first outing (it was illegally parked in front of Hermès, where he had gone to buy a cravat); he burned out the engine soon afterwards. (Stravinsky also bought Vera Sudeikina a Renault in 1926.) His most important composition in 1926 was *Oedipus rex*, some of which was written in Paris. It was first performed privately at the home of the princesse de Polignac on 29 May 1928, with Stravinsky at the piano; the following evening he conducted the official première at the Théâtre Sarah-Bernhardt. On 18 October 1927, Stravinsky (conducting the *Firebird Suite*) and Ravel (conducting *La valse*) shared a concert to inaugurate the new Salle Pleyel, 252 rue du Faubourg-Saint-Honoré, 8e (Métro: Ternes).

From the end of 1931 on, Stravinsky was resident in Paris. In 1933, he began to make official enquiries about becoming a French citizen. Writing to the prefect of police on 27 December, he gave his address as 21 rue Viète, 17e (D9, Métro: Wagram). On 7 June 1934 he entered the Maison de Santé at 29 avenue Junot, 18e (C13, Métro: Lamarck-Caulaincourt), where he stayed for eight days to have his appendix removed. By 1935, Stravinsky had moved to an apartment at 25 rue du Faubourg-Saint-Honoré, 8e (G11, Métro: Madeleine), where he lived for the next five years. He composed several major works here, including the ballet *Jeu de cartes*, *Dumbarton Oaks*, and the first two movements of the Symphony in C. He left for New York at the end of September 1939. Immediately before leaving he stayed at 31 rue de l'Assomption, 16e (J4, Métro: Ranelagh), the home of Vera Sudeikina from 1936 and Stravinsky's last address before he sailed on 25 September 1939 aboard the SS *Manhattan*, from Bordeaux to New York.

Ambroise Thomas (5 August 1811–12 February 1896)

Thomas came to Paris from his native Metz and entered the Conservatoire in 1828. He won the Prix de Rome in 1832 and while in Italy became a friend of the artist Ingres. On his return to Paris in 1835 he began a long series of stage works. Before 1855, Thomas lived at 8 rue Taitbout, 9e (F13, Métro: Richelieu-Drouot), but that year he moved to 8 rue Saint-Georges, 9e (F13, Métro: Le Peletier), the address where, coincidentally, Edgar Degas had been born in 1834. The following year, Thomas became a professor of composition at the Conservatoire. His greatest operatic success was *Mignon*, first performed at the Opéra-Comique on 17 November 1866. The title role was sung by Galli-Marié, who was later to be the first Carmen. A little over a year later, Thomas had another resounding success with *Hamlet*, at the Opéra on 9 March 1868. Despite his age, the patriotic Thomas joined the National Guard during the Franco-Prussian War. He became director of the Conservatoire in 1871 and remained in the post for twenty-five years. His inflexibility and conservatism earned him some notoriety among a younger generation of musicians. Chabrier observed that "there are three kinds of music: good, bad, and that of Ambroise Thomas" (Myers 1969, 3). His failure to appear at Franck's funeral was deplored by d'Indy (who, incidentally, was not there either). Thomas was implacably hostile to Fauré, whom he considered to have modernist tendencies. He refused to appoint him to teach composition at the Conservatoire, with the remark: "Fauré? Never. If he's appointed, I resign" (Nectoux 1991, 224). Thomas was buried in Montmartre Cemetery.

Charles Tournemire (22 January 1870–4 November 1939)

Tournemire was a composer of striking originality, and an inspiration to Olivier Messiaen, Jehan Alain, Maurice Duruflé, and Jean Langlais, among others. He was born in Bordeaux but arrived in Paris as a student in 1886. He joined Franck's organ class in 1889 and, following Franck's death in 1890, continued his studies with Widor. He won a first prize for organ in 1891. The same year he began his career as organist at Saint-Médard, moving to Saint-Nicolas du Chardonnay in December 1897. From April 1898 until his death in 1939, Tournemire was titulaire at Sainte-Clotilde, where his predecessors had been César Franck and

Gabriel Pierné. In addition to a large output of vocal and instrumental music (including eight symphonies), Tournemire's most enduring achievement is his vast and extraordinary output for organ, notably the liturgical organ cycle *L'orgue mystique*, composed from 1927 to 1932. At a concert in Sainte-Clotilde on 25 April 1932, fourteen movements from this work were performed by Noëlie Pierront, Maurice Duruflé, André Fleury, Olivier Messiaen, Jean Langlais, Daniel-Lesur, and Gaston Litaize. For many years (up to the time of his death) Tournemire lived at 4 rue Milne-Edwards (figure 1.57), 17e (D7, Métro: Péreire).

Edgar Varèse (22 December 1883–6 November 1965)

Varèse was born at 12 rue de Strasbourg (now rue du Huit-Mai 1945), 10e (E16, Métro: Gare de l'Est). He spent much of his childhood in Villars (Burgundy) and Turin. His father was a brutal man implacably opposed to Varèse's following a career in music, but after years of domestic violence and strife, Varèse returned to Paris in 1903 to study. At first he lived in a small apartment on the rue Saint-André-des-Arts, 6e (Métro: Saint-Michel). In 1904 Varèse entered the Schola Cantorum, where he studied composition and conducting with d'Indy and fugue with Roussel. Varèse found d'Indy's teaching repressive and later recalled that d'Indy "conceived a tenacious enmity" towards him (Ouellette 1973, 14). Meanwhile, Varèse found his studies of medieval and Renaissance music with Charles Bordes a revelation. He also studied at the Conservatoire with Widor and Massenet (who did much to encourage the young composer), and he met a good many original thinkers who became friends, including Satie, Picasso, and Apollinaire. In about 1905 Varèse was living at 41 rue Monge, 5e (L15, Métro: Cardinal-Lemoine). On 5 November 1907, he married Suzanne Bing, a drama student at the Conservatoire; they lived in an unheated room on the rue Descartes, 5e (L15, Métro: Cardinal-Lemoine). In 1908 he left for Berlin to study with Busoni, remained there for most of the next few years, but returned to Paris by 29 October 1908, when he met Debussy (and was given an inscribed score of *La mer*). In December 1908, Varèse also met Ravel. His marriage to Suzanne broke up in 1913, and Varèse returned from Berlin to Paris, where he attended the first performance of *Le sacre du printemps*. During the months before World War I, Varèse was living at 49 rue de Seine, 6e (J13, Métro: Mabillon). In April 1915, he was mobilised, but his military service was brief: he contracted double pneumonia and left the army soon afterwards. He stayed briefly at 12 avenue du Maine, 15e (L11, Métro: Faulgière), before embarking for New York on 18 December 1915. There, in 1917, he met Louise Norton, who was to become his devoted second wife. In 1921 he finished *Amériques*, his earliest surviving work, and wrote *Octandre* during 1923. Varèse was back in Paris from March to December 1924, staying at Fernand Léger's studio, 86 rue Notre-Dame-des-Champs, 6e (M13, Métro: Vavin). It is likely that he worked here on *Intégrales*, which was given its première on 1 March 1925 when Varèse was back in New York. During August–December 1926, Varèse stayed in Paris (at an address on the Île Saint-Louis), where he worked on *Arcana*. He returned for a much longer stay in October 1928. At first he took a room at the Hôtel Jacob, 44 rue Jacob, 6e (J13, Métro: Saint-Germain-des-Prés), then at the Hôtel Paris–New York, before finding an apartment at 31 rue de Bourgogne, 7e (J11, Métro: Varenne). Several of Varèse's major works were heard for the first time in Paris during this stay, including a concert on 14 March 1930 in which he conducted *Offrandes* and *Octandre*. In June 1931, he moved to 3 villa des Camélias, 14e (P9, Métro: Porte de Vanves). Here he composed his extraordinary percussion masterpiece *Ionisation*, before moving in 1932 to 7 rue Bellini, 16e (H6, Métro: Trocadéro). At the end of

1933, Varèse left Paris and was only to return twenty-one years later: in October 1954 he stayed at the Hôtel de Versailles, 60 boulevard Montparnasse, 15e (L11, Métro: Montparnasse-Bienvenue), where he worked on the electronic tapes for *Déserts*. During this visit, Varèse led a simple and solitary existence, often eating at a small bistro for taxi drivers behind the Gare Montparnasse. The première of *Déserts*, conducted by Hermann Scherchen, was at the Théâtre des Champs-Elysées on 2 December 1954, and it caused perhaps the greatest uproar there since *Le sacre du printemps*. The critic in *Le Monde* (4 December 1904) described the scene: "Murmurs at first, then, crescendo, waves of vociferous protests mingled with wavering applause.... Shouts of 'That's enough,' 'Shame'.... The seats in the Théâtre des Champs-Elysées are, thanks be to heaven, solidly screwed to the floor" (Ouellette 1973, 185–86).

In 1957, Varèse came to Europe to prepare the *Poème électronique*, created with Le Corbusier and Xenakis for the Philips Pavilion at the 1958 Brussels World Fair. On his way back from Brussels in July 1958, Varèse paid his last visit to Paris: a brief stay at the Hôtel Madison, near Saint-Germain-des-Prés.

Ralph Vaughan Williams (12 October 1872–26 August 1958)

Following the success of his choral work *Toward the Unknown Region* at the 1907 Leeds Festival, Vaughan Williams went to Paris in December of that year to study with Ravel for three months. During this stay, his address was Hôtel de l'Univers et du Portugal, 10 rue Croix-des-Petits-Champs, 1er (H13–G14, Métro: Palais Royal). The meetings with Ravel had a lasting influence: "I learned much from him.... 'Complexe mais pas compliqué' was his motto. He showed me how to orchestrate in points of colour rather than in lines. It was an invigorating experience to find all artistic problems looked at from what was to me an entirely new angle" (Vaughan Williams 1964, 79).

The two composers remained friends for the rest of Ravel's life and corresponded regularly. Immediately after returning home from his studies, Vaughan Williams composed the song cycle *On Wenlock Edge* (for voice, string quartet, and piano), perhaps his most overtly Impressionist work, and certainly the one which owes most to the music of his distinguished teacher.

Giuseppe Verdi (9 October 1813–27 January 1901)

Verdi paid his first visit to Paris in June 1847, before travelling to London for the première of *I Masnadieri* (22 July 1847). He was back in Paris by 27 July 1847, making preparations for the first performance of *Jérusalem* (the revised version of *I Lombardi*) at the Opéra (26 November 1847). Verdi himself was dubious about the quality of the company: "I have never heard worse singers and more mediocre choristers," he wrote to Clarina Maffei in a letter of 8 June 1847 (Weaver 1977, 171). He took lodgings on the rue Saint-Georges, 9e, but it is probable that he lived for some of the time with Giuseppina Strepponi in her nearby apartment at 13 rue de la Victoire, 9e (F13–F14, Métro: Le Peletier), where another well-known tenant was the singer Rosina Stoltz. He remained in the city over the winter, probably to spend more time with Strepponi, to whom he dedicated *Jérusalem*. Verdi finished *Il corsaro* in Paris in February 1848 and took a lively interest in the 1848 revolution which overthrew King Louis-Philippe. While Verdi was able to view political developments in France with a certain amused detachment, he was alarmed to learn of similar developments in Italy. He returned to Milan on 5 April, as soon as he heard about Austrian troops' firing on a peaceful crowd. By mid-May 1848, Verdi was back in Paris, spending the summer with Strepponi in Passy, where they lived together openly. He finished *La battaglia di Legnano* in December 1848, then left to prepare for the première in Rome (27 January 1849). In January 1849, Verdi's song "L'abandonnée" was published by Escudier in *La France Musicale*, with a dedication to Strepponi. Verdi was back in Paris by 1 February. On 17 May, he wrote to the librettist Cammarano thanking him for the outline of *Luisa Miller*, which was to be Verdi's next operatic project. He left Paris at the end of July.

Verdi's next visit to Paris was in December 1851. He lived with Strepponi at 24 rue Saint-Georges, 9e (F13, Métro: Le Peletier), and worked on *Il trovatore*. They sometimes went to the theatre together, probably, for example, to see *La dame aux camélias* at the Théâtre du Vaudeville (it opened on 2 February 1852). It was to inspire one of his most enduringly popular works: he told relatives that he began composing *La traviata* immediately after seeing the play, before he even had a libretto. The couple left Paris in early March.

Following the premières in Italy of *Il trovatore* and *La traviata*, he left for Paris with Strepponi on 15 October 1853, full of plans to compose an opera on King Lear (never realised). The main purpose in going to Paris was for *Les vêpres siciliennes*, written to a libretto by Scribe and due for performance at the Opéra in December 1854. Verdi's Paris address during this period was 4 rue Richer, 9e (F14–F15, Métro: Cadet). Work progressed slowly, and by the end of May Verdi and Strepponi had taken a country house at Mandres-les-Roses, where a place Verdi now celebrates its famous visitor. The couple remained there until 1 October, the date on which rehearsals for *Les vêpres siciliennes* began. These did not start well: by the end of the first week the unpredictable soprano Sophie Cruvelli had vanished. She was eventually tracked down on the Côte d'Azur with Baron Vigier (whom she was later to marry), and rehearsals restarted at the end of November. Verdi hoped the opera could now open in February, but in January things were so unsatisfactory that he wrote to Crosnier (director of the Opéra) threatening to cancel the contract altogether. At last the work was ready by the end of May. Berlioz described the rehearsal he attended on 1 June 1855 in a letter to Auguste Morel of 2 June: "Verdi is at loggerheads with all the people at the Opéra. He made a terrible scene at the dress rehearsal yesterday. I feel sorry for the poor man; I put myself in his place. Verdi is a worthy and honourable artist" (Weaver 1977, 195). The première on 13 June was a greater success than Verdi had expected. He took time later in the month to visit the Exposition universelle. Apart from short visits to London, he remained in Paris until just before Christmas. He arrived in Bussetto on 23 December 1855.

Verdi next travelled to Paris on 31 July 1856 and again stayed at 4 rue Richer. After a brief visit to Compiègne in October as the guest of Napoléon III, Verdi moved into a new apartment with Strepponi at 20 rue Neuve-des-Mathurins (now rue des Mathurins), 9e (F12, Métro: Havre-Caumartin). Here Verdi worked on revisions to *Le trouvère* (the French version of *Il trovatore*), which was given its première at the Opéra on 12 January 1857. He left for Italy the next day. On 29 August 1859 Verdi and Strepponi were secretly married in the village of Collange-sous-Salève, near Geneva.

Verdi had been asked to write *L'inno delle nazioni* for the London international exhibition in May 1862. He chose the twenty-year-old poet Arrigo Boito to write the text, and the two met for the first time in March 1862 at the Hôtel Britannique (possibly the hotel listed in the 1903 Baedeker at 20 avenue Victoria, 1er), the start of a long and immensely productive partnership. Verdi spent Christmas 1862 in Paris, leaving for Madrid in January 1863. In mid-March 1863 Verdi returned to Paris, to prepare a revival of *Les vêpres siciliennes*, meanwhile staying at the Hôtel Europa. The rehearsals were fraught with difficulties, and after three months of patient preparation, Verdi finally lost his temper when the orchestra complained about the number of rehearsals. Verdi picked up his hat and walked out of the theatre. He left Paris in July 1863. Despite these unhappy scenes, Perrin, the director of the Opéra, asked Verdi for a new work. The composer wrote robustly to Escudier on 19 June 1865: "You are joking?! Write for the Opéra!!! Don't you think I would be in danger of having my eyes scratched out, after what happened two years ago at the rehearsals of *Vêpres?*" (Phillips-Matz 1993, 500). Nevertheless, he agreed to write a new opera. This was to be *Don Carlos*, a work he described in a letter to Léon Escudier (18 June 1866) as "born in fire and flames." Verdi arrived in September 1865 and stayed at 67 avenue des Champs-Elysées, 8e (F9, Métro: Franklin D. Roosevelt), the house where the ballerina Fanny Cerrito lived. Evidently the location left Verdi more favourably disposed towards the city, and Haussmann's developments seemed to please him. He wrote to Giuseppe Piroli on 31 December 1865: "Paris becomes more beautiful every day. There is a new Paris constructed in the last two years around the Arc de l'Etoile which is truly marvellous. The inhabitants are no crazier than usual" (Weaver 1977, 215). He finished Act 1 of *Don Carlos* in Paris but was back in Italy during summer 1866, looking for a winter residence in Genoa. Returning in September (again staying at 67 avenue des Champs-Elysées), Verdi wrote to Ricordi with depressingly familiar news: "We must not speak for the present of *Don Carlos:* it will not go on in October, or in November, or in December, and perhaps not even in January." On 7 December 1866, Strepponi wrote to Mauro Corticelli: "*Don Carlos*, God and the tortoises of the Opéra willing, will perhaps be put on at the end of January. What a punishment for a composer's sins is the staging of an opera in that theatre, with its machinery of marble and lead!" (216). The death of Verdi's father on 14 January 1867 distressed the composer still further. A dress rehearsal finally took place on 24 February 1867, after which Verdi made a number of cuts. The première was given at the Opéra on 11 March 1867 and Verdi left immediately for Genoa, in despair. He wrote to Count Arrivabene on 12 March: "Last night *Don Carlos*. It was not a success!!"

(217). Despite this pessimistic verdict, *Don Carlos* did well at the Opéra: it ran for forty-three performances.

Verdi and Strepponi were back in Paris in March 1870, attending Patti's performances of *Rigoletto* and *La traviata* at the Théâtre Italien. During this stay they took rooms at the Hôtel de Bade, 32 boulevard des Italiens, 9e (F13, Métro: Opéra). This was where Verdi was to stay for all his Paris visits before 1894, and his life here was vividly described by Jacopo Caponi in an article published in *Le Figaro* on 17 April 1886:

> Verdi, following his well-established habit of twenty years, stayed at the Hôtel de Bade, which, although lacking the lavishness of the modern caravanserais, has the advantage of being situated in the heart of Paris. The Maestro occupies four little rooms on the mezzanine from where he can at any moment plunge into the sea of Parisian life. When visiting Verdi you do not have to wait in antechambers, and there is absolutely no sign of clients and courtiers. You knock, and almost immediately, having crossed the first drawing-room, you hear the Maestro's familiar voice: "Entrez!"—and very often he will open the door himself. More often than not Verdi is quite alone, reading the latest Parisian news, the latest novel, or skimming through the compositions that rain in on him with the customary "as a token of esteem." One day I found him browsing through Gevaert's *Traité de composition* and heard him say: "That is an excellent work, useful and practical." In a corner of the room is a piano which, could it but speak, would tell you more than I.... There is always manuscript paper on the piano.
>
> To all those people who, after a thousand circumlocutions, finish by asking Verdi the aim of his trip to Paris, he replies good-naturedly and very shrewdly: "I come from time to time to keep in touch. One cannot afford to neglect Paris for long. And also—I simply had to talk to my tailor." Sometimes he ends with a confession: "I do not deny that I was curious to hear some of the artists who are presently in fashion." (Conati 1984, 177–88)

In 1873 he wrote some of the Requiem in his rooms at the Hôtel de Bade, and on subsequent visits to Paris he conducted several sensationally successful performances of this work and of *Aida*. On most of these trips, Verdi was accompanied not only by Strepponi but also by Theresa Stolz, with whom the composer was widely rumoured to be having an affair. In

November 1878, Verdi and Strepponi visited Paris for the Exposition universelle. Later the composer returned to the city to sort out the chaos caused by the financial collapse of Escudier's publishing house. In April 1894 Verdi was in Paris for the French premières of *Falstaff* at the Opéra-Comique. On this occasion he stayed in a suite at the Grand Hôtel, 12 boulevard des Capucines, 9e (F13, Métro: Opéra), having been told that his favourite Hôtel de Bade had seen better days (in 1903, Baedeker stated that the Hôtel de Bade was a "maison de vielle réputation" with two hundred rooms priced at 5 francs; meals cost 1.50, 3.50, and 5 francs excluding wine; *pension* was available from 12 francs. The hotel had a side entrance at 6 rue du Helder). During the summer, when Verdi was back in Italy composing the new ballet music for the Paris production of *Otello*, he arranged to stay in the same suite at the Grand Hôtel. He arrived at the Gare de Lyon early on the morning of 26 September 1894, and *Otello* opened at the Opéra on 12 October 1894, a few days after Verdi celebrated his eighty-first birthday. This was his last visit to the city. Plans to attend the première of the *Quattro pezzi sacri* at the Opéra four years later (7 April 1898) had to be abandoned on the orders of Verdi's doctor.

Pauline Viardot (18 July 1821–18 May 1910)

The sister of the legendary Maria Malibran, Pauline Viardot (Viardot-Garcia) was a member of an important musical dynasty. She was born at 83 rue de Richelieu, 2e (F13, Métro: Richelieu-Drouot). A celebrated mezzo-soprano, composer, and teacher, she was also a fine pianist, having studied the instrument with both Liszt and Chopin. She lived for a time in the square d'Orléans, 9e (F13, Métro: Trinité), where Chopin, George Sand, and Marie Taglioni also had apartments. In 1840 she married Louis Viardot (1800–83), director of the Théâtre Italien and founder of the *Revue Indépendante*. In 1848, they made their home in a newly built town house at 50 rue de Douai, 9e (D12, Métro: Blanche); this imposing building, on a corner site, is currently in a poor state of repair. The role of Fidès in Meyerbeer's *Le prophète* (first performed at the Opéra in 1849) was written especially for Pauline Viardot. Following the performance, Berlioz described her as "one of the greatest artists in the past and present history of music," and in 1859 she scored an immense success in Berlioz's

version of Gluck's *Orfeo*, giving 150 performances in the space of three years. She retired from the stage in 1863 and moved for several years to Baden-Baden. Her musical tastes were all-encompassing, ranging from a lively interest in baroque to contemporary music. In Baden-Baden she became a friend of Brahms (who composed a *Morgenständchen*, now lost, for her forty-fourth birthday in 1865). In 1870, she gave the first performance of Brahms's *Alto rhapsody*, composed at Baden-Baden in September 1869. Viardot returned to Paris in 1871.

Viardot was admired by many writers who visited her Thursday salons. On those occasions genius mingled freely with genius (figure 1.58): it was in the Viardot apartment that Charles Dickens met George Sand in 1856, and other literary giants who frequented the rue de Douai salon included Flaubert, the young Henry James, and, most famously, Ivan Turgenev, who fell in love with her in the 1840s, and lived more or less permanently on the second floor of the Viardot home until his death (at Bougival) on 3 September 1883, a few months after Louis Viardot himself died in the rue de Douai house on 5 May 1883. Several generations were encompassed in the galaxy of musicians who came to Pauline Viardot's house, among them Chopin, Liszt, Berlioz, Verdi, Bizet, Gounod, Massenet, Franck, and Fauré.

In May 1860, Wagner gave a truly extraordinary private performance of *Tristan und Isolde*, singing Tristan himself opposite Viardot's Isolde, with Karl Klindworth as the accompanist. They had an audience of two: Wagner's benefactor Marie de Kalergis and Berlioz. Saint-Saëns, a frequent guest, said of Viardot: "What made her even more captivating than her talent as a singer was her personality—one of the most amazing I have ever known.... Madame Viardot was as learned a musician as anyone could be" (Saint-Saëns 1919, 146 and 149).

Saint-Saëns, who often served as her accompanist, also described the different music rooms in the house: "The Viardots used to give in their apartment on Thursday evenings really fine musical festivals which my surviving contemporaries still remember. From the salon in which the famous portrait by Ary Scheffer was hung and which was devoted to instrumental and vocal music, we went down a short staircase to a gallery filled with valuable paintings, and finally to an exquisite organ, one of Cavaillé-Coll's masterpieces" (Saint-Saëns 1919, 148).

In that organ room Viardot, Julius Stockhausen, and others gave private performances of Bach cantatas as the volumes of the Bach-Gesellschaft began to appear (Viardot was among the first subscribers). The organ described by Saint-Saëns was installed by Cavaillé-Coll in 1851. After Viardot moved, the instrument was sold to the church of Notre-Dame in Melun, south of Paris.

The astonishing array of musical and literary talent present on many occasions was recalled by Fauré, who had first been introduced to the Viardot circle by Saint-Saëns in about 1872: "This was 'something else.' There we performed charades with Turgenev and Saint-Saëns as actors and Flaubert, George Sand, Ernest Renan [author of the sensationally successful *La vie de Jésus*], and even Louis Blanc [the politician and historian] as spectators. George Sand was at this time a grand old lady. Turgenev was the great panjandrum himself, handsome and with a gentleness that was even more attractive. I still remember the sound of his voice to the extent that, when I read one of his books, it seems to me that I can hear him talking. Gustave Flaubert took great delight in our jesting, but it was Renan who amused him most" (Orledge 1979, 10).

On Sundays, the Viardot household was given over to specifically musical events. In July 1877, Fauré was engaged briefly to Pauline's youngest daughter Marianne, but she broke off the engagement in October (and subsequently married the pianist Victor Duvernoy). Following the deaths in 1883 of her husband Louis and her lover Turgenev, Pauline Viardot moved across the river from the house on the rue de Douai to 243 boulevard Saint-Germain, 7e (J11–H11, Métro: Solférino). She was buried in Montmartre Cemetery.

Louis Vierne (8 October 1870–1 June 1937)

Vierne was born in Poitiers. The family moved to Paris in April 1873, settling first at 4 passage de l'Elysée-des-Beaux-Arts (now rue André-Antoine), 18e (D13, Métro: Pigalle), then moving to a larger apartment at 11 bis rue Geoffroy-Marie, 9e (F14, Métro: Rue Montmartre). In 1880, the Viernes moved to 4 place Dancourt (now place Charles-Dullin), 18e (D14, Métro: Anvers), which was to remain the family home for many years. In 1880 also, Vierne heard Franck playing during a Mass in Sainte-Clotilde, a revelatory experience for the younger man. Vierne was almost blind, and the following year he entered the Institution des Jeunes Aveugles, 56 boulevard des Invalides, 7e (L10, Métro: Duroc). Vierne studied and lived here (except during vacations) until 1890. In 1883–84 he reported excitedly on the installation of "the finest concert organ in Paris," a large new three-manual Cavaillé-Coll organ in the school hall (elsewhere in the institution were two smaller instruments by Cavaillé-Coll). Vierne was apprehensive but thrilled at the prospect of the revered Franck serving as the visiting adjudicator for his violin and piano examinations, but the composer was charming, and beginning in 1888 he gave Vierne weekly lessons. Vierne enrolled at the Conservatoire in October 1890 and attended four classes with the ailing Franck, who died on 8 November. Widor was appointed the new professor of organ in December, and in February 1892, he invited Vierne to be his deputy at Saint-Sulpice. In 1894, Widor asked Vierne to assist with teaching duties at the Conservatoire, and Vierne took his commitment seriously, meeting Widor for dinner each week to discuss the progress of the class. His pupils in 1897 included the volatile Henri Mulet and Charles Quef (Messiaen's predecessor at the Trinité). While at Caen in July 1898, Vierne met Arlette Taskin, whom he married in April 1899. He moved with his new bride to 3 rue Coëtlogon, 6e (K12, Métro: Sèvres-Babylone). On 21 May 1900 Vierne won the competition for the organist's position at Notre-Dame-de-Paris. He moved in about 1905 to a large new

1.59 Vierne arriving at Notre-Dame in 1928.

apartment at 60 rue des Saints-Pères, 7e (K12, Métro: Sèvres-Babylone). In May 1906 Vierne, who was still able to see just enough to go out alone, fell into a ditch on the quai Voltaire and broke his leg in three places. A long convalescence followed, and he was not able to return to duties at Notre-Dame until January 1907. His marriage was becoming increasingly unhappy, and the couple were divorced on 4 August 1909. (Vierne was assured by the church authorities that such a course of action was acceptable provided he did not remarry.) Misfortune continued to dog Vierne: his mother died on 25 March 1911, and Guilmant died less than a week later. In 1914, Vierne moved to rooms in the magnificent Passy home of his pupil Marthe Braquemond and her husband at 1 rue Louis-David, 16e (H6, Métro: Rue de la Pompe). He continued to teach—Marcel Dupré, Nadia Boulanger, Maurice Duruflé, and André Fleury were among his pupils. Following a diagnosis of glaucoma, Vierne left Paris in 1916 to live in Switzerland for four years, and his sight, already very poor, continued to deteriorate gradually. The death in combat of his brother René in 1918 was a terrible blow. He returned to Paris in April 1920, and after a year in temporary lodgings, his friends the Richepins found him a small apartment in 1921 at 37 rue Saint-Ferdinand, 17e (E6, Métro: Porte Maillot), which was to be his address for the rest of his life. During the next ten years he made a number of highly successful foreign recital tours. He died at the console,

during a recital in Notre-Dame. Vierne had begun with the first performance of his own *Triptyque* op. 58 and then prepared to start an improvisation
on *Alma Redemptoris Mater*. He was seen to stumble, and a low pedal note
sounded. Vierne had been titulaire at Notre-Dame for thirty-eight years
(figure 1.59). He was buried in Montparnasse Cemetery.

Heitor Villa-Lobos (5 March 1887–17 November 1959)

Villa-Lobos first visited Paris in 1923 on a Brazilian government grant.
During that stay he wrote *Chôros* no. 2 and *Chôros* no. 7. He returned to
Rio de Janeiro in 1924. In 1927 he visited Paris for a second time, accompanied by his wife Lucília Guimarães. The couple settled at an apartment
at 11 place Saint-Michel, 6e (J14, Métro: Saint-Michel), that had been lent
to Villa-Lobos by his friend Carlos Guinle. During this three-year stay,
he worked as an editor for the firm of Max Eschig, which was to publish
much of his music. The premières of *Chôros* no. 8 and *Chôros* no. 10 (both
composed in Rio in 1925) were given in Paris in 1927 and enthusiastically
reviewed by Florent Schmitt, who became one of Villa-Lobos's closest
friends. For long periods between 1952 and 1959, Villa-Lobos was again
based in Paris. He always stayed during these years at the Bedford Hôtel,
17 rue de l'Arcade, 8e (F11, Métro: Madeleine), and his residence there is
commemorated by a plaque, which was unveiled in 1971. During the later
years in Paris Villa-Lobos conducted the celebrated series of recordings
of his works. He gave a concert in February 1952 at the Théâtre des
Champs-Elysées, where he conducted the first complete performance of
The Discovery of Brazil, and between 1954 and 1958 he recorded for the
Pathé-Marconi company this score, all the *Bachianas Brasileiras*, four of
the *Chôros*, and several other works.

Richard Wagner (22 May 1813–13 February 1883)

Between 1839 and 1867, Wagner visited Paris on several occasions and
had two long stays in 1839–42 and 1859–61. Seldom has a composer had
such an uneasy relationship with the city or its people. Wagner and his
wife Minna arrived on French soil for the first time in August 1839. (He
was fleeing from creditors in Riga and had just made an abortive visit to
London.) He visited Meyerbeer, who was taking his summer holiday at

Boulogne. Meyerbeer introduced the young Wagner to Moscheles, gave him letters of introduction to the publisher Schlesinger and the conductor Habeneck, and wrote a personal letter of recommendation for him to Pauline Viardot. Following his arrival in Paris on 17 September 1839, Wagner earned a meagre living making piano arrangements for Schlesinger of operas by Donizetti and Halévy. Meyerbeer's kindness was soon to be repaid with bitter hostility from Wagner, who was convinced that the older composer harboured a grudge against him. During this visit, Wagner, Minna, and their dog Robber lodged first in a fourth-floor apartment at 3 rue de la Tonnellerie (now 31 rue du Pont-Neuf), 1er, the alleged birthplace of Molière (H14, Métro: Châtelet). In April 1840 the Wagners moved to an apartment on the fourth floor of 25 rue du Helder, 9e (F13, Métro: Opéra), now demolished. According to a letter from Minna in October 1840, Wagner was sent for a short while to a debtors' prison, but this story may have been a ruse to extract money from friends. At the end of April 1841, Wagner moved to 3 avenue de Meudon, now 27 avenue du Château, Meudon (SNCF: Bellevue), where he worked on *Der fliegende Holländer*. At the end of October 1841, he moved back to the city. He lodged at 14 rue Jacob, 6e (J13, Métro: Saint-Germain-des-Prés), staying there until the following April. It was a time of important musical encounters for Wagner: he met Berlioz and Liszt, and the Orchestre de la Société des Concerts du Conservatoire played his Faust Overture at an open rehearsal (in March 1840). The philologist Samuel Lehrs, a fellow German living in Paris, introduced Wagner to the legends of Lohengrin and Tannhäuser, and he heard performances of Beethoven's Ninth Symphony and the *Symphonie fantastique* of Berlioz. During 1840–41 Wagner was active as a critic for the *Revue et Gazette Musicale*, and he wrote some scathing attacks on French music in general (and on Berlioz and Meyerbeer in particular) for the German periodical *Europa*. His main preoccupation during 1841, however, was the composition of *Der fliegende Holländer*, written while Wagner was living in Paris and Meudon.

Because of Wagner's participation in the May 1849 uprising in Dresden, a warrant was issued for his arrest. He fled first to Zurich, but Liszt encouraged him to go to Paris in June 1849 and indeed financed the trip. Wagner stayed this time with Liszt's secretary Gaetano Belloni at 36 rue des Martyrs, 9e (E14, Métro: Saint-Georges), later moving out of the city in June to La Ferté-sous-Jouarre near Rueil, to escape the cholera epidemic. Wagner arrived on 1 February 1850 for another visit to France. He stayed until April before travelling to Bordeaux, where he hatched a particularly ill-advised (and unsuccessful) scheme to elope to the Orient with Jessie Laussot. In August 1850, back in Zurich, he took the opportunity to renew his attack on Meyerbeer by writing the essay *Das Judenthum in der Musik*.

His next visit to Paris he made with Liszt in October 1853. Wagner met Cosima (then fifteen) for the first time while dining with Liszt and his family. Wagner stayed briefly in the city in 1855, on his way to London to conduct a series of concerts for the Philharmonic Society, and visited Paris again in January 1858. On the second occasion he found that critical reaction to his music had become increasingly antagonistic. Following Minna's discovery in April 1858 of a letter from Wagner to Mathilde Wesendonck, he left Zurich for Venice and then Lucerne, where he finished *Tristan* in August 1859. He travelled to Paris the following month and stayed until July 1861. During this extended stay, his first address was at 4 avenue Matignon, 8e (G10–F10, Métro: Franklin D. Roosevelt), but by mid-November 1859 he had moved to 16 rue Newton, 16e (F8, Métro: Kléber). By 15 October 1860, Wagner was at a new address: 3 rue d'Aumale, 9e (E13, Métro: Saint-Georges), where he stayed until the end of July 1861. It was an important visit, during which he gave three concerts on 25 January and 1 and 8 February 1860 (the first was attended by Auber, Berlioz, Gounod, Rossini, Thomas, and Fantin-Latour, among others). In 1860 too, Wagner sang the male lead in a private performance of *Tristan*

1.60 The Hôtel du Quai Voltaire, where Wagner spent the winter of 1861–62.

und Isolde, opposite Pauline Viardot as Isolde. The sojourn culminated in the scandalous première of *Tannhäuser* at the Opéra on 13 March 1861, at which the Jockey Club, up to its customary mischief, supplied its members with small whistles. The inevitable hisses, boos, and whistling ensued; the contemptuous behaviour was repeated at the two subsequent performances, after which Wagner withdrew the work. Among Wagner's defenders were the poet Baudelaire, the artist Fantin-Latour, and the publisher Flaxland, who issued the vocal score of *Tannhäuser* in its Paris version.

After a trip to Vienna, Wagner returned to Paris by 3 December 1861 and settled at the Hôtel du Quai Voltaire (figure 1.60), 19 quai Voltaire, 7e (J12–H12, Métro: Rue du Bac), the same address at which Baudelaire had written *Les fleurs du mal* a few years earlier, in 1856–58. Here Wagner wrote the libretto of *Die Meistersinger von Nürnberg*. (Sibelius and Oscar Wilde were later guests at the hotel.) Wagner left for Germany on 1 February 1862.

His last visit to Paris was for the Exposition universelle in October 1867, but his subsequent absence from the city did nothing to lessen the enthusiasm of his French supporters. Judith Gautier, Ernest Reyer, and others wrote passionate articles in support of Wagner and his music, and in 1869 Cosima (by then his wife) brought a quartet led by Pierre Maurin (who ran the Société des Derniers Quatuors de Beethoven) from Paris to Tribschen to play late Beethoven quartets for Wagner on his birthday. Later the same year, Judith Gautier and her husband Catulle Mendès visited the Wagners. In June 1870 a large French contingent, including Saint-Saëns and Duparc, went to Munich for the première of *Die Walküre*. Less than a month later, the Franco-Prussian War broke out. For some time afterwards, many French musicians expressed hostility to Wagner's music, though there was a substantial French pilgrimage to the first Bayreuth Festival in August 1876. From 1879 onwards, Pasdeloup, Lamoureux, and Colonne offered Wagner on their programmes in Paris, and audiences treated the events with a kind of awed reverence.

The artist Pierre-Auguste Renoir visited Wagner in Palermo (where the composer was just finishing *Parsifal*) on two consecutive days in January 1882. They met at the Hôtel des Palmes, and Renoir described the sitting in entertaining detail in a letter to an unidentified correspondent dated 14 January 1882:

> The most absurd conversation begins, strewn with uhs and ohs, half
> French, half German with guttural endings.... In the end I had time

enough to say all the silly things you can imagine.... Next day [14 January] I was there at noon. You know the rest. He was very cheerful, but I was very nervous and sorry not to be Ingres. In short, I think my time was well spent, 35 minutes, which is not much, but if I had stopped sooner, it would have been excellent, because my model ended by losing a little of his cheerfulness and getting stiff. I followed these changes too much—anyway you'll see. At the end Wagner asked to have a look, and he said, "Ach! Ach! I look like a Protestant minister"—which is true. Anyway, I was very glad not to have failed too badly; I now have a little souvenir of that splendid head. (Distel 1995, 135–36)

Renoir's portrait of Wagner now hangs in the Musée d'Orsay, a gift from Alfred Cortot in 1947, and a copy (made by Renoir in 1893) hangs in the Bibliothèque-Musée de l'Opéra.

Kurt Weill (2 March 1900–3 April 1950)

On 21 March 1933, Weill fled Germany by crossing the border in a car with Caspar and Erika Neher. By 1 April 1933 he was staying at the Hôtel Splendide, 1 bis avenue Carnot, 17e (F7–E7, Métro: Charles de Gaulle–Etoile). Shortly afterwards he went to live with Charles and Marie-Laure de Noailles at 11 place des Etats-Unis, 16e (G7, Métro: Boissière). Here he renewed work on his Symphony no. 2, commissioned by the princesse de Polignac, which he had started before fleeing Berlin. In April–May 1933, Weill wrote *Die sieben Todsünden*, first performed on 7 June at the Théâtre des Champs-Elysées with choreography by Georges Balanchine. The work is dedicated to his hosts, the Vicomte and Vicomtesse Charles de Noailles. After a holiday in Italy, Weill returned to the Hôtel Splendide and wrote *La grande complainte de Fantômas*, a "ballad for radio," first performed on 3 November. By 9 November 1933 Weill had moved to his new apartment on the first floor of 9 bis place Ernest-Dreux, Louveciennes (SNCF: Louveciennes). After finishing the Symphony no. 2 in February 1934, he wrote to Lotte Lenya on 20 February, about the princesse de Polignac, who had given him the commission and invited him to dine the following Sunday: "I'm ready to string her up on one of the pipes of her organ if she doesn't give me my money" (Symonette and Kowalke 1996, 112). After visiting Max Reinhardt in Salzburg during May, Weill composed two songs for Lys Gauty and, in September, wrote *Marie Galante,* first performed at the Théâtre de Paris on 22 December. In October he was in Amsterdam for the première of the Symphony no. 2, conducted by Bruno Walter. In January 1935, Weill was in London preparing *A Kingdom for a Cow,* but he was back in Paris in August, working on the epic *Der Weg der Verheissung,* later entitled *The Eternal Road.* At the end of August 1935, Weill left Europe. He arrived in New York on 10 September.

Charles-Marie Widor (21 February 1844–12 March 1937)

Widor came to Paris in 1870 to take up a one-year appointment as Lefébure-Wély's successor at Saint-Sulpice. He was to stay in this post for the next sixty-four years. Widor's first home in Paris was near Saint-Sulpice, at the Hôtel de Sourdéac, 8 rue Garancière, 6e (K13, Métro: Mabillon or Saint-Sulpice). During his first decade in the city he wrote the eight numbered organ symphonies which took full advantage of the magnificent Cavaillé-Coll instrument in Saint-Sulpice. In 1893 Widor moved to 3 rue de l'Abbaye (now part of the Institut Catholique), 6e (J13, Métro: Saint-Germain-des-Prés). Following the death of César Franck in 1890, Widor became professor of organ at the Conservatoire and six years later succeeded Théodore Dubois as professor of composition. His organ pupils included Tournemire, Vierne, Dupré, and Albert Schweitzer, and his composition pupils Varèse, Milhaud, and Honegger. Milhaud recalled his classes with Widor: "That charming teacher, a most brilliant conversationalist, would utter cries of alarm at every dissonance he came across in my works; as he listened he would exclaim: 'The worst of it is that you get used to them!'" (Milhaud 1995, 55).

In 1915 Widor moved into rooms at the Institut de France, place de l'Institut, 6e (J13, Métro: Pont-Neuf or Saint-Michel). He had been elected to the Académie des Beaux-Arts in 1910 and later became its energetic "secrétaire perpétuel." On 26 April 1920, at the age of 76, he married Mathilde de Montesquiou-Fezeusac and moved into a new home (now demolished) at 3 rue de Belloy, 16e (G7, Métro: Boissière). At eighty-nine Widor finally retired from his post at Saint-Sulpice on the last Sunday of 1933, to be succeeded by his pupil Marcel Dupré. He was buried in the crypt of Saint-Sulpice.

2 · Churches

Since at least the seventeenth century, the tradition of French organist-composers has been an important feature of Parisian musical life. Perhaps the most remarkable dynasty was the Couperins, including François Couperin "le Grand." For 175 years, from 1653 until 1828 (when the male line died out), members of this extraordinary family in unbroken succession worked at the church of Saint-Gervais. Rameau, the greatest and most innovative French composer of the high baroque, was also recognised as the foremost organist in France during the 1730s, when he worked at Sainte-Croix de la Bretonnerie (demolished in 1790).

During the nineteenth century the great French organ-builder Aristide Cavaillé-Coll constructed many new instruments. From the late 1830s to the end of the century, these were installed in a number of Paris churches, including Notre-Dame-de-Paris, Sainte-Clotilde, the Madeleine, the Trinité, Saint-Sulpice, and Saint-Vincent-de-Paul, as well as in the concert hall of the Trocadéro. It was partly owing to Cavaillé-Coll's brilliantly designed instruments that French organ playing, improvising, and composing enjoyed a magnificent renaissance during the second half of the nineteenth century: Franck, Saint-Saëns, and Fauré were all church organists (coincidentally all with Cavaillé-Coll instruments), as were composers whose names are forever associated with the organ, such as Gigout, Guilmant, Tournemire, Vierne, and Widor.

During the nineteenth and twentieth centuries, extremely long service was a recurrent feature of the titulaire (the title given to the principal organist) in many Parisian churches: Widor was organist at Saint-Sulpice from 1870 until the end of 1933 and was succeeded by Marcel Dupré, who worked there until his death in 1971. Vierne was appointed at Notre-Dame in 1900 and remained there until 1937, when he died at the console. Saint-Saëns served at the Madeleine from 1857 until 1876: on hearing him improvise, Franz Liszt declared him to be the greatest organist in the world.

Messiaen almost matched Widor for length of tenure. An undisputed genius of twentieth-century music, he was appointed organist at the

Trinité in 1931 at the age of twenty-two, and he worked there until the time of his death in April 1992. Almost all his organ works, including *La Nativité du Seigneur* and *Les corps glorieux*, were specifically written for the Cavaillé-Coll instrument which he played for sixty-one years.

La Madeleine (Sainte-Marie-Madeleine)

place de la Madeleine, 8e (G11, Métro: Madeleine)

Aristide Cavaillé-Coll and his father, Dominique, completed the organ in 1846, though the makers' plaque reads "Cavaillé-Coll Père et Fils, Facteurs d'Orgues du Roi, 1845." The first organist at the Madeleine (figure 2.1) was Alexandre-Charles Fessy, appointed in 1846. Fessy moved to Saint-Roch in 1847, to be replaced by Louis-James Lefébure-Wély. For a time his deputy was the young Eugène Gigout, who went on to become organist at Saint-Augustin. Organists and choirmasters have included two very distinguished composers: Camille Saint-Saëns was organist from 1857 to 1877; from 1874 his favourite pupil Gabriel Fauré deputised while Saint-Saëns was away. When Saint-Saëns resigned in April 1877, Théodore Dubois succeeded him as organist and Fauré was appointed choirmaster. On 2 June 1896, Fauré was appointed organist when Dubois left his post at the Madeleine to become director of the Conservatoire, as Fauré was himself to do in 1905, when he was succeeded by Henri Dallier.

2.1 The Madeleine.

2.2 Fauré's funeral
at the Madeleine
on 8 November
1924.

It was here that the first performance of Fauré's Requiem took place
on 16 January 1888, at the Requiem Mass for a parishioner (Joseph Le
Soufaché), and the work was given again on 1 February 1888. At this
stage, it consisted of only five movements (without the "Offertoire" or
"Libera me") and was scored for very modest forces: violas, cellos,
organ, harp, and timpani, with a solo violin in the Sanctus. Fauré added
parts for two horns in time for a performance in May 1888.

Fauré's Requiem was also performed at the composer's own funeral in
the Madeleine on 8 November 1924. The church was draped in black;
Philippe Gaubert conducted a chorus from the Opéra and the orchestra of
the Société des Concerts du Conservatoire. Henri Dallier was the organist,
and the soloists were Jane Laval and Charles Panzéra (figure 2.2). Among
more recent organists at the Madeleine are Jeanne Demessieux (1962–68),
Odile Pierre (1969–79), and François-Henri Houbart (since 1979).

The service at Chopin's funeral, which took place here on 30 October
1849, included a performance of Mozart's Requiem. Fauré was the
organist at the funerals of Gounod (27 October 1893) and Verlaine (10
January 1896).

According to a radio interview given by Stravinsky in March 1936,
the Madeleine, especially its interior, was his favourite building in Paris
(figure 2.3).

2.3 The interior of the Madeleine.

Notre-Dame-de-Clignancourt

place Jules-Joffrin, 18e (B14, Métro: Jules-Joffrin)
The population of the Clignancourt district grew rapidly in the mid-nineteenth century and the foundation stone for a new church was laid (by Baron Haussmann) in 1859. Notre-Dame-de-Clignancourt was opened in 1863, and for a few months in 1870 Gabriel Fauré was assistant organist. It was his first appointment in Paris.

Notre-Dame-de-Lorette

18 bis rue de Châteaudun, 9e (E13, Métro: Notre-Dame-de-Lorette)
Work began on this church in 1823, and it was consecrated on 15 December 1836. The organ by Cavaillé-Coll was installed in 1838 and is almost certainly the firm's earliest instrument in Paris. In 1845 César Franck dedicated an *Ave Maria* to the parish priest, Abbé Dancel, who admired the young composer. In about 1846 Franck was appointed assistant organist (he was also married in the church on 22 February 1848; *see* César Franck under "Musicians"). Abbé Dancel was appointed to Saint-Jean–Saint-François in late 1851 and arranged the transfer of Franck to his new parish in 1853.

parvis Notre-Dame, 4e (K15, Métro: Cité)

The musical tradition at Notre-Dame extends back at least eight hundred years, to the great Notre-Dame school of Léonin (who flourished from about 1163 to 1190) and Pérotin (around 1200). Léonin, also known as Magister Leoninus, is credited with the creation around 1163–82 of the *Magnus Liber,* the single most important collection of two-part organum. Pérotin is said to have revised it, and his own additions to the collection, two astonishing examples of four-part organum, *Viderunt omnes* and *Sederunt principes,* written for the Christmas season in 1198 and 1199, respectively—reveal him as a composer of startling originality. Léonin could not have been choirmaster at Notre-Dame when he compiled the *Magnus Liber* (building began in 1163 but services were not held in the church until 1185); still, there is little doubt that the collection was compiled for use in the new cathedral. Pérotin is associated in one thirteenth-century source (the mysterious "Anonymous IV") with "the great church of the Blessed Virgin in Paris." Shadowy figures they may be, but the significance of Léonin and Pérotin for the development of music at the time was immense. The innovations of the Notre-Dame school also included some of the first attempts to notate rhythm accurately.

During the baroque era, André Campra (1660–1744), who was appointed master of music in 1694, achieved some reforms to a very conservative regime (he was, for instance, permitted to introduce string instruments). But the success of *L'Europe galante* led Campra to try his luck in the theatre, and he left Notre-Dame on 1 October 1700. Among his successors in the eighteenth century were Louis-Claude Daquin (from 1755) and Claude-Bénigne Balbastre (from 1760). In 1784 the celebrated organ builder François-Henri Clicquot undertook a major restoration of the instrument. Jean-François Le Sueur (later to be the teacher of Berlioz, Thomas, and Gounod) was appointed in 1786 but lasted only a little more than a year in the post. His first major work was a *Te Deum* written for the Assumption (15 August 1786) and he followed this with Christmas and Easter oratorios. Le Sueur was dismissed for using large orchestras and opera singers on feast days, and for his novel view of the liturgy: he saw the Mass more or less as a theatrical presentation. Like Campra before him, Le Sueur subsequently turned to opera, and he was to become one of the most important French musicians active during the Revolution.

In 1862, Cavaillé-Coll began a comprehensive restoration of the organ, a task he completed by 1867, in time for the Exposition universelle that year. One of the more unexpected visitors to perform on this instrument was Anton Bruckner, who gave a recital at Notre-Dame in May 1869. César Franck was lost in admiration for Bruckner's playing on this occasion, a view shared by other composers in the audience, including Saint-Saëns, Gounod, and Auber.

At the turn of the century, Louis Vierne was appointed organist, a post he held until 1937. Most of his greatest works for organ were composed with the Notre-Dame instrument in mind, including the six organ symphonies and the four books of *Pièces de fantaisie*.

Saint-Augustin

place Saint-Augustin, 8e (E11, Métro: Saint-Augustin)
Designed by Victor Baltard, this striking domed church with its innovative iron structure was built in 1860–68. Eugène Gigout (1844–1925) was appointed organist in 1863. He inaugurated the new Cavaillé-Coll organ in 1868 and remained the organist there for the rest of his life. A noted performer, Gigout gave the first performance of Franck's Choral no. 3. On Fauré's insistence, he was appointed professor of organ at the Conservatoire in 1911, in succession to Guilmant.

Saint-Etienne-du-Mont

place Sainte-Geneviève, 5e (L15, Métro: Cardinal-Lemoine)
The organ was completely rebuilt by Aristide Cavaillé-Coll in 1863, the year in which it was inaugurated by César Franck. In 1930 Maurice Duruflé was appointed organist at Saint-Etienne-du-Mont (figure 2.4), a post he held until 1975, when he was obliged to give up the post following a road accident. He was succeeded by his wife, Marie-Madeleine Duruflé.

Saint-Eugène

4 bis rue Sainte-Cécile, 9e (F14, Métro: Bonne-Nouvelle)
The church was built in the 1850s. For twenty years (1872–92) the organist here was Raoul Pugno (1852–1914), one of the greatest French pianists

2.4 The Cavaillé-Coll organ at Saint-Etienne-du-Mont.

of his generation, famous not only for his solo playing, but also for his chamber music partnership with Ysaÿe.

Saint-Eustache

place du Jour, 1er (H14, Métro: Les Halles)

After an earlier instrument had been damaged by fire, the firm of Ducroquet installed a new organ, inaugurated on 26 May 1854 (one of the players was César Franck). On 30 April 1855, Saint-Eustache was the venue for the first performance of Berlioz's Te Deum, at the opening ceremony for the Exposition universelle. Berlioz asked both Liszt and the young Saint-Saëns whether they would play the organ part on this occasion, but neither was available, and in the end it was played by Edouard Batiste (organist at Saint-Eustache at the time).

From the early 1870s it was clear that further work needed to be done on the organ, and this was carried out by Merklin. His extensive restoration (greeted at the time as a spectacular success) was finished in February 1879 and celebrated by a concert given by many of the finest Parisian organists of the day: César Franck, Alexandre Guilmant, Théodore Dubois, Eugène

Gigout, and Franck's pupil Henri Dallier, who was appointed organist. He remained in the post until 1905, when he succeeded Fauré at the Madeleine.

Twentieth-century organists at Saint-Eustache included Joseph Bonnet (from 1906 until his death in 1944), André Marchal (1945–63; he made a famous recording of Franck's organ works for Erato at Saint-Eustache in 1958), and Jean Guillou. The organ was extensively restored in 1967.

Saint-Germain-des-Prés

place Saint-Germain-des-Prés, 6e (J13, Métro: Saint-Germain-des-Prés)
André Marchal served as organist here for thirty years, 1915–45, before taking up the post at Saint-Eustache.

Saint-Germain-l'Auxerrois

place du Louvre, 1er (H14, Métro: Pont-Neuf or Louvre-Rivoli)
In the 1660s the choir included two young singers who were later to achieve renown as composers: Michel-Richard Delalande (1657–1726) entered the choir school in about 1666 and remained until his voice broke in about 1672. He went on to be acclaimed as the leading composer of French baroque motets (written for performance in the royal chapel at Versailles). Another chorister at the time was Marin Marais (1656–1728), the greatest virtuoso on the bass viol of his time and one of the most important composers for the instrument.

Alexandre-Pierre-François Boëly (1785–1858) was appointed organist here in 1840, after a few years working at Saint-Gervais. A serious and gifted musician, he is of particular interest as one of the earliest French exponents of Bach's organ works. From 1845 he also taught the piano at the Notre-Dame choir school. He was dismissed as organist of Saint-Germain-l'Auxerrois in 1851, as the clergy and parishioners found his sophisticated musical taste to be unduly austere.

Saint-Gervais

place Saint-Gervais, 4e (J15, Métro: Hôtel-de-Ville)
Members of the Couperin family were organists from 1653 until 1826 at Saint-Gervais (figure 2.5). On 1 November 1685, when he was still only

sixteen, François "le Grand" was appointed, and he held the post until his death in 1733. François's cousin Nicolas Couperin served as his assistant from December 1723 and was the first member of the Couperin family to be buried beneath the organ in the church (*see* Couperin Family under "Musicians"). In 1834–38 Alexandre-Pierre-François Boëly was provisional organist here before moving to Saint-Germain-l'Auxerrois.

Charles Bordes (1863–1909) is best remembered as a cofounder with d'Indy and Guilmant of the Schola Cantorum. A Franck pupil, Bordes became maître de chapelle at Saint-Gervais in 1890. He had a passionate interest in Renaissance polyphony and in plainchant (he later took his students, including Varèse and Séverac, to visit Solesmes). This led him to establish the Semaines Saintes de Saint-Gervais in 1892. Programmes of French and Italian polyphony were sung by his choir, the Chanteurs de Saint-Gervais, whose fame soon spread: Debussy attended concerts of Palestrina and Vittoria in 1893 and the artist Maurice Denis was a regular visitor. The elderly Gounod was another strong supporter of Bordes's activities. (Half a century earlier Gounod had introduced Palestrina to puzzled congregations at the Eglise des Missions étrangères.)

The Société Nationale gave a concert in Saint-Gervais on 28 January 1892. Described as an "Audition de Musique Religieuse," it featured the first performance anywhere of Fauré's "Libera me" (figure 2.6), before the movement was given in a complete performance of the Requiem.

2.6 Programme for the first performance of Fauré's "Libera me" at Saint-Gervais on 28 January 1892.

The programme reads:

218e AUDITION   EGLISE St. GERVAIS

Jeudi 28 Janvier 1892   derrière l'Hôtel de Ville
à 4 heures 1/2 du soir

AUDITION DE MUSIQUE RELIGIEUSE

(Soli, Chœurs et Orchestre)
(AVANT LE SALUT)

1 — LE SYMBOLE DE NICÉE . . . . P. de BRÉVILLE
   (extrait de la messe à 3 voix)   (1re aud.)
   Ténor solo: M. MAUGIÈRE

2 — PATER NOSTER . . . . . . E. CHAUSSON
   Ténor solo: M. MAUGIÈRE   (1re aud.)

3 — DEUX OFFERTOIRES (inédits) . . . C. FRANCK
   a, DOMINE NON SECUNDUM *(pour le carême)* (1re aud.)
      Trio
  Soprano: M. R... Ténor: M. MAUGIÈRE Baryton: M. DIMITRI
   b. QUARE FREMUERUNT GENTES *(pour la fête de Ste Clotilde)*
      Solo et Chœurs
  Basse solo: M. DIMITRI.

4 — TOTA PULCHRA ES. , ... R. SCHUMANN
   Solo M. R.— Violoncelle Solo: M. DRESSEN

5 — LIBERA ME . . . . G. FAURÉ
      Solo et chœurs   (1re aud.)
  Baryton solo: M. BALLARD

(PENDANT LE SALUT)

O JESU DULCIS . . . . . Th. da VITTORIA
   (Motet à 4 voix)   (1570 — 1640)
AVE VERA VIRGINITAS . . . . Josquin DE PRÈS
   (Motet à 4 voix)   (1450 — 1521)
Antienne pour le Souverain Pontife (Chant grégorien)
TANTUM ERGO . . . . . . J. S. BACH
   (Choral à 4 voix)   (1685 — 1750)
     (APRÈS LE SALUT)
SUSCEPIT ISRAEL . . . . . . PALESTRINA
   (Verset du Magnificat)   (1524 — 1590)

CE PROGRAMME SERVIRA D'ENTRÈE POUR DEUX PERSONNES

Le 219e Audition aura lieu le samedi 6 Février: SALLE PLEYEL

Apart from the vocal soloists, no performers are indicated on the programme for this concert; however, the choice of music by Vittoria, Josquin, and Palestrina strongly suggests that Bordes and the Chanteurs de Saint-Gervais were involved.

The church authorities were less than supportive of Bordes's work, and his Chanteurs began to sing more often elsewhere, including trips abroad. Debussy wrote about Bordes as follows in *Gil Blas* on 2 February 1903: "Charles Bordes, choirmaster of Saint-Gervais in Paris, organised the series of Holy Week concerts at that church. It was such a success that the highest-ranking clergy were riled: they considered the concerts to have distracted the faithful! (Though the Lord above never complained that *He* was shocked!). This made Bordes decide to found the Association des Chanteurs de Saint-Gervais, a society for the promotion of old choral music. His enthusiastic campaign dates from this time: there are few towns left where he has not preached his gospel. You can be sure that one day he will be preaching it on the North Star! It would not surprise me" (Lesure and Langham Smith 1977, 110).

Saint-Honoré-d'Eylau

place Victor-Hugo, 16e (G6, Métro: Victor-Hugo)
The church was built in 1855 (it should not be confused with the newer church at 66 bis avenue Raymond-Poincaré, built in 1897 to cope with the growing population). In March 1871, Gabriel Fauré was named organist. The appointment was short-lived, as Fauré fled Paris a few weeks later during the Commune.

Saint-Jean–Saint-François,
now the Cathédrale Sainte-Croix-de-Paris (Armenian rite)

6 rue Charlot, 3e (H16, Métro: Saint-Sébastien-Froissart)
The organ was exhibited by Cavaillé-Coll in 1844 and installed in the church two years later. Franck was organist here in 1853–58 before moving to Sainte-Clotilde. One of his most illustrious successors was Léo Delibes, who served as organist from 1862 until 1871. During the twentieth century the instrument was somewhat neglected. The choir organ is also by Cavaillé-Coll (from about the same period as the larger instrument).

Saint-Louis-des-Invalides

Hôtel des Invalides, 7e (J10, Métro: Latour-Maubourg or Varenne)
Perhaps the most remarkable musical event to have taken place in les Invalides was the first performance of the *Grande messe des morts* by Berlioz on 5 December 1837. The circumstances surrounding this performance included a good deal of bureaucratic muddle, as Berlioz himself recounted in his *Memoirs:* "My Requiem was to be performed at government expense on the day of the annual service commemorating the dead of the 1830 revolution. As July, the month of the ceremony, approached, I

had the separate orchestral and chorus parts copied; and, at the word from the Director of Fine Arts, the rehearsals began. Almost at once an official letter from the Ministry informed me that the memorial service would be taking place without music" (1969, 229).

Five months later, it was decreed that there would be a state funeral in les Invalides for General Damrémont and the other Frenchmen killed at Constantine. Berlioz learned (not without some pleasure) that Cherubini was in a rage at being passed over for this occasion, but was disturbed to learn that Habeneck—an old enemy—would be conducting, as was his custom at big state ceremonies. Berlioz served as assistant conductor and in his *Memoirs* described what happened at one moment in the "Tuba mirum": "With my habitual mistrust I had stayed just behind Habeneck. Standing with my back to him, I supervised the group of timpani (which he could not see), as the moment approached for them to join in the general tumult. There are perhaps a thousand bars in my Requiem. In the very bar I have been speaking of, the bar in which the tempo broadens and the brass proclaim their tremendous fanfare—the one bar, in fact, in which the conductor's direction is absolutely indispensable—Habeneck laid down his baton and, calmly producing his snuff-box, proceeded to take a pinch of snuff" (1969, 231). Happily, Berlioz was able to intervene and rescue the situation. The performance was a great success. The *Grande messe des morts* was the first of Berlioz's major works to be published in full score, with a dedication to Count Adrien Gasparin, the man who had commissioned it.

Saint-Merry

78 rue Saint-Martin, 4e (H15, Métro: Hôtel-de-Ville)
During the seventeenth and eighteenth centuries, Saint-Merry had two outstanding organists: Nicolas-Antoine Lebègue held the post from 18 December 1664 until his death in 1702. The great harpsichord composer Jean-François Dandrieu took over the duties of organist in January 1704 (though he was not formally appointed until 19 July 1705). In the nineteenth century, the most famous organist at Saint-Merry was Camille Saint-Saëns, appointed in December 1852. From 1855 to 1857 extensive rebuilding work on the organ was undertaken by Cavaillé-Coll. Saint-Saëns left in 1857 to take up his appointment at the Madeleine.

Saint-Philippe-du-Roule

154 rue du Faubourg-Saint-Honoré, 8e (F10, Métro: Saint-Philippe-du-Roule)
In the twentieth century, the most important organist was Henri Mulet, appointed in 1922 when he moved from Saint-Roch. A pupil of Guilmant and Widor, he was considered a fine improviser by no less a figure than Tournemire. Evidently viewed as a rather enigmatic personality by many of his contemporaries, Mulet remained at Saint-Philippe-du-Roule until 1937, when he destroyed most his manuscripts. He bitterly renounced life in the capital for the southern French town of Draguignan, where he played the organ at the cathedral until 1958. Ill health and poverty obliged him to move into a convent for his last years, until his death in 1967.

Saint-Pierre-de-Montrouge

place Victor-et-Hélène-Basch, 14e (P12, Métro: Alésia)
Finished just before 1870, this church was used during the siege of Paris as a hospital, and during the Commune it served as a munitions store. The unusual bell tower was used as a lookout post. The wayward but gifted Henri Mulet was organist here at the turn of the century, and later Jean-Jacques Grunenwald held the post (1955–70).

Saint-Roch

296 rue Saint-Honoré, 1er (G13, Métro: Tuileries)
Louis-Alexandre Clicquot and his son François-Henri built the magnificent organ here in the early 1750s: a large instrument with four manuals and thirty-five stops, it was finished in 1755, and Saint-Roch's most famous organist arrived shortly afterwards: Claude-Bénigne Balbastre was appointed on 26 March 1756, following studies with Rameau (1750) and an impressive Paris debut at the Concert Spirituel in 1755. In 1770 Charles Burney went to hear Balbastre playing at Saint-Roch and wrote about it in his *Present State of Music in France and Italy* (1771): "He performed in all styles in accompanying the choir. When the *Magnificat* was sung, he played likewise between each verse several minuets, fugues, imitations, and every species of music, even to hunting pieces and jigs, without surprising or offending the congregation, as far as I was able to discover."

Large crowds came to hear Balbastre's improvisations on Noëls, and such was their popularity that the archbishop of Paris forbade him to play for a time. Balbastre was also famous for his improvised evocations of storms ("Tonnerres"). In 1760, Balbastre was also appointed to Notre-Dame-de-Paris, but he continued to play at Saint-Roch.

Saint-Roch was the venue for the première of the *Messe solennelle* by the young Berlioz. Scheduled for performance on 28 December 1824 (an occasion for which printed invitations were sent out announcing a "Mass for full orchestra composed by M. H. Berlios"!), the rehearsal the previous day was a calamity: several players failed to turn up, and the parts (hastily copied by the choirboys) were riddled with errors and omissions. Six months later, Berlioz was able to reassemble the necessary forces (by borrowing the money to pay them), and the work was given a successful first performance on Sunday, 10 July 1825, the Feast of the Sacred Heart. The funeral of Cherubini took place here on 22 March 1842, the same year in which Cavaillé-Coll undertook a major restoration of the organ which was left more or less intact by subsequent repairs. In the twentieth century, organists included Henri Mulet (for ten years, 1912–22), who composed his best-known work, the *Carillon-sortie*, while at Saint-Roch. In 1922, Mulet moved to Saint-Philippe-du-Roule.

Saint-Séverin

rue des Prêtres-Saint-Séverin, 5e (K14, Métro: Saint-Michel)
Camille Saint-Saëns was organist here for a few months in 1852, while still in his teens. He left the same year to take up his appointment at Saint-Merry.

Saint-Sulpice

place Saint-Sulpice, 6e (K13, Métro: Saint-Sulpice or Mabillon)
Louis-Nicolas Clérambault was the most distinguished organist at Saint-Sulpice (figures 2.7 and 2.8) before the nineteenth century. In 1776–81 an organ was installed by Clicquot. The present instrument, one of Cavaillé-Coll's finest (and largest), is reached by a long spiral staircase in one of the towers. Alexandre Guilmant was organist here from 1862. He was succeeded in 1870 by Charles-Marie Widor, who remained in the post for

sixty-four years, until the end of 1933. Gabriel Fauré, appointed Widor's assistant in October 1871, stayed until January 1874, when he left to be Saint-Saëns's deputy at the Madeleine. He was followed by his friend (and fellow pupil at the Ecole Niedermeyer) André Messager. Widor's other assistants included Louis Vierne, from 1892 to 1900, when he left to take up his post at Notre-Dame. Following Widor's retirement (he found it increasingly difficult to climb the stairs up to the organ), his illustrious pupil Marcel Dupré was appointed organist; he remained in the post until his death in 1971. His assistants included Jean-Jacques Grunenwald, who became organist in 1973. He was succeeded by Daniel Roth.

Saint-Vincent-de-Paul

place Franz-Liszt, 10e (E15, Métro: Poisonnière)
A small chapel of Saint-Vincent-de-Paul was built on the rue Montholon in spring 1802, but soon the congregation had grown too numerous (it sometimes included the young Liszt, who lived nearby). Building work started on the present church in 1824, but it was not finished until 1844. The architect was Jakob Ignaz Hittorff, who also designed the Cirque d'Hiver (see "Theatres and Concert Halls") and the Gare du Nord. The Cavaillé-Coll organ was inaugurated by Jacques Nicolas Lemmens in

1852. From 1863 to 1874, the organist was the publisher Auguste Durand. Durand's most famous successor was Léon Boëllmann, composer of the *Suite gothique*, who held the post until his early death in 1897. Reputed to have been one of Cavaillé-Coll's most remarkable instruments, it was rebuilt in the twentieth century, an exercise which has been described as a mutilation.

La Sainte-Chapelle

boulevard du Palais, 1er (J14, Métro: Cité)
One of the marvels of the Gothic age, the Sainte-Chapelle was built by Saint-Louis (Louis IX) to house relics of the Holy Cross. Consecrated in 1248, it has had a patchy musical tradition, with some impressive highlights. In June 1698 Marc-Antoine Charpentier was appointed choirmaster, a post he held, despite much squabbling with his superiors, until his death in 1704 (*see* Marc-Antoine Charpentier under "Musicians"). Among the organists were members of the Couperin family. The fine Clicquot organ, installed in 1771, was moved to Saint-Germain-l'Auxerrois. The nineteenth century was the low point in the history of this great chapel: it was used as a granary, then as a government archives, and in 1837 it bore a sign reading "National Property: For Sale." The building was restored in the 1860s. On 24 May 1871 it was doused in petrol by the Communards, but somehow it avoided destruction.

More recently, the Sainte-Chapelle was the setting for the private first performance of Messiaen's *Et exspecto resurrectionem mortuorum* on 7 May 1965. As a young man Messiaen was bowled over by the stained glass in the Sainte-Chapelle and often spoke of the inspiration it gave him: the chapel was thus a singularly appropriate venue for the première of this work, scored for a large orchestra consisting only of woodwind, brass, and percussion instruments.

Sainte-Clotilde

23 bis rue Las-Cases, 7e (J11, Métro: Solférino)
This neo-Gothic basilica has had a distinguished musical tradition since its completion. The church (figures 2.9 and 2.10) was inaugurated on 31 November 1857; an orchestra conducted by Pasdeloup provided the

2.9 Sainte-Clotilde.

music. The following year César Franck was appointed organist and by 12 July 1858 work on building the organ was in progress. On the evening of 19 December 1859 Franck and Lefébure-Wély inaugurated the new Cavaillé-Coll organ, which was widely acclaimed as one of the firm's finest instruments to date. Soon Franck's improvisations after Mass were attracting considerable public interest. In 1866 Liszt visited the church to hear his former protégé; he was moved by Franck's music and by his playing, and, as he left the church, Liszt is said to have likened Franck to Bach. Franck was to hold the post of organist for more than three decades, until his death on 8 November 1890. His successor was his pupil Gabriel Pierné, who served from 1890 until 1898.

Pierné was followed by one of the finest French organist-composers of the twentieth century: Charles Tournemire (a pupil of Franck and Widor at the Conservatoire), who held the post from 1898 to 1939, during which time he wrote numerous works for the Sainte-Clotilde organ, of which the greatest is his monumental *L'orgue mystique* (1927–32), consisting of fifty-one offices, each making use of the appropriate plainchant melodies. Tournemire can be heard playing his great predecessor

Franck's *Cantabile* (1878) on a Polydor recording made at Sainte-Clotilde in 1929 before the organ was restored. During Tournemire's tenure, his colleagues included Maurice Emmanuel (maître de chapelle 1904–1907), Maurice Duruflé (assistant organist in the 1920s), and Daniel-Lesur (assistant organist 1927–37). The organist from 1945 until his death in 1991 was Tournemire's pupil Jean Langlais.

Sainte-Croix-de-la-Bretonnerie

square Sainte-Croix-de-la-Bretonnerie, 4e (J15, Métro: Hôtel-de-Ville)
The church was demolished in 1790. Jean-Philippe Rameau was organist here from 1732 until 1738.

La Trinité (Sainte-Trinité)

place d'Estienne-d'Orves, 9e (E12, Métro: Trinité)
Recently restored to its original splendour, the Trinité (figure 2.11) was designed by Théodore Ballu and completed in the 1860s. The first organ was installed by Cavaillé-Coll in 1868 but was damaged during the Commune; a second Cavaillé-Coll instrument was built in 1871. The first organist was Charles-Alexis Chauvet (1868–71), who died young and was succeeded by Alexandre Guilmant, who held the post for thirty years, from 1871 until 1901. Guilmant was almost alone among the major organist-composers at the end of the nineteenth century in having an abiding interest in Gregorian chant and based many pieces on chant melodies. He was a deeply religious man who took his duties as a church musician very seriously. He resigned from his position at the Trinité in 1901, after the organ was rebuilt during his absence.

The Trinité's greatest (and longest-serving) organist was unquestionably Olivier Messiaen. At the time of his appointment in September 1931 (in succession to Charles Quef, a Vierne pupil), Messiaen had already been the ailing Quef's deputy for two years. He remained in the post until his death in April 1992. Messiaen described his work at the Trinité in an interview with Claude Samuel: "For the High Mass on Sunday, I played only plainsong, harmonised or not according to circumstances; for the eleven o'clock Mass on Sundays, classical and romantic music; for the Mass at noon, I was allowed to play my own music; and finally, for the

2.11 The Trinité,
where Messiaen
was organist for
more than sixty
years.

five o'clock Vespers, I was obliged to improvise." As Messiaen observed in the same interview, the parishioners were sometimes "startled" by his music, and he stated that the *Messe de la Pentecôte* (1950) was "a résumé of all my collected improvisations," at least those which were not in the style of earlier composers.

It was for the organ of the Trinité that Messiaen's greatest organ works were conceived: *Apparition de l'église éternelle* (1932), *L'Ascension* (1934), *La Nativité du Seigneur* (1935), *Les corps glorieux* (1939), *Messe de la Pentecôte* (1950), *Livre d'orgue* (1951), *Méditations sur le Mystère de la Sainte Trinité* (1969), and *Livre du Saint Sacrement* (1984). Collectively, these works constitute perhaps the most significant and original contribution to the organ repertoire by any twentieth-century composer. Messiaen recorded all his organ works up to the *Livre d'orgue* at the Trinité in 1956 (reissued on CD by EMI as *Messiaen par lui-même*), and he later recorded the *Méditations sur le Mystère de la Sainte Trinité* (for Erato).

During Messiaen's tenure, the Cavaillé-Coll organ was restored and considerably expanded: seven stops were added in 1934, and a further eight in 1962–65, when both the stop and note actions were electrified and a new console was installed. Messiaen was succeeded by Naji Hakim, formerly organist at the Sacré-Coeur and a pupil of Jean Langlais.

The funerals of Rossini (21 November 1868), Bizet (5 June 1875), and Lili Boulanger (19 March 1918) took place at the Trinité.

Saint-Leu-la-Forêt

at the southwest end of the Forêt de Montmorency, outside Paris (SNCF: Saint-Leu-la-Forêt)

The church was built by Napoleon III in 1851 as a resting-place for the tomb of his father, Louis Bonaparte. Charles Bonaparte (father of Napoleon I) was also buried here until his body was moved in 1951 to Corsica. In 1873 Vincent d'Indy was appointed organist. He remained in the post until 1878.

Saint-Nicolas

rue du Fossé, Maisons-Laffitte, twenty kilometres northwest of Paris (RER: Maisons-Laffitte)

The fabulously gifted Jehan Alain, killed in battle in 1940, was organist here from 1935 to 1939.

3 · Theatres and Concert Halls

Paris has had a bewildering array of theatres and concert halls over the last three hundred years, including buildings which have been home to opera and ballet companies, or which have been the venue for important premières of works by composers such as Lully, Rameau, Mozart, Berlioz, Rossini, Bellini, Donizetti, Berlioz, Verdi, Wagner, Fauré, Debussy, Ravel, Stravinsky, and Messiaen. The various homes of the Opéra, as of the Opéra-Comique and the Théâtre Italien, since 1673 are described under names of the relevant buildings (for details see the section that follows, "Opera Companies and Their Theatres"). The concert halls of the Conservatoire, Schola Cantorum, and Ecole Normale are listed here; for their role as teaching institutions see "Institutions and Orchestras." As several buildings were used for both staged and concert performances, theatres and concert halls are listed in a single sequence. Terminology is anyway uncertain, *Salle* often being applied to opera houses (Salle Favart, Salle Le Peletier, Salle Ventadour) as well as to concert halls (Salle Gaveau, Salle Pleyel). A number of the buildings described below no longer exist. Destruction by fire was something of an occupational hazard for Parisian theatres during the eighteenth and nineteenth centuries. The Opéra was less fortunate than most in this respect, and the Salle Favart, which housed both the Opéra-Comique and the Théâtre Italien at various times, burnt down twice. Other buildings have been included even though they have since been put to another use (such as the Salle Ventadour, which was converted into offices at the end of the nineteenth century).

Opera Companies and Their Theatres

(i) The Opéra

The Académie d'Opéra was founded in 1669 by Pierre Perrin and set up its first home on a converted tennis court (on the site of 43 rue de Seine, 6e). In 1672 financial difficulties landed Perrin in debtor's prison, and the royal privilege for the company was taken over by the ambitious and entrepreneurial Lully. It was renamed Académie Royale de Musique the same year and was soon referred to informally as the Opéra. Lully opened a new theatre, on the site of another tennis court, the Bel Air on the rue de Vaugirard (between the Odéon and the Jardin du Luxembourg). It was here that his *Cadmus et Hermione* was first given on 27 April 1673. Following Molière's death that year, the Opéra moved into the Palais Royal, where it remained until the theatre was destroyed by fire in 1763. For a few years the Opéra was based in the Salle des Machines at the Palais des Tuileries, before moving in 1770 to the new theatre at the Palais Royal. Like its predecessor, this also burnt down, in 1781. The Opéra's next home was the Théâtre de la Porte Saint-Martin in 1781–94, followed by the Théâtre National de la rue de la Loi, on the rue de Louvois, where it remained from 1794 until 1820 (when the theatre was destroyed by order of the king, following the assassination there of the duc de Berry). For more than fifty years, the Opéra was based in the Salle Le Peletier, from 1821 until it burnt down in 1873. After a year at the Salle Ventadour, the company moved in 1875 to the Palais Garnier, where it remains to this day, with a second home at the Opéra Bastille since 1989. Though it has always been known as the Opéra, the formal title in most general use from Lully's time until well into the nineteenth century was Académie Royale de Musique. At various times during the nineteenth century it was also known as the Théâtre des Arts and the Académie Impériale de Musique. The poster announcing the first performance at the Palais Garnier (5 January 1875) gives the company as the Théâtre National de l'Opéra (though the facade of the building still describes it as the "Académie Nationale de Musique"). Subsequent twentieth-century titles included Opéra de Paris, and Opéra National de Paris.

For theatres used by the Opéra see Opéra (Palais Garnier), Opéra Bastille, Palais Royal, Palais des Tuileries, Salle Louvois, Salle Le Peletier, Salle Ventadour, Théâtre National de la rue de la Loi, and Théâtre de la Porte Saint-Martin.

(ii) The Opéra-Comique
In 1714 the actors and musicians who provided entertainments at the Lenten fairs in the Foire Saint-Germain and the Foire Saint-Laurent came to an agreement which enabled them (for payment of a fee to the Opéra) to put on plays with music and call themselves the Opéra-

Comique. The Comédie-Italienne, established in 1716, was initially a fierce competitor (sometimes stepping in to provide plays at the fairs when pressure from the Opéra or from the Comédie-Française caused the Opéra-Comique to be banned). The Opéra-Comique and Comédie-Italienne companies amalgamated in 1762 and moved to the Théâtre de l'Hôtel de Bourgogne (on the site of 29 rue Etienne-Marcel, 1er, commemorated with a plaque). For almost half a century, the most important librettist (and part-time composer) of comic opera was Charles-Simon Favart (1710–92), whose vast output of parodies, vaudevilles, and other comedies stretches from *Polichinelle* (Foire Saint-Germain, 14 March 1732) to *Les rêveries renouvelées des Grecs*, a parody of Gluck's *Iphigénie en Tauride* (Hôtel de Bourgogne, 26 June 1779). In 1783 the company moved into the Salle Favart. It remained here until July 1801, when it transferred to the Salle Feydeau as a result of a merger with the resident company there. Apart from a season (1804–1805) back in the Salle Favart, the Opéra-Comique remained at the Salle Feydeau until 12 April 1829. From April 1829 until March 1832, it performed at the Salle Ventadour, then moved to the Salle de la Bourse from September 1832 to April 1840. The Opéra-Comique moved into the second Salle Favart in 1840 and remained there until the building burnt down in May 1887. Its new home for eleven years was at the Théâtre Lyrique (ii). In December 1898, the Opéra-Comique inaugurated the third Salle Favart, and the company has remained there ever since.

For theatres used by the Opéra-Comique see Salle de la Bourse, Salle Favart (i)–(iii), Salle Feydeau, Salle Ventadour, and Théâtre Lyrique (ii).

(iii) The Théâtre Italien
Initially known as the Opera Buffa (or, informally, as the Bouffons), this company was founded in 1801, and in 1807 it was given exclusive rights to present opera in Italian on the Paris stage. In its early years the company led an itinerant existence. It was based at the first Salle Favart in 1802, then moved in 1804 to the Salle Louvois and in 1808 to the newly reopened Théâtre de l'Odéon, where it remained until 1815. The company was once more in the Salle Louvois in 1819–25. From November 1825 until the theatre burnt down in 1838, the Théâtre Italien was back in the Salle Favart. A three-month stay in the Salle Ventadour was followed by three further years at the Théâtre de l'Odéon. In 1841 the Théâtre Italien settled once

again at the Salle Ventadour, where it remained until a series of financial crises forced the closure of the company in 1878. The company was variously known as the Théâtre Italien, the Théâtre Royal Italien, the Théâtre Royal Italien et Anglais (when seasons were split between Paris and the Theatre Royal, Drury Lane), the Théâtre Impérial Italien and, unofficially (but almost universally), as the Théâtre des Italiens.

For theatres used by the Théâtre Italien see Salle Favart (i), Salle Louvois, Salle Ventadour, and Théâtre de l'Odéon.

Cirque d'Hiver

place Pasdeloup, rue Amelot, 11e (H17, Métro: Filles-du-Calvaire)
This striking circular building (figure 3.1), designed by Jakob Ignaz Hittorff, was opened by the emperor on 11 December 1852 as the Cirque Napoléon (it acquired its present name in 1870). Jules Pasdeloup (1819–87) gave the first of his Sunday Concerts Populaires de Musique Classique here on 27 October 1861, and such was the success of the event that he booked the hall on an annual basis for more than twenty years. These were remarkable concerts for the time: low ticket prices drew huge audiences (of up to five thousand), made up largely of working people who had not previously had the opportunity of hearing orchestral music. The Franco-Prussian War interrupted the concerts briefly, but Pasdeloup resumed them during the siege of Paris (only to suspend them again dur-

3.1 The Cirque d'Hiver at the end of the nineteenth century.

ing the Commune). During the 1870s, the rival (and technically superior) concerts provided by Colonne and especially Lamoureux caused Pasdeloup considerable financial problems, and in 1884 he abandoned the Concerts Populaires. In 1886 Franck's pupils organised a festival of his works at the Cirque d'Hiver, one of which was the accident-prone première (on 1 May 1886) of the *Variations symphoniques*, a woefully under-rehearsed performance in which the soloist (Louis Diémer) and the orchestra (under Pasdeloup) parted company during the finale. John Singer Sargent evoked the musical life of the building in his magnificent *Rehearsal of the Pasdeloup Orchestra at the Cirque d'Hiver* (Museum of Fine Arts, Boston).

Cité de la Musique

221 avenue Jean-Jaurès, 19e (C21, Métro: Porte de Pantin)
The Cité de la Musique at La Villette opened in phases during the 1990s, in a striking series of buildings designed by Christian de Portzamparc, who was announced as the winner of a competition to design the Cité de la Musique on 16 January 1985. The Conservatoire moved here from the rue de Madrid, and from the start there has been an active programme of orchestral and chamber concerts. A speciality has been concerts which make use of period instruments, and some programmes have featured instruments from the collection of the Musée de la Musique, housed in the same complex. Concerts of contemporary music are also a significant aspect of the programming, and the Ensemble Intercontemporain is one of the resident ensembles. The scope of the concert series at the Cité de la Musique has established this complex as one of the most important and innovative venues for music in Paris (*see* Conservatoire under "Institutions and Orchestras" and Musée de la Musique under "Museums and Libraries").

Opéra (Palais Garnier)

place de l'Opéra, 9e (F12, Métro: Opéra)
In 1861 Charles Garnier was chosen from 171 entrants in a competition to find the architect for a new Paris opera house; construction began the same year. The Opéra (figures 3.2, 3.3, and 3.4), the single most expensive building conceived under the Second Empire (the cost was thirty-three million francs), was unfinished at the time of the collapse of the

3.2 The Opéra
Garnier in 1997.

3.3 The auditorium
of the Opéra Gar-
nier (*L'Illustration*,
16 January 1875).

regime in 1870. Work was resumed after the Commune, and the building
which is perhaps the supreme monument to Napoléon III was actually
opened during the Third Republic. Following the fire at the Salle Le
Peletier, there was greater urgency to complete the new theatre, and by
March 1874 more than 250 men were working on the site. On 17 October
1874 the orchestra met in the empty theatre to test the acoustics. On 2
December the orchestra and chorus undertook another acoustic trial,
which was attended by members of the company, journalists, and guests.
The corps de ballet tried out the theatre on 12 December, and six days

3.4 The inaugura-
tion of the Opéra
Garnier (*L'Illustra-
tion,* 9 January
1875).

later the famous chandelier was lit for the first time. The keys were
handed over by Garnier on 30 December (Charles Nuitter's official statis-
tics from 1875 state that the building had 2,531 doors and 7,593 keys, so
Garnier's gesture was presumably an entirely symbolic one).

Bickering over the programme had already made it difficult for the
conductor, Deldevez, to prepare for the opening night. The problems
were exacerbated by the outrageous behaviour of Christine Nilsson,
whose unsuccessful last-minute attempt to extort an astronomical fee
inevitably led to her withdrawal from the performance (in breach of contract). A rather chaotic public dress rehearsal took place on 4 January,
and new playbills, without Nilsson's name, were hastily printed for the
inauguration. The Opéra finally opened on 5 January 1875 with a gala
attended by the president of the republic and numerous foreign notables,
including the Lord Mayor of London. The spectacle of the magnificent
staircase on this glittering occasion is documented in Edouard Detaille's
painting *Inauguration du Nouvel Opéra,* and there are two models of the

building in the Musée d'Orsay, including a fine one of the interior made for the 1900 Exposition universelle. The opening performance included extracts from Halévy's *La Juive*, Meyerbeer's *Les Huguenots*, and the Delibes and Minkus ballet *La source*. The first complete opera, *La Juive*, was given on 8 January (it was the only work on the programme for the next three weeks). Electric lighting was installed in 1881, and six years later a new generator in one of the Opéra's basements made possible further electrification.

Delibes's ballet *Sylvia* (14 June 1876) and many operas—Massenet's *Le roi de Lahore* (27 April 1877), Gounod's *Polyeucte* (7 October 1878), d'Indy's *La légende de Saint Christophe* (6 June 1920), Roussel's *Padmâvatî* (1 June 1923), Milhaud's *Maximilien* (4 January 1932), Canteloube's *Vercingétorix* (26 June 1933), Messiaen's *Saint François d'Assise* (28 November 1983)—were first performed in the Palais Garnier.

The theatre was used by the Ballets Russes for several seasons and premières given by Diaghilev's company in the Palais Garnier included five major works by Stravinsky: *The Firebird* (25 June 1910), *Le rossignol* (26 May 1914), *Pulcinella* (15 May 1920), *Renard* (18 May 1922), and *Mavra* (3 June 1922), as well as the French premières of Respighi's Rossini arrangement *La boutique fantasque* (24 December 1919) and Falla's *Le tricorne* (23 January 1920).

Opéra Bastille

120 rue de Lyon, 12e (K18, Métro: Bastille)
The idea of a new opera house was first considered in 1968, but it was only in 1982 that François Mitterand made the decision to build it at the place de la Bastille, on the site of the Gare de Vincennes (demolished 1984). One of the largest ever architectural contests was launched to find the best design: 756 projects from forty countries were submitted to President Mitterand. The eventual choice was the Canadian architect Carlos Ott. The latest home of the Opéra opened officially with a concert on Bastille Day 1989, and the inaugural production (of Berlioz's *Les Troyens*) was given on 17 March 1990. The auditorium has a capacity of 2,700. Envisaged as an "opera house for the people," and equipped with impressive technology, the Opéra Bastille was intended to house most opera performances from the Palais Garnier; the older house was to be

used mainly for ballet. In fact, performances of ballet and opera are staged at both houses. Even before the house opened, it was a source of politically motivated squabbling over artistic matters, notoriously over the appointment of a music director: Daniel Barenboim was sacked before the house opened, and Myung-Whun Chung left amidst a storm of recrimination in 1994. Enormously impressive productions have taken place at the Opéra Bastille, but the building has not as yet endeared itself to the public: it appears regularly at or near the top in any list of buildings the Parisians would most like to see demolished.

Palais Royal

place du Palais Royal, rue Saint-Honoré, 1er (H13, Métro: Palais Royal)
Two theatres stood on this site in 1641–1763 and in 1770–81. Both of them burnt down.

(i) Cardinal Richelieu started to build a theatre at the Palais Royal in 1639, and it was inaugurated on 14 January 1641 with *Mirame*, a play by the Cardinal himself which even his most fervent admirers found it hard to praise. Molière used the theatre from 1661, and a number of his late plays were first performed here, including the last, *Le malade imaginaire*, in 1673. Following Molière's death, Lully somehow persuaded Louis XIV to let him use the theatre for the Opéra rent-free. His productions were noted for their scenic magnificence and special effects. Lully's premières at the Palais Royal included several of his grandest *tragédies en musique*, such as *Alceste* (19 January 1674), *Amadis* (18 January 1684), and *Armide* (15 February 1686). Performances at the Opéra began in the late afternoon (the starting time was fixed by decree at 5:15 P.M. in 1714). Here Rameau scored his first operatic triumph, with *Hippolyte et Aricie* on 1 October 1733, followed by such works as *Les Indes galantes* (23 August 1735), *Castor et Pollux* (24 October 1737), *Dardanus* (19 November 1739), and *Zoroastre* (5 December 1749). After the theatre was destroyed by fire on 6 April 1763, the Opéra moved to the Salle des Machines in the Palais des Tuileries.

(ii) The second theatre at the Palais Royal, built next to the site of the old theatre, opened on 26 January 1770 with a revival of Rameau's *Zoroastre*. It was a larger building than the earlier theatre, with a capacity of two thousand. Despite the additional safety precautions against fire, the theatre was engulfed in flames, near the end of a performance on 8 June 1781. The fire claimed twenty-one victims, mostly dancers and technicians. The Opéra moved later in the year to the Théâtre de la Porte Saint-Martin.

Palais des Tuileries

(i) Salle des Suisses
(ii) Salle des Machines
Destroyed during the Commune (23 May 1871) on the site of the present avenue du Général-Lemonnier, Jardin des Tuileries, 1er (H12, Métro: Palais Royal)
Following the death of Louis XIV in 1715, the Regency installed the young Louis XV in the Palais des Tuileries, but he decided to move the court back to Versailles in 1722. The palace was thus left unused as a royal residence. The Salle des Suisses (i) was rented by the king to the Concert Spirituel as the first public concert hall in Paris, and later in the century the vast Salle des Machines (ii) was converted into a temporary home for the Opéra.

(i) The Salle des Suisses (sometimes known as the Salle des Cent-Suisses) was sited on the first floor of the Palais des Tuileries and was the venue until 1784 for the Concert Spirituel, the famous series founded by Philidor. The first concert took place on 18 March 1725 and featured a performance of Corelli's "Christmas" Concerto, the first of many Italian works to which French audiences were introduced by the Concert Spirituel. Leclair caused a sensation with his playing here in 1728, and Boccherini appeared in March 1768 to perform one of his cello sonatas. On 18 June 1778, Mozart's "Paris" Symphony K297/300a was first performed in the Salle des Cent-Suisses. The work had been commissioned by Joseph Legros, a distinguished singer at the Opéra and director of the Concert Spirituel (1777–91). In 1784 the Concert Spirituel moved to the Salle des Machines.

(ii) Following the fire which destroyed the first theatre at the Palais Royal in 1763, the Opéra moved to the Salle des Machines, in the Palais des Tuileries. Originally a vast space able to hold eight thousand people, the hall was adapted by Soufflot, who used the area of the old stage to create a new stage and auditorium, with dimensions similar to those of the Palais Royal. The Opéra remained here until it could move into the new theatre at the Palais Royal in 1770. The Comédie-Française took the

Opéra's place, before moving in 1782 to the Odéon. It was in the Salle des Machines that Beaumarchais's *Le barbier de Séville* was performed for the first time in 1775. The Concert Spirituel took place here in 1784–91.

Salle de la Bourse

27 rue Vivienne, 2e (G14, Métro: Bourse)
Built in 1827 by Bérard (director of the Théâtre des Nouveautés in boulevard Poissonière), the theatre at the Salle de la Bourse opened on 1 March 1827. After moving here in September 1832, the Opéra-Comique remained until April 1840, when it relocated to the new Salle Favart. It was in the Salle de la Bourse that the ailing Ferdinand Hérold had his last and greatest triumph, with the première on 15 December 1832 of *Le pré aux clercs,* but the composer was too ill to take a curtain call (the work was performed more than fifteen hundred times by the Opéra-Comique during the nineteenth century). The new repertory was dominated during the 1830s by Adam (including *Le postillon de Longjumeau,* 13 October 1836) and Auber (notably *Le domino noir,* 2 December 1837). Perhaps the greatest opera to be given its first performance here by the Opéra-Comique was Donizetti's *La fille du régiment* (11 February 1840).

After the Opéra-Comique moved to the Salle Favart, the Salle de la Bourse became home to the Théâtre du Vaudeville company, whose production of *La dame aux camélias* opened in February 1852. It was almost certainly seen by Verdi (and was the inspiration for *La traviata*). The company moved in 1868 to the new theatre at 2 boulevard des Capucines.

Salle du Conservatoire (Salle de l'Ancien Conservatoire)

2 rue Bergère, 9e (F15, Métro: Bonne-Nouvelle)
The concert hall of the Conservatoire (figure 3.5), designed by Delannoy and inaugurated on 7 July 1811, was the location for the series of concerts started by François Habeneck in 1828 as the Société des Concerts du Conservatoire. Berlioz first rehearsed the *Symphonie fantastique* (16 May 1830) here but was forced to abandon plans for a performance until later in the year. The première took place in the Conservatoire hall on Sunday, 5 December 1830, with an orchestra of more than a hundred players, drawn from the Théâtre des Nouveautés, the Théâtre Italien, and the

Société des Concerts. The day before, Liszt had visited Berlioz for the first time; he was immensely enthusiastic about the concert. Also in the audience were Spontini, Meyerbeer, and Fétis. Several further performances of the *Symphonie fantastique* followed at the Salle du Conservatoire over the next few years, as did other important Berlioz premières: *Harold en Italie* (23 November 1834) and *Roméo et Juliette* (24 November 1839, conducted by Berlioz). On 25 April 1841 Berlioz conducted an all-Beethoven programme, with Liszt as soloist in the "Emperor" Concerto. The hall continued to be used for important concerts (and recordings) in the twentieth century, after the Conservatoire itself moved to the rue de Madrid in 1911. Generally known after the move as the Salle de l'Ancien Conservatoire, this was the setting for most of the concerts of the Société Nationale from 1917 until 1923, including the first public performance of Satie's *Socrate* (14 February 1920) and the première of Fauré's *L'horizon chimérique* (13 May 1922). Later the première of Messiaen's *Trois petites liturgies de la Présence Divine*, conducted by Roger Désormière, was given here on 21 April 1945 (*see also* Conservatoire under "Institutions and Orchestras").

Salle de l'Ecole Normale de Musique

78 rue Cardinet, 17e (D9, Métro: Malesherbes)

The Ecole Normale was founded in 1919 under the direction of Alfred Cortot and Auguste Mangeot (Cortot remained director until 1962). The hall (with a capacity of five hundred) was an important venue for concerts of contemporary music, including virtually all of the remarkable series given by Triton beginning in 1932. This contemporary music society was founded by Pierre-Octave Ferroud and had on its honorary committee Ravel, Roussel, Schoenberg, Richard Strauss, Stravinsky, Bartók, and Szymanowski. Its *comité actif* (executive committee) was made up of composers—Poulenc, Milhaud, Honegger, Martinů, Prokofiev, and others. Premières of works by Roussel, Honegger, Milhaud, and Ibert were offered by Triton at the Ecole Normale, as well as first performances in France of works by Prokofiev, Bartók, and Hindemith. The first performance of Messiaen's *Chants de terre et de ciel* took place at a Triton concert presented under the title "Prismes" (Marcelle Bunlet and Olivier Messiaen, 23 January 1939). On 1 June 1943 a work improbably entitled "Mous-Arechac," composed by the mysterious "Hamid-al-Usurid," was performed here. Such were the restrictions in Nazi-occupied Paris on performances of music by non-Aryan French composers, that the anagrammatic ruse perpetrated on this occasion was necessary to enable Darius Milhaud's *Scaramouche* to be performed (*see also* Ecole Normale de Musique under "Institutions and Orchestras").

Salle Erard

13 rue du Mail, 2e (G14, Métro: Sentier)

Used for recitals and some orchestral concerts, the Salle Erard (figure 3.6) was part of the complex of buildings on the rue du Mail belonging to the Erard piano and harp manufacturing firm. Among the many concerts of the Société Nationale, premières were given of Debussy's *Pour le piano* (11 January 1902) and *Estampes* (9 January 1904), and Ravel's *Miroirs* (6 January 1906) and *Gaspard de la nuit* (9 January 1909), all played by Ricardo Viñes. Later, Messiaen had one of his earliest successes, when the *Préludes* were given their first public performance here (by Henriette Roget, 1 March 1930).

Salle Favart

place Boieldieu, 2e (F13, Métro: Richelieu-Drouot)
Three theatres have stood on this site since 1783. The first and second
burnt down in 1838 and 1887. The Salle Favart (figures 3.7, 3.8, and 3.9)
has served at different times as the home of the Théâtre Italien and the
Opéra-Comique.

(i) The first Salle Favart was inaugurated on 28 April 1783. Among the
resident companies in the earlier nineteenth century were the Opéra-
Comique and, from 1825, the Théâtre Italien, famous for its introduction of
Rossini, Bellini, and Donizetti to the Paris stage and for recruiting singers
such as Pasta, Malibran, Sontag, Lablache, Rubini, Tamburini, Malibran,
and Grisi. Here the Théâtre Italien gave the earliest Paris performance of
any opera by Rossini (*L'italiana in Algeria* on 1 February 1817), an occasion
notable for the vituperativeness of the critics. The *Gazette de France*
asserted that "this production of Signor Rossini's does not justify the title of
Celebrated Maestro which the libretto accords him," and the *Journal des
Débats* declared the second act to be "completely worthless." Later, under
Rossini's direction, the company gave the first Paris performance of *Semi-
ramide* (8 December 1825). There were two important premières in 1835: of
Bellini's *I puritani* (25 January) and Donizetti's *Marino Faliero* (12 March).
The first Salle Favart was destroyed by fire on the night of 14–15 January

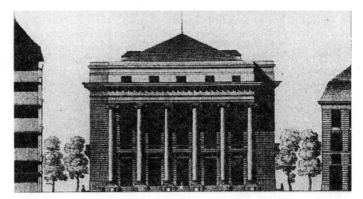

1838, following a performance of *Don Giovanni*. The fire claimed the life of Carlo Severini, one of the directors, who lived in an apartment in the eaves of the theatre. He tried to escape the flames by jumping from a window but was killed in the fall.

(ii) Following reconstruction, the second Salle Favart opened on 16 May 1840 as the home of the Opéra-Comique, which performed new works by Adam, Auber, Halévy, Thomas, and others. Meyerbeer's *L'étoile du Nord* was given here for the first time on 16 February 1854, as was his *Le pardon de Ploërmel* (4 April 1859). Félicien David's *Lallah-Roukh*, an immense success, was first performed on 12 May 1862. The work was welcomed by Berlioz, though Auber reacted to its misty evocations of Kashmir with the memorable remark, "I wish he'd get off his camel." During the 1870s, the Opéra-Comique gave important premières of Bizet's *Djameleh* (22 May 1872), Delibes's *Le roi l'a dit* (24 May 1873), and, most famously, *Carmen* (3 March 1875). The 1880s saw first performances in the Salle Favart of Delibes's *Jean de Nivelle* (8 March 1880), Offenbach's *Les contes d'Hoffmann* (10 February 1881), Delibes's *Lakmé* (14 April 1883), and Massenet's *Manon* (19 January 1884). On 25 May 1887, during the first act of Thomas's *Mignon*, another fire broke out at the Salle Favart, causing a number of deaths and destroying the building for the second time.

(iii) The third Salle Favart, designed by Bernier, was completed in 1898. Under the leadership of Albert Carré (with André Messager as musical director until 1904), the Opéra-Comique returned, after several seasons at the Théâtre Lyrique. It continued to promote a rather bolder

repertory than that favoured by the Opéra. Charpentier's *Louise* (2 February 1900), Debussy's *Pelléas et Mélisande* (30 April 1902), Dukas's *Ariane et Barbe-Bleue* (10 May 1907), Bloch's *Macbeth* (30 November 1910), Ravel's *L'heure espagnole* (19 May 1911), and Milhaud's *Le pauvre matelot* (16 December 1927) were all first performed there.

Salle Feydeau

19–21 rue Feydeau, 2e (G14, Métro: Bourse)
Originally called the Théâtre de Monsieur when it opened in 1790, it soon became known by the street in which it is situated (named, incidentally, after Claude-Henri Feydeau de Marville, lieutenant-general of the Paris police in 1740–47). The company of the Théâtre de Monsieur was largely Italian, and its music director was Cherubini. Over the next decade he produced a succession of works that were given their premières in the Salle Feydeau—*Lodoïska* (18 July 1791), *Médée* (13 March 1797), and *Les deux journées* (16 January 1800). In 1801 the resident company merged with the Opéra-Comique, which performed here from September 1801 until July 1804, then from September 1805 until financial problems necessitated the theatre's closure in April 1829. During this period the Opéra-Comique introduced some significant operas, among them two of

Méhul's most interesting works: *Uthal* (17 May 1806), an opera notable for its dark orchestral colours, due to the omission of violins, and *Joseph* (17 February 1807). Boieldieu's *La dame blanche* was given its première on 10 December 1825.

Salle Gaveau

45 rue La Boétie, 8e (F10, Métro: Miromesnil)
Designed by Jacques Hermant, the Salle Gaveau was built in 1906 as a concert hall (capacity approximately one thousand), with a number of studios attached. In its inaugural season (1907–1908) Ysaÿe and the Cortot-Thibaud-Casals Trio gave concerts, and d'Indy and Messager conducted orchestral programmes. The concerts of La Jeune France took place in the Salle Gaveau (3 June 1936 and 4 June 1937), as did the premières of Ravel's *Ma mère l'oye* (20 April 1910, played by two children, Jeanne Leleu and Geneviève Durony), several Debussy preludes (including four from Book 1, played by the composer on 25 May 1910), and Ravel's *Valses nobles et sentimentales* (Louis Aubert, 9 May 1911) in a concert where the audience had to guess the identities of the composers (for the *Valses nobles* the audience suggested Ravel, Satie, or Kodály); another important Ravel première was the Piano Trio (on 28 January 1915, with Casella at the piano). On 5 May 1916 Debussy gave his last concert in Paris, the première of the Violin Sonata, with Gaston Poulet. More recently the Salle Gaveau has been the venue for the first performances of works such as Poulenc's *Tel jour, telle nuit* (by Pierre Bernac and Poulenc on 13 February 1938) and Messiaen's *Vingt regards sur l'Enfant-Jésus* (26 March 1945) and *Catalogue d'oiseaux* (15 April 1959), both played by their dedicatee, Yvonne Loriod.

Salle Herz

48 rue de la Victoire, 9e (F13, Métro: Le Peletier)
This concert hall was built by the piano virtuoso Henri Herz and his brother Jacques in 1842. At one of the first notable concerts in the Salle Herz, the young Offenbach gave a recital of his newly composed settings of fables by La Fontaine. Though the audience response was cool, another concert Offenbach put on in the same hall in the following

spring was a success, largely thanks to the participation of the tenor Gustave Roger (who was later to create the title role of Roméo in Berlioz's *Roméo et Juliette* and the part of John of Leyden in Meyerbeer's *Le prophète*).

Berlioz conducted the première of *Le carnaval romain* in this hall on 3 February 1844, and the following year (10 April 1845) Glinka gave a concert here (figure 3.10). Of the major works which received their first performances in the Salle Herz, perhaps the most notable was Berlioz's *L'enfance du Christ*, first given on 10 December 1854 and quickly followed by two further performances (on 24 December 1854 and 28 January 1855). These three concerts were a considerable financial success for Berlioz as well as an artistic triumph. In the audience were Verdi, and Liszt's daughters Cosima and Blandine. Adolphe Adam wrote to Berlioz that the work was a "truly grand and beautiful thing," and Berlioz recalled the evening in his *Memoirs:* "Its success was immediate, and so great as to be positively insulting to my earlier works" (Berlioz 1969, 416). As for the work's seemingly characteristic serenity, Berlioz declared: "Some people imagined they could detect in this work a complete change in my manner and style. Nothing could be more mistaken. The subject naturally lent itself to a mild and simple kind of music" (474).

Salle Le Peletier

12 rue Le Peletier, 9e (F13, Métro: Richelieu-Drouot)
Following the destruction of the Théâtre National de la rue de la Loi in 1820, a new house was built for the Opéra in 1820–21 (which made use of some materials from the demolished theatre) and inaugurated on 16 August 1821. On 6 February 1822, the theatre used gas lighting for the first time (appropriately in a production of *Aladin ou la Lampe*

3.11 The Salle Le Peletier on its opening night, 16 August 1821. Lithograph.

merveilleuse). For the next fifty years, the Salle Le Peletier (figures 3.11
and 3.12) was the scene of many important premières, foremost among
which were Rossini's last operatic masterpiece, *Guillaume Tell* (3 August
1829), Meyerbeer's *Robert le Diable* (21 November 1831), Halévy's *La
Juive* (23 February 1835), Berlioz's *Benvenuto Cellini* (10 September
1838), and two operas by Verdi composed specifically for the Opéra: *Les
vêpres siciliennes* (13 June 1855) and *Don Carlos* (11 March 1867).

Verdi was left frustrated and exhausted by the six-month rehearsal
period for *Don Carlos*. *La France Musicale* reported on 23 December 1866:
"There has been talk of incidents and a curious anecdote concerning the
preliminary rehearsals for Verdi's new opera. The composer's patience
has been most sorely tried; but finally, thanks to the ever conciliatory
intervention of Perrin [director of the Opéra], all difficulties have been
resolved, and we are assured that all the artists are now satisfied. It has to
be admitted that the composers who work for the Opéra do not always
tread on rose-strewn paths. More often than not, alas, they encounter
thorns instead of flowers. Happy are they who can reach their goal without losing patience and having to fight some great battle."

Verdi was still bitter about his Parisian experiences in a letter he wrote
to Camille Du Locle on 8 December 1869, nearly three years after the
première: "It's neither the toil of writing an opera nor the judgements of
the Parisian public that deter me; it's the certainty of never being able to
have my music performed in Paris according to my own wishes. It is very

strange that a composer must always see his ideas thwarted and his concepts misrepresented.... I should be most upset if I were to write an opera for you, my dear Du Locle, which you might have to withdraw after some dozen performances, as Perrin did with *Don Carlos*."

Perhaps the most celebrated première at the Opéra during the 1860s was the Paris version of Wagner's *Tannhäuser* (13 March 1861), an evening made notorious by the disruptive behaviour of the Jockey Club, whose members brought whistles to the performance. Surprisingly, perhaps, the production ledgers of the Opéra record that Napoléon III (who had invited Wagner to stage *Tannhäuser* in Paris) was "satisfied" with the performance, which began at 7:45 P.M. and ended at 11:50 P.M. The uproar continued during the two remaining performances (18 and 24 March), before Wagner withdrew his work in disgust.

Ballet premières in the Salle Le Peletier included three works destined to become classics of the repertory: Hérold's *La fille mal gardée* (17 November 1828), Adam's *Giselle* (28 June 1841), and Delibes's *Coppélia* (2 May 1870). The ballet company had long been a part of the Opéra (and was, of course, regularly used to provide the *divertissements* in opera performances). A ballet rehearsal in the Foyer de la danse is depicted in the famous painting by Degas, *Le Foyer de la danse à l'Opéra de la rue le Peletier* (circa 1873, Musée d'Orsay). But there was a seedier side to the Foyer de la danse as a place for subscribers ("abonnés") to meet girls (figure 3.13). This was illustrated by

3.13 The Foyer de la danse at the Opéra. Engraving after E. Guérard, 1843.

such artists as Eugène Lami, Jean-Louis Forain, and Degas. The freedom that men had to roam the corridors and rehearsal rooms was deplored by the dancers themselves even before the Salle Le Peletier was opened, but this disreputable custom continued throughout the nineteenth century, even after the move to the Palais Garnier.

The Salle Le Peletier was completely destroyed by a fire which started on the night of 28–29 October 1873 and lasted for almost twenty-four hours. The cause was never discovered.

Salle Louvois

rue de Louvois, 2e (G13, Métro: Quatre-Septembre)

Two theatres stood in the rue de Louvois by the end of the eighteenth century, following the sale of several large plots of land in 1784: the Salle Louvois, built in 1791, and the Théâtre National de la rue de la Loi. The Salle Louvois was also known as the Théâtre de Louvois and, for a time, as the Théâtre de l'Impératrice. It was used briefly in 1821 by the Opéra (following the destruction of the Theatre National de la rue de la Loi) but achieved greater importance as the home of the Théâtre Italien in 1804–1808 and 1819–25. The company gave the first Paris performance of Rossini's *Otello* here (31 May 1821), and the première of his *Il viaggio a Reims* (19 June 1825), composed to celebrate the coronation of Charles X. The theatre closed the same year and was demolished in 1899.

Salle du Nouveau Théâtre

15 rue Blanche, 9e (E12, Métro: Trinité)

Until 1891, this was the site of a skating rink. It was replaced that year by the Nouveau Théâtre, which gave regular concerts. Both Ravel's works entitled *Shéhérazade* had their premières here: the overture (Ravel's conducting debut, 27 May 1899), and the famous song cycle with Jane Hatto (soprano), conducted by Alfred Cortot (17 May 1904). On 26 February 1905, Camille Chevillard conducted the Lamoureux Orchestra in the earliest Paris performance of any major work by Mahler (the original programme calls him Malher): three of the *Lieder eines fahrenden Gesellen*, with Nina Faliéro-Dalcroze as the soloist. The Nouveau

Théâtre was also a very important venue for contemporary drama, and it staged performances by the Théâtre de l'Oeuvre from 1894 onwards. One of the notable productions was of Ibsen's *Peer Gynt,* using Grieg's incidental music, on 12 November 1896 (with a poster designed by Edvard Munch), and, one month later, the Théâtre de l'Oeuvre gave the première of Alfred Jarry's *Ubu roi* (10 December 1896). The building became the Théâtre Réjane in 1906, and later the Théâtre de Paris.

Salle Pleyel

(i) *9 rue Cadet, 9e (F14–E14, Métro: Cadet) 1830–1839*
(ii) *22 rue de Rochechouart, 9e (E14, Métro: Cadet) 1839–1927*
(iii) *252 rue du Faubourg-Saint-Honoré, 8e (E8, Métro: Ternes) 1927 onwards*

(i) The first Salle Pleyel, opened in 1830 at 9 rue Cadet, was described as "Les Salons de MM. Pleyel et Cie." Chopin gave his first Paris recital here on 26 February 1832.

(ii) By 1839 Camille Pleyel had opened a much larger hall at 22 rue de Rochechouart. Here Chopin, Liszt, Thalberg, Franck, Saint-Saëns, and numerous other distinguished musicians gave recitals. Many of the concerts of the Société Nationale took place in the Salle Pleyel, and among the works first performed there by the society were Fauré's *La bonne chanson* (20 April 1895) and Ravel's *Pavane pour une Infante défunte* and *Jeux d'eau* (both played on 5 April 1902 by Viñes). For several years in the 1920s, Stravinsky rented a studio in the Pleyel building, where he worked on the piano rolls of his music issued by the firm.

(iii) On 18 October 1927, the new Salle Pleyel opened at 252 rue du Faubourg-Saint-Honoré, with a special concert in which Ravel conducted his *La valse* and Stravinsky his *Firebird Suite.* Among notable premières in the new hall was Ravel's Piano Concerto in G major, played by Marguerite Long, with Ravel conducting the Lamoureux Orchestra (14 January 1932). The hall was completely renovated in 1981. The main hall had a seating capacity of 2,500.

The Salle Chopin adjoining the large hall (500 seats) was used extensively for chamber concerts by organisations such as the Société Nationale. The smallest of the three halls was the Salle Debussy (150 seats).

3.14 The Salle Ventadour. Lithograph by Arnout père, after Chapuy, 1851.

Salle Ventadour

rue Méhul, 2e (G13, Métro: Pyramides), now used by the Banque de France
This handsome theatre, with a facade graced by nine arches (figure 3.14), was built in 1826. In April 1829 the Opéra-Comique moved to the Salle Ventadour, where it remained until its move to the Salle de la Bourse in 1832. Financially very unstable during the period, the company nevertheless gave some successful premières—for example, of Auber's *Fra Diavolo* (28 January 1830) and Hérold's *Zampa* (3 May 1831). Following the destruction of the first Salle Favart in 1838, the Théâtre Italien moved to the Salle Ventadour for January–March 1838, then spent three years at the Théâtre de l'Odéon before settling permanently in the Salle Ventadour on 2 October 1841. On 3 January 1843 the Théâtre Italien presented the première of Donizetti's *Don Pasquale,* and several of Verdi's works were introduced to Parisian audiences (it was said to be his favourite opera house in Paris): *Il trovatore* (23 December 1854), *La traviata* (6 December 1856), *Rigoletto* (19 January 1857), and *Un ballo in maschera* (13 January 1861). On 25 January and 1 and 8 February 1860, Wagner conducted three concerts of his works in the Salle Ventadour. The Opéra used the building for the 1874 season, after the fire in the rue Le Peletier and before the opening of the Palais Garnier in January 1875. Following the collapse of the Théâtre Italien company in 1878, the theatre was sold and converted into offices, occupied since 1893 by the Banque de France.

Salle Wagram

39 avenue de Wagram, 17e (E18, Métro: Ternes)

A building which has been used for a variety of purposes, though not as a concert hall, the Salle Wagram is an important recording venue, particularly for Pathé Marconi (EMI). Sessions from the Salle Wagram include Jean Martinon's recordings of Debussy orchestral works (1973–74), all the Fauré chamber music played by Jean-Philippe Collard and others (1975–78), Michel Béroff's recording of Messiaen's *Vingt regards sur l'Enfant-Jésus* (1969), Poulenc's *Gloria*, under the supervision of the composer (1961), and the Ravel piano concertos, played by Samson François (1959).

Schola Cantorum

269 rue Saint-Jacques, 5e (M14, RER: Luxembourg)

The Schola Cantorum moved to the rue Saint-Jacques in 1900, and the old chapel of the Benedictine convent which had stood on this site since 1632 was converted into a concert hall. The Société Nationale gave a number of concerts here in the early 1900s, including the première of Ravel's String Quartet (5 March 1904) and the first performance in Paris of his *Sonatine* (31 March 1906). On 28 April 1937 (at a concert given by La Spirale), Marcelle Bunlet and the composer gave the première of Messiaen's *Poèmes pour Mi* (*see* Schola Cantorum under "Institutions and Orchestras").

Théâtre des Bouffes-Parisiens

4 rue Monsigny, 2e (G13, Métro: Quatre-Septembre or Pyramides)

In 1855, Offenbach had a highly successful summer season in a makeshift theatre in the Marigny gardens on the Champs-Elysées which he called the Bouffes-Parisiens. The theatre in the rue Monsigny, with a stage door at 73 passage Choiseul, was built by Louis Comte in 1818 and was taken over by Offenbach in time for the opening night of *Ba-ta-clan* on 29 December 1855: this one-act *chinoiserie musicale*, with words by Ludovic Halévy, offers a delightful parody of Meyerbeer and an outrageous setting of "Ein feste Burg ist unser Gott." A string of hits for Offenbach followed in this theatre, most famously *Orphée aux enfers* on 21 October

1858. Despite frequent quarrels and changes of management, many of Offenbach's subsequent works were introduced here. Messager's operetta *Véronique* was first performed at the Bouffes-Parisiens (10 December 1898), as was Maeterlinck's play *Pelléas et Mélisande,* in a performance by the company of the Théâtre de l'Oeuvre (17 May 1893), attended by Debussy with far-reaching consequences. The theatre was restored in 1918 and again in 1960.

Théâtre des Champs-Elysées

13 avenue Montaigne, 8e (G9, Métro: Alma-Marceau)
Designed by the innovative architect Auguste Perret, built largely of reinforced concrete, and decorated by Maurice Denis, Edouard Vuillard, and others, the Théâtre des Champs-Elysées (figure 3.15) opened on 2 April 1913 with a magnificent gala concert. The impresario whose vision it was to build the new theatre was the larger-than-life Gabriel Astruc (figure 3.16), who ran into financial difficulties almost at once, but whose inaugural season was nothing short of dazzling. At the opening concert five great French composers conducted their own works: Debussy (*Prélude à l'après-midi d'un faune*), Dukas (*L'apprenti sorcier*), Fauré (*La naissance de Vénus*), d'Indy (*Le camp de Wallenstein*), and Saint-Saëns (*Phaéton* and extracts from *La lyre et la harpe*). The following day, Weingartner conducted Berlioz's *Benvenuto Cellini,* an occasion which also included a dance spectacular by Anna Pavlova. In addition to a

3.15 The Théâtre des Champs-Elysées, avenue Montaigne.

Beethoven cycle by Weingartner (with Alfred Cortot, Louis Diémer, and Lilli Lehmann as soloists), in the first few weeks at the new theatre two concerts by Mengelberg and the Amsterdam Concertgebouw Orchestra (Beethoven's Ninth Symphony and Bach's *St. Matthew Passion*) were given, as well as the Paris première of Fauré's opera *Pénélope* (10 May).

The fifth season of Diaghilev's Ballets Russes opened on 15 May 1913 with a gala: *The Firebird, Scheherazade*, and the world première of Debussy's *Jeux* (choreographed by Nijinsky and designed by Bakst); on Thursday, 29 May 1913, the theatre offered the first performance of Stravinsky's *Le sacre du printemps*, choreographed by Nijinsky, designed by Nicholas Roerich, and conducted by Pierre Monteux. The opening night has acquired legendary status as the occasion of the most celebrated riot in musical history. Two weeks earlier, traditionalists had been disturbed by the depiction of a tennis game in *Jeux*, but the audience were outraged by the ritual sacrifice in *Le sacre*. According to Louis Vuillemin's account (in *Commoedia*, 31 May 1913): "People sang, whistled, applauded and shouted ironic bravos even before the curtain went up." Once the performance began, the music was soon inaudible. Carl van Vechten wrote that "the orchestra played unheard, except occasionally when a slight lull occurred" (White 1979, 214). Soon fights were breaking out all over the theatre. As the Chosen Victim began to tremble at the start of the Sacrificial Dance, Marie Rambert recalled hearing the gallery call out: "Un docteur... un dentiste... deux docteurs!" (215). The second performance, on 4 June, passed off without incident and drew the wry observation from Ravel to Stravinsky of 6 June that "at any rate, the whole work was heard" (Stravinsky and Craft 1979, 101).

The first part of Astruc's season ended with a performance of Fauré's *Pénélope* on 26 June 1913. By the time of the reopening on 2 October (with the same work) Astruc was in severe financial trouble, but the new season contained several highlights: On 9 October, d'Indy conducted a gala performance of Weber's *Der Freischütz*, and on 15 October, Debussy conducted his *Ibéria* in a programme of the Société des Nouveaux Concerts, and *La damoiselle élue* a week later. But on 20 November the bankrupt Astruc was expelled from the theatre, and the sets and costumes were seized. Astruc's downfall was greeted gleefully by his many enemies (some motivated by antisemitism), but others, including Marcel Proust, wrote to offer support. The following season was given by two visiting opera companies: Covent Garden and the Boston Opera Company. The outbreak of war led to the closing of the theatre, which did not open again for regular performances until 1919, when Pavlova's ballet company played a short season.

In 1920 the postwar fortunes of the theatre revived when Rolf de Maré took a seven-year lease, as a home for the Ballets Suédois. This remarkable company (its regular conductors included Inghelbrecht and Désormière), revived Debussy's *Jeux* with a ravishing new set by Pierre Bonnard and costumes by Jeanne Lanvin (25 October 1920), and it gave the première of Milhaud's *La création du monde* (25 October 1923), with sets and costumes by Fernand Léger. The following season the company provoked a tremendous scandal with the première of Satie's last work, *Relâche* (4 December 1924). Devised by Francis Picabia, *Relâche*—the word means "no performance today"—was described by him as a "ballet instantanéiste" (Instantanéisme was Picabia's private offshoot of Dadaism). The performance was conducted by Roger Désormière; at the end Satie took a curtain call in Désormière's car. The work included a film interlude by René Clair (shot in June 1924 on the roof of the theatre), accompanied by Satie's new and astonishing film score *Cinéma*.

The Ballets Russes returned to the theatre for their 1924 season, with the premières of Poulenc's *Les biches,* choreographed by Bronislava Nijinska and designed by Marie Laurencin (26 May), Auric's *Les fâcheux*, designed by Braque (4 June), and Milhaud's *Le train bleu*, to a scenario by Cocteau, with costumes by Coco Chanel (20 June).

3.16 "Gabriel Astruc Drinking Champagne with Vaslav Nijinsky." Cartoon by Sem, 1911.

The subsequent history of the theatre has been extremely distinguished, whether one considers staged performances of ballet and opera or concerts by Chaliapin, Toscanini, Bruno Walter, Heifetz, or other visiting artists. A cutaway model of the building as it appeared when it opened can be seen in the Musée de la Musique.

Théâtre du Châtelet

1 place du Châtelet, 1er (J14, Métro: Châtelet)
Building work on Gabriel Davioud's handsome theatre started on 1 May 1860, and it was inaugurated on 19 August 1862. Many of the Concerts Colonne took place here, and the theatre has been used regularly for concerts ever since. On 19 April 1903, Grieg conducted a programme at the Châtelet which included *Peer Gynt* (first suite) and the Piano Concerto, in which Raoul Pugno was the soloist. Another notable event took place on 17 April 1910: the first performance in France of Mahler's Second Symphony, conducted by the composer at the Concerts Colonne (figure 3.17). The Ballets Russes had four seasons here (1909, 1911, 1912, and 1917), and the Châtelet hosted the premières of two of the greatest ballets of the twentieth century: Stravinsky's *Petrouchka* (13 June 1911) and Ravel's *Daphnis et Chloé* (8 June 1912). In 1980, the theatre was taken over by the City of Paris as a venue for opera productions. As a consequence, it has since also been known as the Théâtre Musical de Paris. It was extensively restored in 1998–99.

Théâtre de la Gaîté-Lyrique

3–5 rue Papin, 3e (G15, Métro: Réaumur-Sébastopol)
Designed by Hittorff and Cuzin, the theatre was built 1861–62 and inaugurated on 3 September 1862. On 15 January 1872 Offenbach's *Le roi Carotte* was given its première here, and it subsequently ran for 149 performances. With its ballet of insects and a scene depicting the fall of Pompeii, it was a spectacular show with a sharp satirical edge (the libretto was by Victorien Sardou). Offenbach took over the management of the theatre, and his greatest success here was the première of the revised (and expanded) *Orphée aux enfers* (7 February 1874). The composer himself conducted the hundredth performance of a long run during which two

3.17 Programme for the first Paris performance of Mahler's Second Symphony on 17 April 1910 at the Théâtre du Châtelet, conducted by the composer.

million francs were taken at the box office, but by the end of the next year Offenbach was in financial trouble and had to give up the theatre. During the seasons of the Ballets Russes in 1921, 1923, and 1925, Prokofiev's *Chout* and Stravinsky's *Les noces* had their premières here (on 17 May 1921 and 13 June 1923, respectively).

Théâtre Lyrique

(i) *1851–62: 72 boulevard du Temple (now part of place de la République), 11e (G17, Métro: République)*

(ii) *1862–70 and 1874 onwards: 2 place du Châtelet, 4e (J15, Métro: Châtelet)*

Théâtre des Nations (known as Théâtre Lyrique when the Opéra-Comique used the theatre in 1887–98); renamed Théâtre Sarah-Bernhardt in 1898, Théâtre de la Ville in 1968, and Théâtre Municipal de Paris in 1979.

(i) The first Théâtre Lyrique was at 72 rue du Temple (now part of the place de la République). It was demolished in 1863. The Théâtre Lyrique company gave the premières here of Adam's *Si j'étais roi* (4 September 1852) and, memorably, Gounod's *Faust* (19 March 1859).

(ii) The second Théâtre Lyrique opened in 1862 in the place du Châtelet. Designed by Gabriel Davioud, it faces his very similar Théâtre du Châtelet, across the square. The Théâtre Lyrique company gave the premières here of Bizet's *Les pêcheurs de perles* (30 September 1863) and *La jolie fille de Perth* (26 December 1867), and Gounod's *Mireille* (19 March 1864) and *Roméo et Juliette* (27 April 1867). The house also staged important revivals, of Mozart operas and Wagner's *Rienzi*, for instance. The theatre was badly damaged by fire on 21 May 1871, as a consequence of the fighting which raged between the Communards and Thiers's troops. The costumes, music, and archives survived. Rebuilt in 1874, it became the home from 1887 until 1898 of the Opéra-Comique. The repertoire was dominated by works of Massenet—premières of *Esclarmonde* (14 May 1889) and *Sapho* (27 November 1897) and the first Paris performance of *Werther* (16 January 1893, a year after the première in Vienna).

The Ballets Russes gave several premières at the Théâtre Sarah-Bernhardt, including Stravinsky's *Apollon musagète* (12 June 1928), and two ballets by Prokofiev, *Le pas d'acier* (27 May 1927) and *L'enfant prodigue* (21 May 1929).

Théâtre National de la Rue de la Loi

rue de Louvois, 2e (G13, Métro: Quatre-Septembre)

This large theatre (with a seating capacity of 2,800) was the home of the
Opéra for quarter of a century (rue de la Loi was the name given to the rue
de Richelieu from 1793 to 1806). The Opéra was based here from 7 August
1794 until 13 February 1820, and premières were given of Paisiello's *Proser-
pine* (29 March 1803, setting a text first used by Lully), Cherubini's *Anacréon*
(4 October 1803), and Spontini's *La vestale* (16 December 1807) and *Fernand
Cortez ou La conquête du Mexique* (28 November 1809). There were vigorous
complaints from audience and management alike about some aspects of the
theatre. Despite its large seating capacity, the building was cramped, the
backstage facilities were miserable, and the lighting and ventilation were
highly unsatisfactory. Various proposals were made for a new theatre during
the first decade of the nineteenth century, but they came to nothing. The
theatre was refurbished in 1808, however, and some structural repairs were
made in 1811. Perhaps the most celebrated event connected with this theatre
was the one which resulted in its destruction: the assassination of the duc de
Berry (son of the future Charles X) on 13 February 1820 at the hand of Louvel, a Parisian saddle-maker who remained fanatically loyal to Napoléon
and who considered the Bourbons to be the enemies of France. Louvel mur-
dered the duke outside the royal entrance to the theatre (level with 5 rue
Rameau) by stabbing him in the chest. The Opéra lost several of its homes
as a result of fires, but the demolition of this theatre was by royal decree:
Louis XVIII wished to obliterate the scene of Louvel's crime and planned to
erect a large memorial (never built) to the duc de Berry.

Théâtre de l'Odéon

place de l'Odéon, 6e (K13, Métro: Odéon)

The first theatre on this site opened on 9 April 1782. Used mostly for spoken drama, the Odéon had perhaps its most notorious first night on 26
April 1784, when Beaumarchais's *Le marriage de Figaro* caused a scandal.
On 18 March 1799, the theatre was completely destroyed by a fire so
intense that it is said to have illuminated most of Paris. A new building,
which was not put up until eight years later, reopened on 16 June 1808 as
the home of the Théâtre Italien, which remained here until September

3.18 The Théâtre de l'Odéon in 1900.

1815. This theatre, too, burnt down on 20 March 1818; the building which reopened on 1 October 1819 is the one that survives to this day (figure 3.18). Again used mostly for plays, the present theatre gave several opera seasons in the 1820s, and the Théâtre Italien was back at the Odéon from October 1838 to March 1841, following the destruction of the first Salle Favart and before settling at the Salle Ventadour.

On Sunday, 2 March 1873, Edouard Colonne conducted the first Concert National, in the series that later became the Concerts Colonne, in the theatre (figure 3.19). The soloists were Pauline Viardot (singing Schubert) and Saint-Saëns (playing his Second Piano Concerto and accompanying Viardot).

In 1888 Fauré composed incidental music for a revival of the play *Caligula* by Alexandre Dumas *père*. He conducted the first performance (in its original version for small theatre orchestra) on 8 November 1888. The following year he was asked to write another work for the Odéon, incidental music to Edmond Haraucourt's *Shylock*. Once again, Fauré conducted the first performance, on 17 December 1889.

In the twentieth century the Odéon served as the venue for concerts, notably those of the Domaine Musical. Founded in 1953–54 by Pierre Boulez, while he was musical director for the Renaud-Barrault Company, the Domaine Musical has often been acclaimed as perhaps the most progressive concert-giving organisation in Europe at the time, and its list of premières is formidable. Among those given at the Odéon were three of Messiaen's most important works from the 1960s: *Sept haïkaï* (world première, 30 October 1963), *Couleurs de la Cité céleste* (French première, 16 December 1964), and *Et exspecto resurrectionem mortuorum* (first concert

3.19 Programme
for the first Con-
cert National on 2
March 1873 at the
Théâtre de
l'Odéon.

performance, 12 January 1966), all conducted by Boulez. Boulez relin-
quished the musical direction in 1967 to Gilbert Amy, and the Domaine
Musical gave its last concert in 1973.

Théâtre de la Porte Saint-Martin

16 boulevard Saint-Martin, 10e (G16, Métro: République)
Following the fire which destroyed the second opera house at the Palais
Royal on 8 June 1781, Nicolas Lenoir built a new theatre for the Opéra on

the orders of Marie-Antoinette, on the boulevard Saint-Martin site (used by the Opéra since 1767 for storing sets). Work was carried out at great speed, around the clock (clergy were outraged that building work even continued on the Feast of the Assumption), in order for Lenoir to avoid a heavy penalty for not completing the theatre by October. It opened on 27 October 1781 with a new opera by Niccolò Piccini, *Adèle de Ponthieu*, written to celebrate the dauphin's birthday (22 October). The Opéra remained here until 1794, when it moved to the Théâtre de la rue de la Loi. The theatre was sold in 1799 and opened under new management in 1802 as the Opéra du Peuple, which closed in 1807. In 1810 it reopened as the Théâtre des Jeux Gymniques (including ballet productions with real horses), then in 1814 as Théâtre de la Porte Saint-Martin, where a number of ballets were successfully produced. Although it was destroyed by fire during the Commune, a new theatre opened on the same site in 1873.

Théâtre des Variétés

7 boulevard Montmartre, 2e (F14, Métro: Rue Montmartre)
The Théâtre des Variétés opened on 24 June 1807, and the buildings were expanded in 1833 to include offices and storage space for sets and costumes. Its most remarkable successes were two works by Offenbach. *La belle Hélène* opened here on 17 December 1864 with Hortense Schneider in the title role (figure 3.20). This was the first operatic collaboration between the librettists Henri Meilhac and Ludovic Halévy (who went on to write three more successful libretti for Offenbach, as well as *Carmen* for Bizet). Schneider struck a hard bargain to sing Hélène, and she was difficult and argumentative during rehearsals. But the first night was a complete success. The ancient Auber wrote that he went to see *La belle Hélène* "whenever I want to fill my ears with delight." In 1866 *Barbe-Bleue* was given here for the first time (5 February 1866). A little over a year later, during the 1867 Exposition universelle, Offenbach, Meilhac, and Halévy produced *La Grande Duchesse de Gérolstein* for the Théâtre des Variétés (12 April 1867). Again Schneider's tantrums were a problem during rehearsals, but the first night was a success, and a steady stream of monarchs visiting the exposition followed the French emperor's example by attending performances of a work which was openly satirical about monarchy and introduces the ludicrous figure of Général Boum (General

Boom), who takes gunpowder as snuff, as the personification of war. The following year, the première of *La Périchole*, another collaboration with Meilhac and Halévy, was given here (6 October 1868). The theatre has continued a tradition of comic drama to this day.

Théâtre du Vaudeville

2 boulevard des Capucines, 9e (F13, Métro: Opéra)
This building was completed in 1868 and was inaugurated on 23 April 1869 by the company which had previously been at the Salle de la Bourse. The management was taken over by Léon Carvalho, who had been forced by bankruptcy to abandon the Théâtre Lyrique in 1868. Determined to revive the reputation of the mélodrame (play with music), Carvalho pre-

sented Alphonse Daudet's *L'Arlésienne*, with music by Bizet, on 1 October 1872. The public's response was chilly: the audience was bored by the music and talked over it. Théodore de Banville recalled that his neighbours would complain, "Another overture!" each time a piece of music was played. By the end of the play, the theatre was almost empty, though some of Bizet's friends, including Jules Massenet and Ambroise Thomas, were present and greatly admired the music. Ernest Reyer reviewed *L'Arlésienne* in the *Journal des Débats:* "The twenty-six musicians played this charming score with rare perfection and irreproachable ensemble, the most sensitive variations and exquisite feeling. No one is more skilful nor more ingenious than M. Bizet. What other composer would have made better use of such slender resources?" The play closed after only twenty-one performances, played to almost empty houses, though the orchestral suite by Bizet was an immense success in November 1872.

In the twentieth century, the theatre was the venue for the posthumous première of Debussy's delightful ballet *La boîte à joujoux*, orchestrated by Caplet and conducted by Inghelbrecht (10 December 1919). It was only when the Ballets Suédois took up the work three years later (giving 280 performances at the Théâtre des Champs-Elysées) that it began to enjoy real success.

The Théâtre du Vaudeville became the Paramount Cinema in 1927.

Trocadéro

Palais de Chaillot, 16e (H7, Métro: Trocadéro)
In 1876 a competition was announced for a new building to stand on the Chaillot hill above the Seine for the 1878 Exposition universelle. The winner was Gabriel Davioud (1823–81), whose design was for an extravagant, Moorish edifice with twin towers. Architecturally, the Trocadéro was always considered something of a curiosity (figure 3.21). Despite its unruly acoustics (including a cavernous echo), the immense Salle des fêtes was the scene of numerous important musical events (figure 3.22). These included the concerts given as part of the Expositions universelles: Russian music conducted by Rimsky-Korsakov in 1878 and 1889, and three concerts given by Mahler and the Vienna Philharmonic Orchestra on 20, 21, and 22 June 1900, the first of which included a performance of the *Symphonie fantastique*. A few weeks later, on 12 July 1900, the final

3.21 The Tro-
cadéro. The ani-
mal statues are
now in front of the
Musée d'Orsay.

3.22 The Salle des
fêtes at the Tro-
cadéro.

version of Fauré's Requiem had its première, conducted by Paul Taffanel, at the Trocadéro. In writing to his friend Ysaÿe about the performance, Fauré mentioned one of its more remarkable features: Mlle. Torrès had such a success with the "Pie Jesu" that it was encored.

The magnificent Cavaillé-Coll organ inaugurated in 1878 had the distinction of being the first large instrument to be installed in a concert hall rather than a church. During August–October 1878 there was a remarkable series of recitals by leading organists—Guilmant (7 August), Gigout (13 August), Widor (24 August, including the first performance of his Sixth Symphony), Saint-Saëns (28 September), and César Franck (1 October). At this concert Franck gave the first performance of the *Trois pièces* (including the celebrated "Pièce héroïque"), which had been written especially for the occasion, along with two improvisations, the first on themes by Hector Berlioz, Félicien David, and Georges Bizet (two themes from *L'Arlésienne*), and the second on Russian themes.

The Trocadéro was demolished in 1935 to make way for the Palais de Chaillot, built for the 1937 exposition. A cutaway model of the Trocadéro's vast interior can be seen at the Musée de la Musique.

4 · Institutions and Orchestras

Académie des Beaux-Arts (Institut de France)

Institut de France, 23 quai de Conti, 6e (J13, Métro: Pont-Neuf)

(i) The Prix de Rome

The Prix de Rome for music was awarded annually by the Académie des Beaux-Arts from 1803 until 1968 (awards were also made for painting, sculpture, engraving, and architecture). The prize for composition has attracted controversy and even ridicule. It certainly cannot be considered a roll call of the most distinguished French composers, since the judges failed to award a Prix de Rome to several notable entrants. Four outstanding composers were unsuccessful in the competition: Saint-Saëns in 1852 (while still in his teens) and 1864, Dukas for four years running (1886–89), Ravel on no fewer than five occasions in 1900–1905 (he did not enter in 1904), and Messiaen twice (1930–31). Other major figures never entered at all, among them Franck, Fauré, Duparc, and Chabrier. Nevertheless, winners have included some great composers, notably Berlioz in 1830 (his fourth attempt), and Debussy in 1884 (his third attempt). Other winners of interest were Hérold (1812), Halévy (1819), Thomas (1832), Gounod (1839), Bizet (1857), Massenet (1863), Charpentier (1887), Schmitt (1900), Caplet (1901), Paray (1911), Lili Boulanger (1913, the first woman to win the Prix de Rome for music), Dupré (1914), Ibert (1919), and Dutilleux (1938). Conversely, many winners have lapsed into obscurity. In his article on the Prix de Rome, Gustave Chouqet (*Grove*, 5th ed.) has described it as "interesting and somewhat depressing" that so many winners had musical careers which "came to nothing.... On the other hand the absence of many of the most distinguished French composers is equally striking."

Ravel's fifth failure to win the prize in 1905 (his last possible entry, given the age limit of thirty) provoked the most famous scandal over the Prix de Rome. Having recently enjoyed success with the first performances of the song cycle *Shéhérazade* and the String Quartet, Ravel was now informed by the jury that he lacked basic competence and was eliminated in the first round. When the final results were announced, the front pages of newspapers ran outraged stories about nepotism and intrigue, asserting that the results had been rigged in favour of the Conservatoire teacher Charles Lenepveu. This was a fair assumption: all six finalists were his pupils, and he himself sat on the jury. Lenepveu, however, rather weakly denied that there had been any irregularity; he asserted that it was purely coincidental that only his pupils had won prizes. It was not a persuasive viewpoint. Given Lenepveu's involvement, the Conservatoire was inevitably dragged into the affair and the director, Théodore Dubois, resigned his post as a direct result of the scandal. Through a delightfully ironic twist, it was Ravel's teacher, Fauré, who at once replaced him. Louis Laloy (a friend of Ravel's) and Pierre Lalo (usually a harsh critic of Ravel's music, but on this occasion the composer's advocate) wrote eloquent and understandably gleeful condemnations of the jury's decision making, first in eliminating Ravel in the preliminary stages, and second in awarding the prizes exclusively to finalists who were also Lenepveu pupils. Romain Rolland wrote in a letter to the director of the Académie des Beaux-Arts: "Ravel comes to the competition for the Prix de Rome not as a pupil but as a composer who has already proved himself. I admire the composers who dared to judge him. Who shall judge them in their turn? ... Is there no way for the state (without going against its decision) at least to prove its interest in Ravel?" (Orenstein 1975, 43). Rolland's final question was a pertinent one: Ravel had been defeated by two gifted composers in 1900 and 1901 (Florent Schmitt and André Caplet), but in later attempts, works by Aymé Kunc (1902) and Raoul Laparra (1903) were preferred to his.

Twenty-five years later, Messiaen's case was championed in the press. On his second attempt, in 1931, he reached the final round for a setting of the cantata *L'ensorceleuse*. Reviewing the work in the musical journal *Le Ménestrel*, Paul Bertrand wrote: "If Messiaen was some way from having written the best cantata, it is nevertheless possible to detect in him an unparalleled musicianship. ... Remember his name. It is doubtful whether he will become famous for operatic music, but I shall be surprised if he does not place himself at the highest level as a composer of abstract music."

(ii) Musicians in the Académie des Beaux-Arts
Six members of the Académie des Beaux-Arts represent music. Dukas and his most famous pupil, Messiaen, having each failed to win the Prix de

Rome after more than one attempt, were both subsequently elected to this distinguished group in later life. Fauré, despite several attempts, was never able to garner enough support to be admitted, even though he was director of the Conservatoire for fifteen years. Much more recently, Iannis Xenakis was elected, and Messiaen gave a charming speech of welcome (2 May 1984), which concluded with a witty parody of Mallarmé's "Le tombeau d'Edgar Poe." In 1988 Mstislav Rostropovich, joining Yehudi Menuhin, among others, was elected as a foreign associate of the Académie des Beaux-Arts. The six members of the Musical Composition Section of the Académie des Beaux-Arts on 1 July 1995 were Marcel Landowski (also chancellor of the Institut), Daniel-Lesur, Iannis Xenakis, Serge Nigg (president of the Académie des Beaux-Arts), Marius Constant, and Jean-Louis Florentz.

Conservatoire de Musique

(i) *2 rue Bergère, 9e (F15, Métro: Bonne-Nouvelle)*
(ii) *14 rue de Madrid, 8e (E11, Métro: Europe)*
(iii) *Cité de la Musique, 221 avenue Jean-Jaurès, 19e (C20, Métro: Porte de Pantin)*

(i) In 1784 the Ecole Royale de Chant was founded in Paris on the initiative of François-Joseph Gossec, and in 1792 Bernard Sarrette instituted the Ecole Gratuite de la Garde Nationale. The following year the Ecole Gratuite became the Institut National de Musique and was given the assignment of training military musicians for the bands of the National Guard, partly to satisfy the seemingly insatiable demand for massive outdoor celebrations, which were among the most popular manifestations of the revolutionary government after the Reign of Terror. On 3 August 1795 the Conservatoire de Musique was officially established, and the combined staff of both earlier institutions was put under Sarrette's directorship. The first 351 students arrived in October 1796. In 1800 the Conservatoire staff amounted to a roll call of the finest musicians in Paris, including the composers Cherubini, Gossec, Le Sueur, Méhul, and Monsigny, and the violinists Baillot, Kreutzer, and Rode.

Sarrette retired in November 1815. The director from April 1816 was François-Louis Perne, and the institution was renamed the Ecole Royale de Musique. Perhaps the most famous director of the Conservatoire during the nineteenth century was Luigi Cherubini; appointed on 1 April 1822, he remained in the post until 8 February 1842. When visiting the library, before he became a student, Berlioz first encountered the strict rules imposed by the newly appointed Cherubini. This typically entertaining incident is reported in his *Memoirs:* "The moment Cherubini took over the Conservatoire on the death of his predecessor, Perne, he determined to mark his accession by introducing revolutionary restrictions in the internal régime of the school, which had not been run on exactly puritan principles. In order that the two sexes should not mix except under the supervision of a teacher, he decreed that the men must use the door in the rue du Faubourg-Poissonnière and the women the door in the rue Bergère, the two entrances being at opposite ends of the building. One morning, knowing nothing about this moral edict, which had only just been promulgated, I proceeded to the Conservatoire and entered by the usual door in the rue Bergère—the female door. I was half-way to the library when a porter stopped me in the middle of the courtyard and tried to make me go back and return by the other entrance. I thought this so absurd that I sent the liveried Argus about his business and went on. The rogue, wishing to get in well with his new employer by showing that he could be just as strict, refused to admit defeat, and hurried off to report the matter to the director. I had been absorbed in *Alceste* for a quarter of an hour and had thought no more of the incident, when Cherubini, with my accuser behind him, stumped into the reading-room, his face more cadaverous and basilisk-eyed, his hair bristling more angrily, than ever. They made the rounds of the table where several students were reading. The porter scrutinised each one in turn, then came to a halt in front of me" (Berlioz 1969, 59).

After a confrontation with the ill-tempered Cherubini, and a chase around the library, Berlioz escaped. He entered the Conservatoire as a student the following year and seems uncertain whether Cherubini remembered this escapade when he was subsequently introduced. Cherubini did much to maintain the highest possible musical standards by employing teachers such as Fétis, Habeneck, Halévy, Le Sueur, Paer, and Reicha.

Daniel-François-Esprit Auber was appointed Cherubini's successor in 1842, and during Auber's tenure Adam, Halévy, and Thomas were among the composition teachers. Louise Farrenc, Henri Herz, and Marmontel taught piano, Alard and Dancla violin, and Chevillard and Franchomme cello. In the 1830s Berlioz had been appointed part-time curator in the library, and he was librarian from 1852 until his death. Thus France's greatest nineteenth-century composer never held a position on the teaching staff of its most prestigious musical institution. His successor as librarian was Félicien David. The instrument museum (now the Musée de la Musique) was founded in 1861.

During the siege of Paris, the Conservatoire was requisitioned as a hospital. The director appointed by the Commune on 13 May 1871 (the day after Auber's death) was the little-known Salvador Daniel. It was not a post Daniel held for long: he was shot ten days later by Thiers's troops in his apartment on the rue Jacob. He was followed by Ambroise Thomas (1871–96), whose twenty-five-year tenure was marked by a rather stolid conservatism, roundly condemned by some of the students at the time, notably Debussy. During that period, Franck's unofficial composition classes (nominally, organ classes) attracted several composers who were later to achieve eminence—Chausson, Ropartz, Lekeu, Bordes, and d'Indy. In 1875, the year of *Carmen*, Bizet joined Franck's class for a few sessions.

After Thomas's death, Théodore Dubois was appointed (1896–1905). Widor, Fauré, and Lenepveu were on his teaching staff for composition, Guilmant for organ, Taffanel for flute, and Diémer and Philipp for piano. Following the "Affaire Ravel" (*see* Académie des Beaux-Arts), Gabriel Fauré succeeded Dubois. The appointment of Fauré, who had taught Ravel, was greeted enthusiastically in *Le Courrier Musical* (15 June 1905): "Gabriel Fauré is an independent thinker: that is to say, there is much we can expect from him, and it is with joy that we welcome his nomination."

(ii) Fauré presided over the move of the Conservatoire to 14 rue de Madrid in 1911 and instigated several reforms, including the establishment of a conducting class in 1914. He appointed progressive figures to the governing council, notably, Debussy, Dukas, and Messager. The repertoire became less restrictive (Schubert's *Gretchen am Spinnrade* caused a sensation when it was set for the singing competition in 1906), and music history became more important part in the curriculum (it was taught by Maurice Emmanuel from 1909). Among Widor's pupils in the composition class during Fauré's tenure were Milhaud, Honegger, and Tailleferre. Lili and Nadia Boulanger also studied at the Conservatoire during this period. Cortot joined the staff to teach piano, and Gigout to teach organ. Fauré's successor was Henri Rabaud (1920–41), director during the years when Messiaen, Langlais, and Jehan Alain were students. Dukas and Roger-Ducasse taught composition, Claire Croiza singing, Marcel Moÿse flute, Louis Laloy music history, and Marcel Dupré organ.

Claude Delvincourt was appointed director in 1941, during the German Occupation of Paris. He was an enlightened reformer who established classes in percussion, saxophone, Ondes Martenot, and harpsichord and secured the services of Messiaen (to teach analysis and aesthetics) and Milhaud (as professor of composition). Delvincourt's death in a car accident in 1954 was a blow to the newly invigorated institution. His immediate successors were Marcel Dupré (1954–56), Raymond Loucheur (1956–62), and Raymond Gallois-Montbrun (1962–83), who appointed Messiaen as professor of composition.

(iii) Under the directorship of Marc Bleuse (1984–86), active planning went on to relocate the Conservatoire to La Villette. By the time the move became a reality, in 1990, the director was Alain Louvier (1986–91). The Conservatoire remained on the rue de Madrid until June 1990, then, during September 1990, opened at its magnificent new site as part of the Cité de la Musique (*see* Orchestre de la Société des Concerts du Conservatoire; also Salle du Conservatoire under "Theatres and Concert Halls" and Musée de la Musique under "Museums and Libraries").

Ecole Niedermeyer

10 rue Neuve-Fontaine Saint-Georges (now rue Fromentin), near place Blanche, 9e (D13, Métro: Blanche or Pigalle)
Founded by Louis Niedermeyer as the Ecole de Musique Religieuse et Classique in 1853, the Ecole Niedermeyer, as it soon became known, had as its express purpose the training of organists and choirmasters. Niedermeyer himself died in 1861, and his successor as director was Saint-Saëns. Among the pupils from those years who were destined to become successful composers were Fauré, Messager, Gigout, and Terrasse (brother-in-law of the artist Pierre Bonnard). A later director of the Ecole Niedermeyer was Henri Büsser.

Ecole Normale de Musique

78 rue Cardinet, 17e (D9, Métro: Malesherbes)

Founded in 1919 by Auguste Mangeot and Alfred Cortot (who had previously taught the piano at the Conservatoire 1907–17), the Ecole Normale was, for a time, a serious rival to the Conservatoire, especially in the field of instrumental teaching (in much the same way as d'Indy's Schola Cantorum was for composition). Cortot, who appointed a distinguished staff, remained the director of the Ecole Normale until his death in 1962. During the 1930s, Messiaen was on the staff here (*see also* Salle de l'Ecole Normale de Musique under "Theatres and Concert Halls").

IRCAM

place Igor-Stravinsky, 4e (H15, Métro: Rambuteau)

Founded in 1975, with Pierre Boulez as director, the Institut de Recherche et de Co-ordination Acoustique-Musique was inaugurated in 1978, a year after the Centre Georges-Pompidou, of which it forms a part. The principal performance area is the *espace de projection*, which measures 375 square metres. This is a flexible space with adjustable acoustic properties, which is intended for recordings, musical and acoustical research, and public concerts and lectures. Leading contemporary composers Amy, Berio, Globokar, and Kagel, as well as Boulez himself, have been involved in projects at IRCAM. The Ensemble Intercontemporain, originally founded in 1976 as part of IRCAM, moved in 1990 to the Cité de la Musique (*see* Cité de la Musique under "Theatres and Concert Halls.")

Orchestre des Concerts Colonne

The series founded by Georges Hartmann in 1873 as the Concert National gave its first concert at the Théâtre de l'Odéon on 2 March 1873, with Saint-Saëns and Pauline Viardot as soloists (see figure 3.19). The conductor was Edouard Colonne (figure 4.1), and the series soon became known as the Concerts Colonne. Its principal conductors were Edouard Colonne (1873–1910), Gabriel Pierné (1910–34), Paul Paray (1934–40 and 1944–56), Gaston Poulet (1940–44), and Charles Münch (1956–58).

Among the notable first performances by the orchestra were

Debussy: *Danse sacrée et danse profane* (6 November 1904, cond. Colonne); *Ibéria* (20 February 1910, cond. Pierné); *Gigues* (26 January 1913, cond. Pierné)

Duparc: *Lénore* (15 May 1875, cond. Colonne; given as "Symphonie Ballade")

Ravel: *Rapsodie espagnole* (15 March 1908, Théâtre du Châtelet, cond. Colonne); *Daphnis et Chloé,* Suite no. 1 (2 April 1911, cond. Pierné; the earliest performance of any part of *Daphnis*); *Tzigane* (30 November 1924, Jelly d'Aranyi, violin; cond. Pierné); *Don Quichotte à Dulcinée* (1 December 1934, Théâtre du Châtelet, Martial Singher, baritone; cond. Paray)

Saint-Saëns: *Danse macabre* (3 February 1875, cond. Colonne)

Orchestre des Concerts Lamoureux

The series was founded in 1881 by Charles Lamoureux (figure 4.2). Principal conductors included Lamoureux (1881–97), Camille Chevillard (1897–1923), Paul Paray (1923–28), Albert Wolff (1928–34), Eugène Bigot (1935–51), Jean Martinon (1951–57), and Igor Markevitch (1957–62).

Among the many premières given by the orchestra were several cornerstones of the French orchestral repertoire:

Chabrier: *España* (4 November 1883, cond. Lamoureux)

Debussy: *Nocturnes* ("Nuages" and "Fêtes": 9 December 1900; complete: 27 October 1901, both cond. Chevillard); *La mer* (15 October 1905, cond. Chevillard)

Fauré: *Pavane* (25 November 1888, cond. Lamoureux)

4.2 Charles Lamoureux. Caricature by C.-L. Léandre (*Le Rire,* 9 November 1895).

Ravel: *Valses nobles et sentimentales* (22 April 1912, Théâtre du Châtelet, cond. Ravel); *La valse* (12 December 1920, cond. Chevillard); *Menuet antique* (11 January 1930, cond. Ravel); Piano Concerto in G (14 January 1932, Salle Pleyel, Marguerite Long, piano; cond. Ravel)

Orchestre des Concerts Pasdeloup

The series was founded in 1861 by Jules Pasdeloup as the Concerts Populaires (*see* Cirque d'Hiver under "Theatres and Concert Halls"). The orchestra ceased its activities in 1884 but re-formed in 1919 as the Orchestre des Concerts Pasdeloup. Principal conductors included Pasdeloup (1861–84), Rhené-Bâton (1919–33), and Albert Wolff (1934–70).

Among the important first performances given by the orchestra were

Ravel: *Alborada del gracioso* (17 May 1919, cond. Rhené-Bâton); *Le tombeau de Couperin* (28 February 1920, cond. Rhené-Bâton)

Roussel: Symphony no. 4 (19 October 1935, cond. Wolff)

Orchestre des Concerts Straram

Founded in 1925 by Walther Straram, the orchestra's principal conductor until his death in 1933, when the orchestra was disbanded. Considered by some musicians to be the finest French orchestra of the interwar years, it was chosen by Toscanini for his French debut and by Stravinsky for his first recording of *Le sacre du printemps* (made in May 1929).

Among the first performances given by the orchestra were two of Messiaen's earliest works: *Les offrandes oubliées* (19 February 1931, Théâtre des Champs-Elysées, cond. Walther Straram) and *Hymne au Saint-Sacrement* (23 March 1933, Théâtre des Champs-Elysées, cond. Walther Straram).

Orchestre des Concerts de la Société du Conservatoire

Founded in 1828, the orchestra was disbanded in 1967 (on the formation of the Orchestre de Paris). Its repertory was rooted in established classics, and its notable first performances were thus rather fewer than might be assumed. Principal conductors included François Habeneck (1828–49),

Narcisse Girard (1849–60), Alexandre Tilmant (1960–68), Georges Hainl (1868–72), Edouard Deldevez (1872–85), Jules Garcin (1885–92), Paul Taffanel (1895–1901), Georges Marty (1901–1908), André Messager (1908–18), Philippe Gaubert (1918–38), Charles Münch (1938–46), and André Cluytens (1949–67).

The following important works were given premières by the orchestra (all in the Salle du Conservatoire, unless otherwise stated):

Berlioz: *Symphonie fantastique* (5 December 1830, cond. Habeneck)

Fauré: Requiem, full orchestral version (12 July 1900, Trocadéro, Mlle Torrès, soprano; M. Vallier, baritone; Eugène Gigout, organ; cond. Paul Taffanel); *Masques et bergamasques,* suite (16 November 1919, cond. Philippe Gaubert)

Franck: Symphony in D Minor (17 February 1889, cond. Jules Garcin)

Messiaen: *Trois petites liturgies de la Présence Divine* (21 April 1945, Yvonne Loriod, piano; Ginette Martenot, Ondes Martenot; Chorale Yvonne Gouverné; cond. Roger Désormière)

Saint-Saëns: Cello Concerto no. 1 (19 January 1873, Auguste Tolbecque, cello)

Schola Cantorum

(i) *rue Stanislas, 6e (L12, Métro: Notre-Dame-des-Champs)*
(ii) *269 rue Saint-Jacques, 5e (M14, RER: Luxembourg)*
During its earliest years, from its opening on 15 October 1896, the Schola Cantorum was located on the rue Stanislas; it moved in 1900 to 269 rue Saint-Jacques, where it has remained to the present day. The buildings include those of the former English Benedictine monastery which occupied this site from the seventeenth century. The original intention of the founders of the Schola Cantorum, Vincent d'Indy, Alexandre Guilmant, and Charles Bordes (*see* Saint-Gervais under "Churches"), was that the institution would serve as a centre for the study of plainchant and Renaissance choral music, but on the move to the rue Saint-Jacques it soon became an important rival to the Conservatoire for the study of composition; a good many students came to attend d'Indy's lengthy *Cours de com-*

position musicale. Other major figures taught there as well: Vierne for organ and Blanche Selva for piano, as well as Roussel, Messiaen, and Nadia Boulanger. Varèse and Satie were among the students who found d'Indy's composition course impossibly prescriptive and dogmatic, and Varèse had a particularly well-developed dislike for his teacher, which was apparently reciprocated. Roussel, Séverac, Canteloube, and Albéniz also studied there. Following d'Indy's death in 1931, the Schola Cantorum fragmented (some of the former staff left to set up the Ecole César Franck at 16 boulevard Edgar-Quinet), and it gradually became a less formidable rival to the Conservatoire for the teaching of composition. It had other distinguished directors in Daniel-Lesur and Jacques Chailley (*see also* Schola Cantorum under "Theatres and Concert Halls").

5 · Some Parisian Music Publishers and Instrument Makers

Ballard

Originally founded as Le Roy and Ballard in 1551, the firm acquired the royal privilege for printing music in 1553, giving it a near monopoly on the publishing of music in France during the second half of the sixteenth century, including works by Lassus, Janequin, and Le Jeune. In 1607 Pierre Ballard took over from his father, Robert, and was in turn made music printer to the king. The business passed down through the family to Robert Ballard (in 1639), who was responsible for publishing several songs by Lully, and then to Christophe (in 1673), who published handsome scores of major works by Lully, Campra, Charpentier, the Couperins, and Marais. The development of music printing from engraved plates was a serious blow to the firm, which continued to use the old system of movable type. The last effective member of this long dynasty was Jean-Baptiste-Christophe Ballard, who issued the first edition of Rameau's *Traité de l'harmonie reduite à ses principes naturels* in 1722. His successor (from 1750) was Christophe-Jean-François Ballard, who received the royal privilege on the death of his father. The reluctance to update the equipment of the firm (it was still using some tools from the sixteenth century) led to its gradual but inevitable demise, although the family continued to publish music until 1825. Partly through the zealous protection of its royal privilege, the firm of Ballard issued a vast range and quantity of the most significant French music for a period of more than two hundred years.

Brandus

Founded in 1846, when Louis and Gemmy Brandus bought Schlesinger's premises and stock, the firm of Brandus rapidly established a reputation as one of the leading publishers of opera, for instance, works by Berlioz

5.1 The premises of the music publisher Brandus on the corner of the rue de Richelieu and the boulevard des Italiens.

(*Béatrice et Bénédict*) and Meyerbeer (*Le prophète*, *L'étoile du Nord,* and *L'Africaine*). In addition to publishing the vocal scores (and sometimes full scores) to many such works, Brandus also issued some unusual souvenir items including a series of "vues au stéréoscope" for operas which provide very valuable photographic evidence of contemporary productions. The firm was based in the rue de Richelieu: no. 97 in 1846, no. 87 in 1848, in 1851 at no. 103, on the corner of the boulevard des Italiens (figure 5.1). Louis Brandus, one of the cofounders, took his own life (by drinking cyanide) on 30 September 1887, and the company was taken over by Philippe Maquet.

Cavaillé-Coll

Aristide Cavaillé-Coll (1811–99) arrived in Paris in 1833, lodging at 11 quai Voltaire, 7e (H12, Métro: Rue du Bac), near the Institut, and the same year he won the competition to design a new organ for the cathedral of Saint-Denis, an instrument which was subsequently built by his father. In 1838 Aristide built his first instrument at Notre-Dame-de-Lorette in Paris, of particular interest now as one of the few Parisian Cavaillé-Coll organs still in its original state. Cavaillé-Coll's factory at the time was at 42 rue Notre-Dame-de-Lorette, 9e (E13, Métro: Saint-Georges). Cavaillé-Coll built almost five hundred organs, and several of his finest instruments are to be found in Paris, though some have been extensively rebuilt. Fortunately, the essential sound of these superlative instruments has usually remained

5.2 Cavaillé-Coll's factory in avenue du Maine (*L'Illustration,* 12 March 1870).

intact, such as those at Saint-Sulpice (see figure 2.8), Saint-Roch, Sainte-Clotilde (see figure 2.10), the Madeleine, and the Trinité. The restoration of the organ at Notre-Dame-de-Paris undertaken during Pierre Cochereau's years as *titulaire* was more controversial. Cavaillé-Coll's influence on French organ composers from Franck to Messiaen was immense, and both Franck and Widor were employed to demonstrate his instruments. Cavaillé-Coll married Adèle Blanc in 1854 (the witnesses at the wedding were Pierre Erard and César Franck). The same year, he moved to new premises at 94–96 rue de Vaugirard, 6e (L12, Métro: Saint-Placide).

In 1866, Cavaillé-Coll moved to a new factory (figure 5.2) at 13–15 avenue du Maine, 15e (L11, Métro: Faulgière). Although he was an organ builder of genius, Cavaillé-Coll was a poor businessman. Faced with financial ruin near the end of his life, he was obliged to sell the business and his house to Charles Mutin and move to 21 rue du Vieux-Colombier, 6e (K12, Métro: Saint-Sulpice), a few steps from Saint-Sulpice, where one of Cavaillé-Coll's greatest instruments was installed. It was here that his funeral was held, with his old friend Widor playing the organ. Cavaillé-Coll was buried in Montparnasse Cemetery.

Choudens

Founded by Antoine de Choudens in 1844 (when he was only nineteen years of age), this firm had the foresight (and later the good fortune) to publish three of the best-known works in the French operatic repertoire: Bizet's *Carmen*, Offenbach's *Les contes d'Hoffmann,* and Gounod's *Faust.* Choudens also published other major works by these composers, and Berlioz's *Les Troyens.* Scores of all these operas were originally issued from 265 rue Saint-Honoré, the firm's address from 1857 to 1885. Antoine de Choudens was particularly lucky with *Faust,* one of his earliest ventures into opera. He purchased the French and Belgian rights outright for 10,000 francs (Gounod received two-thirds of the total: 6,666 francs, 66 centimes), and the work went on to earn him a fortune. However, Choudens does not seem to have cared for the music: his son Antony Choudens told Bizet that his father used to threaten to take his children to see *Faust* again if they did not behave. The threat may have worked, but Antony and his brother Paul took over the running of the business when their father died in 1888. Choudens seldom let a promising composer go,

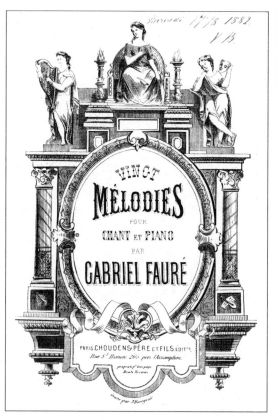

5.3 The earliest collection of Fauré's *Vingt mélodies,* published in 1879 by Choudens.

though Fauré was an exception: in 1879, the firm published the earliest collection of Fauré's *Vingt mélodies* (figure 5.3), but shortly afterwards Choudens sold the rights to these songs (and the original plates) to the recently founded firm of Hamelle.

Durand

According to Durand's own printing records, the firm's plate number 1 was assigned to G. Silvio's *Mignon: Polka très facile,* printed on 1 December 1868, but the business was not fully established until the following year. Durand, Schoenenwerk, et Cie. (as it was first known) opened at 4 place de la Madeleine in January 1870, as the successor to Gustave Flaxland, and remained there for 110 years. Auguste Durand (1830–1909) was organist of Saint-Vincent-de-Paul when the company was founded, and he was able to acquire almost all the works of his friend Saint-Saëns (a fellow-pupil in Benoist's class at the Conservatoire), as well as the organ works of another classmate, César Franck. Auguste Durand (succeeded by his son Jacques) went on to publish most of the greatest works of Debussy (including *La mer*, the *Préludes*, *L'isle joyeuse*, and *Jeux;* Durand acquired *Pelléas et Mélisande* from Fromont) and works by Ravel (including *Daphnis et Chloé*, *La valse*, *L'enfant et les sortilèges*, *Bolero*, and the two piano concertos), as well as Fauré's late song cycles and chamber music. Other composers strongly represented in Durand's catalogue include Dukas (*L'apprenti sorcier*, *La Péri*, and *Ariane et Barbe-Bleue*), and compositions by Roussel, Caplet, d'Indy, and Florent Schmitt. During World War I, Durand issued new, distinctively French, editions of the standard classics, with an extraordinary group of editors, including Saint-Saëns, Debussy, Ravel, Dukas, and Fauré. In 1930 the firm issued the young Messiaen's *Préludes* for piano, and it subsequently published a number of his most important earlier works, culminating in the *Turangalîla-Symphonie*. In May 1980 Durand moved to 21 rue Vernet and later to 215 rue du Faubourg-Saint-Honoré.

Erard

Sébastien Erard founded his celebrated piano and harp firm in 1780, which began by making square pianos, thanks to which the firm enjoyed its first financial success. Erard's patent for the double escapement (1821), improving the instrument's ability to repeat notes, was a significant innovation in piano design. During the later years of the nineteenth century, Erard's reluctance to embrace new technological advances resulted in a considerable loss of international business, though the firm's grand pianos remained the standard instruments at the Conservatoire and in many French concert halls. Erard was also extremely successful as a harp maker. Ravel's *Introduction et allegro* (1906) is dedicated to Albert Blondel, then a director of the Erard firm, which had commissioned the work to demonstrate its instruments. The firm was based in the rue du Mail, 2e, with addresses at no. 37, then nos. 13 and 21 (the shop and the workshop, from 1806). It used no. 13 as its principal address from 1818.

On these premises Erard opened the Salle Erard (*see* Salle Erard under "Theatres and Concert Halls"). Later, Erard also built a large factory at 110 rue de Flandre (now avenue de Flandre), 19e. Erard was amalgamated with Gaveau in 1960.

Heugel

Jacques-Léopold Heugel founded the firm which bears his name on 1 January 1839. A former singing teacher from Nantes, he joined forces with the publisher Antoine Meissonnier. The firm took over publication of the periodical *Le Ménestrel*. Meissonnier retired in 1855 (he died in penury in a mental hospital two years later), and Heugel continued on his own, publishing a vast number of sheet songs, some with covers by such noted artists as Gustave Doré and Honoré Daumier. The firm's theatre catalogue included twenty works by Offenbach, among them *Orphée aux enfers* and *La belle Hélène*, Thomas (*Mignon* and *Hamlet*), and Delibes (*Coppélia*, *Sylvia*, and *Lakmé*). Other composers strongly represented in the firm's nineteenth-century publications were Franck, Lalo, and Massenet. In the twentieth century, Heugel issued a number of later works by Fauré (including *Pénélope*), Milhaud, and Poulenc (including the *Poèmes de Ronsard*, with an illustrated cover by Picasso) and the earliest published works of Boulez. Among the firm's most visually attractive publications are the six *Chants du silence* by Paul Arma, each with an illustrated cover specially drawn by Braque, Chagall, Dufy, Léger, Matisse, or Picasso.

La Sirène

Founded in 1918, Editions de la Sirène published Cocteau's *Le coq et l'arlequin* the same year, with illustrations by Picasso. In 1919 the firm issued the first edition of Stravinsky's *Rag-Time*, with its famous front cover, again by Picasso. The following year Milhaud's *Le boeuf sur le toit* was published with a frontispiece by Dufy (figure 5.4). La Sirène also published important editions of works by Satie (*Socrate*) and Poulenc (*Le bestiare*); it also issued an edition of Apollinaire's original poems illustrated by Dufy. In about 1927 the firm became known as La Sirène Musicale. It was purchased by Max Eschig in 1936.

Leduc

The principal claim to fame of the firm, which was founded in 1841 by Alphonse Leduc, is as the publisher of many important works by Olivier Messiaen: organ works such as *La Nativité du Seigneur* and *Les corps glorieux* and almost all his music since 1950. The production standards for many of these editions are extremely high. Some have fine illustrated covers (*Catalogue d'oiseaux*) and one a cover designed by the composer himself (*Couleurs de la Cité céleste*). The firm's most grandiose undertaking has been the publication of the full score of Messiaen's *Saint François d'Assise* in eight folio volumes, a magnificent achievement and a model of the music engraver's art in the late twentieth century. In recent years the firm has taken over the catalogues of Hamelle and Heugel.

Mustel

Victor Mustel (1815–90) arrived in Paris in May 1844 and set up an independent business in 1853 as a maker of harmoniums, for which he soon acquired an international reputation. Mustel's instruments have long been considered to be among the finest ever made. In 1886 his son Auguste Mustel (1842–1919) invented the celesta. Tchaikovsky was much impressed when he heard the instrument on a visit to Paris, and he is the earliest composer known to have used it in the orchestra (first in the tone poem *Voyevoda*, then in *The Nutcracker*). In 1895 Mustel's address was 168 rue Saint-Maur, 112 (G18, Métro: Goncourt), then the firm moved to 46 rue de Douai, 9e (D12, Métro: Blanche).

Pleyel

In 1795 Ignace Pleyel, a pupil of Haydn, settled in Paris and established a publishing firm which issued French editions of important works by Beethoven, Clementi, Haydn, and others. Pleyel's Bibliothèque musicale, begun in 1802, was the earliest known series of miniature scores, and included symphonies and string quartets by Haydn and, later, works by Hummel and Beethoven. In 1834 the firm abandoned activity as a publisher. In 1807, Pleyel began to make pianos, including some of the earliest uprights. Ignace's son Camille became a partner in the firm in 1815 and developed its new role as a manufacturer of pianos. He opened the first Salle Pleyel in 1830 at 9 rue Cadet (*see* Salle Pleyel under "Theatres and Concert Halls"). Chopin gave his first Paris recital here on 26 February 1832 and became an enthusiastic supporter of Pleyel's instruments. Following the death of Camille Pleyel in 1855, his son-in-law Albert Wolff took over the firm. By the 1870s, Pleyel was producing 2,500 pianos each year. Following Wolff's death, his son-in-law Robert Lyon took control of the business and developed the chromatic harp for which Debussy wrote his *Danse sacrée et danse profane*, though the instrument never replaced the pedal harp as Lyon hoped it would (a fine example can be seen in the Musée de la Musique). In the twentieth century, Robert Lyon encouraged Stravinsky to produce piano rolls of his works, and the composer kept a small apartment on Pleyel's premises on the rue Rochechouart. Another Pleyel innovation was its production of iron-framed harpsichords following a design by Wanda Landowska; she played such harpsichords throughout her career. The firm amalgamated with Gaveau in 1961 (further takeovers followed), but pianos bearing Pleyel's name are still in production today.

Sax

Adolphe Sax (1814–94) was one of the most innovative and creative instrument makers of the nineteenth century, the son of the Brussels maker, Charles Sax. The latter encouraged his son to study music, and Adolphe became an extremely proficient clarinettist. He soon began to experiment with the design of the instrument and by 1838 had developed, with his father's assistance, a new bass clarinet, a vast improvement on any earlier model. Sax arrived in Paris in about 1841. His first instrument

5.5 Adolphe Sax's workshop in the rue Neuve-Saint-Georges, later rue Saint-Georges (*L'Illustration*, 5 February 1848).

factory (figure 5.5) was at 50 rue Saint-Georges (originally 10 rue Neuve-Saint-Georges), 9e (E13, Métro: Notre-Dame-de-Lorette). Among Sax's earliest supporters was Hector Berlioz, and another was Donizetti, who wrote a part for Sax's bass clarinet in *Dom Sébastien*, though its use had to be abandoned, as none of the Opéra's players was prepared to attempt performing on the new-fangled instrument; when Sax offered to play it himself, the entire orchestra threatened to walk out. Another example of Sax's innovative designs was the invention of saxhorns, a completely new family of brass instruments. Berlioz and d'Indy used several different saxhorns in their works, but it is the bass and contrabass instruments which appear most frequently in French orchestral scores, up through Messiaen's time.

Sax's most celebrated instrument, the saxophone, was developed over a long period. An early prototype was to be shown at the 1841 Brussels Exposition, but apparently the instrument was damaged. Berlioz described the instrument in some detail in the *Journal des Débats* on 12 June 1842, but the saxophone appears not to have made its public debut until 3 February 1844 at the Salle Herz, in a concert directed by Berlioz that featured a *Chant sacré* arranged for six instruments designed by Sax. When the saxophone was shown at the Paris Exposition in 1844, Auber was among its admirers. Sax took out a patent for the saxophone in March 1846. Rossini was another composer who admired Sax's instruments, and a band made up entirely of them played at the Italian master's funeral. In about 1858 Sax began to issue music for his various instruments (in all, the firm issued almost two hundred publications), and the same year he was appointed director of the stage band at the Opéra, a post he held until his death. Offenbach's affectionate lampoon of Sax, in the "Couplets des Rois" from Act 1 of *La belle Hélène* (1864), draws attention to the sheer volume of the instruments: "Parmi le fracas immense des cuivres de Sax" (Amid the immense din of Sax's brass).

Despite endless intrigues by rival instrument makers, Sax attracted favourable attention from military musicians and an extraordinary contest of two rival forty-five-piece bands under the direction of Carafa (using traditional instruments) and Fessy (using Sax's instruments) was arranged on the Champ de Mars on 22 April 1845. It took place in front of a crowd estimated at twenty thousand people. Berlioz was only one of many who believed Sax to have triumphed. After several months' deliberation, a government commission decreed that military bands should consist largely of Sax's instruments. Inevitably, the necessary financing was not made available to reequip every band, but this official endorsement enabled Sax to increase his firm's production vastly.

The most magnificent display of Sax's instruments was offered at the Exposition universelle of 1867. Here, every one of his inventions, including entire families of saxhorns and saxophones, was on show, with a gold-plated alto saxophone as the centrepiece. The firm came to a sorry end: after years of financial difficulties and interminable litigation over patents, Sax was declared bankrupt in 1873. The following year the factory ceased production, and in December 1877 Sax's collection of instruments was put up for sale. Many fine examples were acquired by the museum of the Conservatoire and can be seen at the Musée de la Musique.

Schlesinger

Maurice Schlesinger settled in Paris in 1816 and started his publishing business five years later. His catalogue included the first French editions of many of Chopin's piano works, several important editions of Beethoven, and Berlioz's *Symphonie fantastique*, first in Liszt's piano transcription, then in full score. Opera was a central part of Schlesinger's output: he issued Meyerbeer's *Robert le diable* and *Les Huguenots*, Halévy's *La Juive* and Donizetti's *La favorite*. In 1840–42 he employed Wagner to make piano arrangements of operas. Schlesinger was also the publisher of the celebrated *Gazette Musicale* (later *Revue et Gazette Musicale*), one of the most significant musical periodicals in Paris during the nineteenth century. In 1846 he sold his business to Louis and Gemmy Brandus. From 1824 onwards Schlesinger's premises were at 97 rue de Richelieu, 2e (F13, Métro: Richelieu-Drouot).

Troupenas

Eugène-Thomas Troupenas purchased the firm of Nicolo in 1825 and went on to become Rossini's most important French publisher, issuing the first editions of *Le siège de Corinth*, *Le Comte Ory*, and *Guillaume Tell*, for which he employed Berlioz to do the proofreading. Troupenas also published two of the most important works of Rossini's later years, *Soirées musicales* and the *Stabat Mater*. With the active encouragement of Rossini, he also issued Auber's *La muette de Portici*. Such was its success that he went on to publish twenty of Auber's operas. Among his important instrumental publications was a group of piano works by Chopin.

Troupenas was housed at 3 rue de Ménars, 23 rue Saint-Marc, and, from 1835, 40 rue Vivienne. After Troupenas's death, the business was acquired by Brandus.

Vuillaume

Jean-Baptiste Vuillaume (1798–1875) was the most renowned French violin maker and dealer of the nineteenth century. He arrived in Paris in 1818. After ten years working for other makers (during which time he began to sign and number his own instruments), Vuillaume went into business for himself at 46 rue Croix-des-Petits-Champs, 1e (G14, Métro: Palais Royal). This was the site of his workshop for thirty years (in 1858 he moved to a new workshop on the rue Demours, now rue Pierre-Demours, 17e). He is best known for his careful study of Cremonese models and the excellent copies he produced of these. But Vuillaume was also an enthusiastic innovator. His two most remarkable experiments were the Contralto and the Octobass. The first of these was a strange-looking instrument which sought to produce a much more powerful viola sound through the use of a very wide body; the formidable Octobass was a monster of an instrument, standing almost four metres tall, with three immense strings (tuned to C, G, and C), and requiring a pedal mechanism to work the mechanical fingers. Amazingly, this instrument is reputed to have produced a splendid sound. It was much admired by Berlioz, who commented on its "remarkable power and beauty, full and strong without any roughness." According to Vuillaume, only three of these massive instruments were ever made. The Contralto and the Octobass were both exhibited at the Exposition universelle in 1855 and examples of them can be seen in the Musée de la Musique.

6 · Museums and Libraries

Following is a selection of the most important collections of music or musically related materials in Parisian museums and libraries. Of the great Parisian art galleries, only the Musée d'Orsay has been included, as it contains work of the period most thoroughly covered in the present gazetteer, though there are, of course, important paintings and works of art on musical subjects or of musical interest in the Louvre, the Orangerie (for example, a version of Renoir's *Jeunes filles au piano*), and the Centre Georges Pompidou. The Musée d'Art Moderne de la Ville de Paris at the Palais de Tokyo includes two marvellous paintings relating to music and dance which are also remarkable for their vast dimensions: the Paris version of Matisse's *La danse* and Dufy's astonishing *La fée Electricité*, which includes several panels depicting an orchestra. Opening hours, telephone numbers, and other details given below were correct in 1999 but may be subject to change.

Bibliothèque Nationale de France

Département de la Musique
2 rue de Louvois, 2e (G13, Métro: Quatre-Septembre)
Monday to Friday: 10:00–18:00; Saturday: 10:00–17:30. Closed Sunday.
Telephone: 01 47 03 88 62
Charge for reader's card

One of the world's greatest music libraries, with unparalleled holdings of French material (thanks to the *dépôt légal* requiring a copy of every French publication to be lodged at the library). The collection of manuscripts ranges from the twenty-eight volumes of autograph music by Marc-Antoine Charpentier (purchased in 1728) to an astonishingly rich collection of twentieth-century material. Among the outstanding autograph manuscripts are Mozart's *Don Giovanni*, Beethoven's *Appassionata* sonata, Berlioz's *Symphonie fantastique*, Bizet's *Carmen*, Gounod's *Faust*, Ravel's *Bolero*, and Stravinsky's *Les noces*. In addition to printed and manuscript music, the department also has extensive holdings of archives of concert societies (such as the Société Nationale), prints and photographs of musicians, and programmes.

The Département de la Musique has not been affected by the partial relocation of the Bibliothèque Nationale to the site of the Bibliothèque de France in Tolbiac, and it remains in the premises at rue de Louvois, over the road from the main entrance of the Bibliothèque Nationale at 58 rue de Richelieu, where application for a reader's card can be made. New readers should note that a letter of introduction or accreditation is needed and that a modest charge is made for the card. Once a card has been obtained, use of the music library is relatively straightforward, though there are a number of different (and immensely useful) card indexes and a computer catalogue to search. Most items are ordered on slips and are brought promptly to the reader's designated seat. Photocopying is done quickly and efficiently but must be paid for with tickets which need to be purchased in advance from the cashier's desk at 58 rue de Richelieu.

Bibliothèque-Musée de l'Opéra

Opéra Garnier, place de l'Opéra, 9e (F12, Métro: Opéra)
Monday to Saturday: 10:00–17:00. Closed Sunday.
Telephone 01 47 42 07 02

Affiliated with the Bibliothèque Nationale since 1935, the library contains an outstanding collection of material relating to opera and ballet: fifteen thousand scores, thirty thousand librettos, set designs, paintings, programmes, and letters, as well as fascinating items such as Taglioni's ballet shoes. Among the paintings held by the library are a version of Renoir's portrait of Wagner and a large full-length portrait of Galli-Marié as Carmen, a role she created. There are regular special exhibitions relating to works in repertoire at the Palais Garnier and at Opéra-Bastille.

The elegant reading room of the library provides a fine working environment and has a helpful and extremely knowledgeable staff. Apart from the reading room, the physical appearance of the museum is relatively unchanged since the nineteenth century (figure 6.1). Entrance to the library may be difficult at times (it is through the main foyer of the Opéra), and prospective readers are urged to telephone first to confirm opening hours.

Musée Carnavalet

23 rue de Sévigné, 3e (J17, Métro: Saint-Paul)
Tuesday to Sunday: 10:00–17:40. Closed Monday.
Admission charge

The Musée Carnavalet, which documents the history of the city of Paris, has a number of exhibits relating to music and important musical locations. These include a version of Carmontelle's Mozart family portrait, Henri Lehmann's famous portrait of Liszt, Jean-Pierre Dantan's plaster caricature of Rossini, Louis Béroud's *L'escalier de l'Opéra,* Jean Béraud's *La sortie du Conservatoire rue de Madrid, Le boulevard des Capucines devant le théâtre du Vaudeville,* and *Le boulevard des Italiens, la nuit* (showing the facade of the Théâtre des Variétés), Jacques-Emile Blanche's *Jean Cocteau,* Albert Lebourg's *Le Trocadéro vu du quai de Grenelle,* and a large collection of prints (not on general display except as part of special exhibitions), many of which are valuable documents of musical life in Paris. Other exhibits show the topography of Paris in considerable detail, such as the fine series of Parisian views by Nicolas Raguenet painted in the second half of the eighteenth century, depicting the city at the time of Mozart's visits.

Musée de la Musique

Cité de la Musique, 221 avenue Jean-Jaurès, 19e (C21, Métro: Porte de Pantin)
Tuesday to Saturday: 12:00–18:00; open Thursday until 21:30; Sunday:
10:00–18:00. Closed Monday.
Telephone: 01 44 84 46 00
Admission charge

Opened in January 1997, the Musée de la Musique contains the magnificent instrument collection formerly in the Paris Conservatoire. A visit to
this outstanding museum is an immensely enjoyable experience for anyone with an interest in music. Among the many outstanding exhibits are
instruments by Sax, Vuillaume, Taskin, Erard, Pleyel, Ruckers, and
Stradivari. But what makes a visit so rewarding is the considerable imagination with which the collection is presented. On arrival, the visitor is
given a set of headphones. At each significant exhibit, a recorded performance on the instrument(s) in question accompanies the commentary
(which is available in either French or English).

The broadly chronological arrangement of the galleries reflects
important times in musical history—the birth of Italian opera, music at
Versailles, the growth of public concerts, the development of the romantic orchestra, French grand opera, outdoor and military music, and musical innovations at the Expositions universelles. The final gallery, "Les
ruptures instrumentales," includes examples of many of the most exciting musical developments in the twentieth century. A further enhance-
ment is the illustration, with fine cut-away models of each building, of
particular locations and specific events, such as Monteverdi's *Orfeo* in
Mantua, Mozart's *Paris* Symphony in the Palais des Tuileries, Berlioz's
Symphonie fantastique in the Salle de l'Ancien Conservatoire, Wagner's
Parsifal in the Festspielhaus at Bayreuth, Saint-Saëns's Third Symphony
in the Trocadéro, and Stravinsky's *Le sacre du printemps* in the Théâtre
des Champs-Elysées.

Many of Sax's greatest inventions (and a few of the odder ones) can be
viewed; Vuillaume's mighty Octobass and the strangely proportioned
Contralto are also on display. Among more recent instruments on view is
Varèse's own collection of the instruments required to perform his *Ionisation*, complete with New York Fire Department sirens. Other modern
highlights are Django Reinhardt's guitar and an early version of the

Ondes Martenot (accompanied by a recording of Messiaen's *Fête des belles eaux*, for six Ondes Martenot). A guitar which belonged to Berlioz is just one of the instruments on view that have had distinguished owners.

The unusual collection of outdoor and military instruments includes fine examples of so-called Russian bassoons, serpents, and some "omnitonic" horns, the tubes of which resemble spaghetti. In addition to bringing this wonderful collection to life in such an imaginative way, the Musée de la Musique has some fine musical paintings.

The museum's central focus, on music in France, is one of its great strengths, enabling the visitor to experience the musical history of the country, and especially its capital, in a wholly absorbing way. There is an excellent shop which sells books, CDs, and other items of musical interest. The concert halls in the Cité de la Musique building, in which the museum is housed, have a very active programme of concerts, workshops, and lectures, and the Café de la Musique next door is a pleasant and reasonably priced place for light meals and drinks.

Musée d'Orsay

1 rue de Bellechasse, 7e (H12, Métro: Solférino, RER: Musée d'Orsay)
Tuesday to Saturday: 10:00–18:00 (open at 9:00 from mid-June to mid-September); open Thursday until 21:45; Sunday: 9:00 to 18:00. Closed Monday.
Telephone (recorded information): 01 45 49 11 11
Admission charge

Among the world's greatest collections of nineteenth- and early twentieth-century art, this glorious museum contains several major exhibits related to music and dance, of which the following examples are among the highlights:

Gustave Courbet (1819–1877)
Courbet's portrait of Hector Berlioz (1850) was rejected by the composer after its completion; it was exhibited at the salon in 1850 and at the Exposition universelle in 1889 before being acquired for the nation in 1921.

Edgar Degas (1834–1917)
The Musée d'Orsay has a comprehensive collection of Degas's sculptures of dancers, including the only one to be exhibited during the artist's lifetime, *Petite Danseuse de quatorze ans* (and a lovely bronze study for it). In

addition, the museum has some outstanding pastels of ballet dancers, and several of his most important paintings with music or ballet as their subject.

L'orchestre de l'Opéra (circa 1870) shows Degas's friend the bassoonist Désiré Dihau (1833–1909) in the front row, with another friend, the cellist Louis-Marie Pilet (1815–77) to the left, and the double bass player Gouffé to the right. In the top left-hand corner, Degas depicts the head of Emmanuel Chabrier watching from a box. The arrangement of the players is fanciful. The ballet on stage is not identifiable (nor are the dancers, whose heads cannot be seen), but this is one of Degas's earliest paintings of dancers. The opera house is the Salle Le Peletier (destroyed in 1874), and part of the proscenium arch and a box (with Chabrier sitting in it) are clearly visible.

In addition to maintaining a warm friendship with Degas, Dihau knew Toulouse-Lautrec (according to some sources, Degas introduced them; according to others, Dihau and Lautrec were cousins). Toulouse-Lautrec provided some magnificent lithographs to illustrate Dihau's songs, including six for *Les vielles histoires* (Ondet, Paris, 1893), a series of fourteen for his *Mélodies* (Joubert, Paris, 1895), and the charming *La valse des lapins* (Bosc, Paris, 1895).

Louis-Marie Pilet, painted at about the same time (circa 1868–69), is a portrait of the cellist, with his instrument and its case prominent in the foreground. Theodor Reff has written in detail about the picture hanging behind Pilet in this portrait. It shows a large gathering, comprising Chopin at the piano, Heine, Liszt, Delacroix, Berlioz, Balzac, Sand, Hiller, and others. As Reff has noted, many of these figures appear to be looking at Pilet: "The homage that they thus appear to pay him is all the more flattering in that they can be identified as some of the most illustrious musicians and *amateurs* of music of the immediate past" (Reff 1987, 121).

Le Foyer de la danse à l'Opéra de la rue Le Peletier (1872). The ballet master shown in this painting is thought to be Louis Mérante (1828–87), who was appointed to the Opéra in 1853 and thereafter took many leading roles until the mid-1860s. He subsequently created the choreography for Delibes's *Sylvia* (1876), Widor's *La Korrigane* (1880), and Messager's *Les deux pigeons* (1886).

La classe de danse (circa 1873–76) depicts a lesson given by Jules Perrot (1810–92), the original choreographer of Grisi's solos in *Giselle* and one of the most distinguished dancers and, later, choreographers of his time. The scene is notable for the realism of the dancers' poses: stretching, exercising, adjusting ribbons, and chatting. The watering can in the left foreground was used to wet the floor in order to keep the dust down.

Répétition d'un ballet sur la scène (1874) was shown at the first Impressionist exhibition in 1874. It is one of three similar paintings from the same period (another hangs in the Metropolitan Museum of Art in New York). The ballet being rehearsed by dancers on the stage of the Salle Le Peletier appears to be more imaginary than real; it has not been identified.

Henri Fantin-Latour (1836–1904)

Perhaps the most striking portrait of Emmanuel Chabrier, *Autour du piano* (1885), hangs in the museum's splendid Salle des fêtes. Fantin-Latour was an enthusiastic Wagnerite, and this large group portrait depicts friends who shared an admiration for Wagner. The painting was executed in Fantin-Latour's studio and shows the salon of the solicitor and keen amateur musician Antoine Lascoux. The subjects are Emmanuel Chabrier (at the piano) and, from left to right, Adolphe Jullien (critic and biographer of Berlioz and Wagner), Arthur Boisseau (violinist at the Opéra), Camille Benoît (Franck pupil, musician, translator of Wagner and curator at the Louvre), Edmond Maître (artist, musician, and lawyer), Antoine Lascoux (solicitor and ardent Wagnerite), Vincent d'Indy, and Amédée Pigeon (novelist and art critic, an enthusiast of German art and music who wrote for *Le Figaro*). Jullien bought the painting from the artist in 1885 and donated it to the nation in 1915. Mystery surrounds the identity of the indecipherable score on the music desk of the piano. At the 1885 Salon, where *Autour du piano* was first exhibited, it was said by some critics to be Wagner (a fair assumption). In 1907, however, Jullien identified it as a piece by Brahms, and in 1938 Léon Vallas claimed that it was Bizet's *Carmen*.

Edouard Manet (1832–1883)

The Musée d'Orsay owns three important Manets with musical subjects: *Le fifre* (1866) shows a young boy playing the fife. A young musician in the Garde Impériale posed for it, apparently after being brought to Manet's studio by Commander Lejosne. Zola, who was struck by the picture's deliberate simplification, greatly admired the painting, but it was rejected by the Salon jury in 1866. *Madame Manet au piano* (1868) shows the artist's wife Suzanne (née Leenhoff) seated at a grand piano. She was an excellent player, and the Manets' friend Chabrier dedicated his *Impromptu* (1873) to her. *La dame aux éventails* (1873) is a portrait of Nina de Callias, also known as Nina de Villard (1845–84), a good pianist who held one of the most remarkable salons in Paris, first at 17 rue Chaptal and later, after the Commune, at 82 rue des Moines. She died young, having gone insane. Her regular guests included Chabrier, Cézanne, Mallarmé, and Zola.

Pierre-Auguste Renoir (1841–1919)

One of the most popular paintings in the Musée d'Orsay collection is *Jeunes filles au piano* (1892). In late 1891 or early 1892, Renoir was commissioned by the Ministry of Fine Arts to paint a large picture for the Musée du Luxembourg. He painted five large oil versions of the same subject, two girls at the piano. The version selected by the state is the one now hanging in the Musée d'Orsay. Another version (evidently an oil sketch) can be seen in the Walter-Guillaume collection in the Musée de l'Orangerie, and another is in the Metropolitan Museum of Art in New York. A further version shows the standing girl in a red dress with large white polka dots (similar to the Orangerie version). This was owned by the artist Caillebotte and is now in a private collection. The two models used by Renoir for this remarkable series (of which the colour scheme of the Musée d'Orsay version is the warmest) have not been identified.

A few years later, in 1897, Renoir painted another pair of girls at the piano, this time naming the models. *Yvonne et Christine Lerolle au piano* is in the Walter-Guillaume collection, Musée de l'Orangerie. Julie Manet described the painting as "ravishing" when she saw it in October 1897, and the subjects of this fine portrait have important associations with Debussy (see frontispiece and "Envoi"). The first version of Renoir's *Richard Wagner* (1882) is also in the museum's collection, as is his portrait of Mme Georges Hartmann (1874), depicting her standing in front of a grand piano. She was the wife of the music publisher and impresario Georges Hartmann, to whom Debussy later dedicated his *Trois nocturnes* and to whose memory he inscribed *Pelléas et Mélisande*.

Georges Seurat (1859–1891)

Seurat had a passionate interest in music, especially Wagner, and several of his paintings include musicians. *Le cirque* (1890–91), the greatest of Seurat's works in the Musée d'Orsay, shows a circus band in the upper right-hand corner.

Opera Houses and Concert Halls

The Musée d'Orsay has a very large cut-away model of the Opéra Garnier, made in 1982–86, several original set designs, and a fine model of the interior of the building made for the 1900 Exposition universelle. *Glorification de la musique* by Benjamin-Constant (1845–1902) is a design for the ceiling of the newly built (third) Salle Favart executed in 1898. *Loge à l'Opéra-Comique* (1887) by Charles Cottet (1863–1925) shows the interior of the second Salle Favart, painted in the year it was destroyed by fire. The Musée d'Orsay has a large circular design by Maurice Denis (1870–1943) for his interior decorations in the Théâtre des Champs-Elysées, and four sketches for his ceiling panels in the theatre, all painted in 1911–12. Félix Vallotton (1865–1925) painted *La troisième galerie au Théâtre du Châtelet* in 1895. This theatre was the venue for numerous important musical events including concerts by Grieg and Mahler, and the premières of *Daphnis et Chloé* and *Petrouchka* (*see* Théâtre du Châtelet under "Theatres and Concert Halls"). Another concert scene is shown in *Concert Colonne* by André Devambez (1867–1944).

Other Portraits

The Musée d'Orsay has a number of musical portraits in addition to those already mentioned. They include the following, arranged alphabetically by artist:

Paul Baudoüin (1844–1931): portrait of Charles Garnier, architect of the Opéra.

Frédéric Bazille (1841–70): the wonderfully evocative painting of his own studio, *L'atelier de Bazille* (9 rue de La Condamine), painted in 1870 just before Bazille was killed in the Franco-Prussian War at the Battle of Beaune-la-Rolande. It shows, along with Monet, Manet, and Bazille himself, the gifted amateur musician and artist Edmond Maître seated at an upright piano (for another portrayal of Maître, see Fantin-Latour).

Jacques-Emile Blanche (1861–1942): his celebrated full-length portrait of Stravinsky, painted in 1915, belongs to the Musée d'Orsay but has recently been on loan to the Musée de la Musique.

Pierre Bonnard (1867–1947): a portrait of Ravel's friend Cipa Godebski (1895) and *Le compositeur Claude Terrasse et ses fils* (circa 1902). Terrasse (1867–1923) was Bonnard's brother-in-law.

Léon Bonnat (1933–1922): portrait of the great pianist Antoine-François Marmontel (1816–98), painted in 1889.

Jules-Elie Delaunay (1828–91): portrait of *Madame Georges Bizet* (Geneviève Halévy), painted in 1878.

Jean-Louis Forain (1852–1941): *Danseuse debout derrière un portant de coulisse*. An interesting contrast with the more familiar images by Degas discussed earlier.

Frans Masreel (1889–1972): a striking full-length portrait of Romain Rolland (1866–1944), painted in 1938.

Ernest Meissonier (1815–91): *Jeune femme chantant* (circa 1883).

Louis-Gustave Ricard (1823–75): portrait of Stephen Heller, formerly in the collection of Antoine-François Marmontel.

Musical subjects are frequently the focus of temporary exhibitions about musicians or important musical events and locations (Offenbach, Meyerbeer's *Le prophète*, the opening of the Opéra Garnier, the Foyer de la danse, and the Théâtre des Champs-Elysées), and the museum runs a concert series which concentrates on music of the period 1848–1914. Concerts are given either in the auditorium or in the Salle des fêtes.

Musée de Montmartre

12 rue Cortot, 18e (C14, Métro: Lamarck-Caulaincourt)
Tuesday to Saturday: 11:00–18:00. Closed Sunday and Monday.
Telephone: 01 46 06 61 11

This museum features various exhibits relating to musicians who lived in Montmartre and locations of musical interest, such as *Le Chat Noir*. The history and atmosphere of the district is well captured.

Musée Erik Satie (Le Placard d'Erik Satie)

6 rue Cortot, 18e (C14, Métro: Lamarck-Caulaincourt)
The latest information (as of November 1999) is that the museum has closed.

Satie lived in a tiny room at this address in the 1890s. The museum is not in the actual room which Satie rented; the exhibits, however, are curated with expert care by Ornella Volta. Along with some manuscripts (such as Satie's score of *Bon-jour Bi-qui*, written for Suzanne Valadon), the museum contains paintings, drawings, and lithographs as well as some fine examples of Satie's magnificent calligraphy.

Maison Debussy

38 rue au Pain, Saint-Germain-en-Laye (RER: Saint-Germain-en-Laye)
Tuesday to Saturday, 14:00–18:00. Closed Sunday and Monday.
Telephone: 01 34 51 05 12

Debussy's birthplace. The ground floor houses the tourist information office for Saint-Germain-en-Laye, but on the first floor is an exhibition of Debussy memorabilia.

Musée Maurice Ravel

Le Belvédère, rue Maurice-Ravel, Montfort-l'Amaury (SNCF: Montfort-l'Amaury–Méré)
Monday, Wednesday, Thursday: 14:30–17:30; Saturday and Sunday: 10:00–12:30, 14:30–17:30. Closed Tuesday and Friday.
Telephone: 01 34 86 00 89

Ravel purchased Le Belvédère (built by the architect Morel in 1907) on 16 April 1921 for twenty thousand francs. This was where he spent much of the last two decades of his life and composed several of his greatest works, including *Tzigane, L'enfant et les sortilèges, Chansons madécasses, Bolero*, and the two piano concertos. The house is now the Musée Maurice Ravel. The carefully preserved contents and decor reflect Ravel's interests in Japanese prints and in small toys and automata. Ravel's library has been preserved here, as has his furniture and Erard piano. Montfort-l'Amaury is situated forty-five kilometres west of Paris. Trains depart from the Gare Montparnasse (in the direction of Dreux).

7 · Graves and Monuments

In addition to some of the greatest French musicians, including Lully, Rameau, Berlioz, Franck, Bizet, Gounod, Fauré, Debussy, and Ravel, many of those who came to settle in Paris were also buried in the city's cemeteries, including Bellini, Chopin, Rossini, Taglioni, Chaliapin, and Nijinsky.

This list of Parisian cemeteries, arranged alphabetically by their names, gives the whereabouts of the graves of musicians (along with those of some noted dancers and others associated with the world of music). In the case of graves in large cemeteries such as Montmartre, Montparnasse, and Père-Lachaise, the division is given. Musicians buried in churches are listed separately, followed by those known to have been guillotined. An alphabetical index of names follows the listing by cemetery.

Arcueil Cemetery (Cimetière d'Arcueil-Cachan)
avenue Carnot, Arcueil (RER: Arcueil-Cachan)
Erik Satie

Auteuil Cemetery (Cimetière d'Auteuil)
57 rue Claude-Lorrain, 16e (M3, Métro: Exelmans)
Charles Gounod

Batignolles Cemetery (Cimetière des Batignolles)
8 rue Saint-Just, 17e (B10–A11, Métro: Porte de Clichy)
Leon Bakst
Alfred Bruneau
Feodor Chaliapin

Levallois-Perret Cemetery (Cimetière de Levallois-Perret)
rue Baudin, Levallois-Perret (A7, SNCF: Clichy Levallois, or Métro: Pont de Levallois Bécon)
Maurice Ravel
Ravel is buried in a family grave, with his father, mother, and younger brother Edouard.

Berlioz.

Lili and Nadia
Boulanger.

Delibes.

Jolivet.

Nijinsky.

Offenbach.

Viardot.

Montmartre Cemetery (Cimetière de Montmartre)

20 avenue Rachel, 18e (C12–D12, Métro: Blanche or Place de Clichy)

Adolphe Adam (5th division)

Hector Berlioz (20th division), with Harriet Smithson and Marie Récio

Lili and Nadia Boulanger (33rd division), family grave

Léo Delibes (9th division)

Louis Diémer (24th division)

André Jolivet (27th division)

Josef Kosma (20th division)

Charles Lamoureux (29th division)

Emma Livry (31st division)

Victor Massé (26th division)

Sigismund Neukomm (22nd division)

Vaslav Nijinsky (22nd division)

Adolphe Nourrit (22nd division)

Jacques Offenbach (9th division)

Alphonsine Plessis, "La Dame aux Camélias" (15th division)

Henri Sauguet (27th division)

Adolphe Sax (5th division)

Fernando Sor (24th division)

Marie Taglioni (22nd division)

Ambroise Thomas (28th division)

Pauline Viardot (28th division)

Louise Weber, "La Goulue" (31st division)

Montparnasse Cemetery (Cimetière de Montparnasse)

boulevard Edgar-Quinet, 14e (M12, Métro: Raspail)

Emmanuel Chabrier (9th division)

César Franck (26th division)

Clara Haskil (4th division)

Vincent d'Indy (13th division)

Jean de Reszke (26th division)

Camille Saint-Saëns (13th division)

Louis Vierne (13th division)

Chabrier.

Franck.

D'Indy.

Passy Cemetery (Cimetière de Passy)

2 rue du Commandant-Schloesing, 16e (H6, Métro: Trocadéro)

Claude Debussy

Three days after his death, Debussy's body was taken across Paris (despite the cannon fire) to Père-Lachaise Cemetery. Debussy's explicit wish, however, was to rest "among the trees and the birds" of Passy Cemetery, and his body was reburied here in 1919, in a simple black marble grave.

Gabriel Fauré

Fauré was buried in a family grave with his father-in-law (the sculptor Emmanuel Fremiet), Fauré's wife, and his son Philippe.

André Messager

Debussy.

Fauré.

Bellini.

Bizet.

Chausson.

Chopin.

Enesco.

Neveu.

Rossini.

Père-Lachaise Cemetery (Cimetière du Père-Lachaise)

boulevard de Ménilmontant, 20e (H20–H21, Métro: Père-Lachaise)

Marie d'Agoult (54th division)

Marietta Alboni (66th division)

Daniel-François-Esprit Auber (4th division)

Vincenzo Bellini (11th division)

Bellini was buried here in 1835, then reburied (1876) in Catania Cathedral.

Georges Bizet (68th division)

Adrien Boieldieu (11th division)

Marie-Caroline Carvalho (65th division)

Gustave Charpentier (10th division)

Ernest Chausson (67th division)

Luigi Cherubini (11th division)

Frédéric Chopin (11th division)

Chopin's heart was taken back to Poland by his sister and is buried in Warsaw.

Edouard Colonne (89th division)

Paul Dukas (87th division)

Georges Enesco (68th division)

Sébastien Erard (11th division)

Galli-Marié (56th division)

Philippe Gaubert (94th division)

François-Joseph Gossec (13th division)

André Grétry (11th division)

Ernest Guiraud (82nd division)

Reynaldo Hahn (85th division)

Stephen Heller (90th division)

Ferdinand Hérold (13th division)

Rodolphe Kreutzer (13th division)

Edouard Lalo (67th division)

Charles Lecocq (89th division)

Jean-François Le Sueur (11th division)

Etienne Méhul (13th division)

Ginette Neveu (11th division)

Ferdinando Paer (13th division)

Carlotta and Adelina Patti (4th division)

Edith Piaf (97th division)

Gabriel Pierné (13th division)

Ignace Pleyel (13th division)

Francis Poulenc (5th division)

Anton Reicha (7th division)

Gioachino Rossini (4th division)

Rossini was buried here in 1868, then reburied at Santa Croce, Florence, 2 May 1887.

Vanni-Marcoux (56th division)

Saint-Mandé Cemetery (Cimetière de Saint-Mandé, Cimetière Nord)

24 avenue Joffre, Saint-Mandé (Métro: Saint-Mandé-Tourelle)

Georges Thill

Saint-Ouen Cemetery (Cimetière Parisien de Saint-Ouen)

avenue Michelet, Saint-Ouen (Métro: Mairie de Saint-Ouen or Porte de Clignancourt)

Paul Delmet

Louis Ganne

Saint-Vincent Cemetery (Cimetière Saint-Vincent)

rue Lucien-Gaulard, 18e (C13, Métro: Lamarck-Caulaincourt)

Arthur Honegger

Désiré-Emile Inghelbrecht

Honegger.

Musicians Buried in Churches

Couperin family, excluding François "le Grand" and earlier members of the family: Saint-Gervais, place Saint-Gervais, 4e (Métro: Hôtel-de-Ville)

Jean-Baptiste Lully: Notre-Dame-des-Victoires, place des Petits-Pères, 2e (G14, Métro: Sentier or Bourse)

Jean-Philippe Rameau: Saint-Eustache, place du Jour, 1er (H14, Métro: Les Halles)

Charles-Marie Widor: Saint-Sulpice, place Saint-Sulpice, 6e (K13, Métro: Saint-Sulpice or Mabillon)

Musicians Guillotined

Jean-Benjamin De La Borde (22 July 1794)
Jean-Frédéric Edelmann (17 July 1794)
Geoffrey-Louis Edelmann (1794)

Index of Musicians' Graves and Monuments

Abbreviations

Ar	Cimetière d'Arcueil-Cachan	Pa	Cimetière de Passy
Au	Cimetière d'Auteuil	PL	Cimetière du Père-Lachaise
Ba	Cimetière des Batignolles	SMn	Cimetière de Saint-Mandé, Cimetière Nord
LP	Cimetière de Levallois-Perret	SO	Cimetière Parisien de Saint-Ouen
Mm	Cimetière de Montmartre	SV	Cimetière Saint-Vincent
Mp	Cimetière de Montparnasse		

Charpentier, Gustave	PL	Kreutzer, Rodolphe	PL
Chausson, Ernest	PL	Lalo, Edouard	PL
Cherubini, Luigi	PL	Lamoureux, Charles	Mm
Chopin, Frédéric	PL	Lecocq, Charles	PL
Colonne, Edouard	PL	Le Sueur, Jean-François	PL
Couperin family	Saint-Gervais	Livry, Emma	Mm
Debussy, Claude	Pa	Lully, Jean-Baptiste	
De La Borde, Jean-Benjamin			Notre-Dame-des-Victoires
	guillotined	Massé, Victor	Mm
Delibes, Léo	Mm	Méhul, Etienne	PL
Delmet, Paul	SO	Messager, André	Pa
Diémer, Louis	Mm	Neukomm, Sigismund	Mm
Dukas, Paul	PL	Neveu, Ginette	PL
Edelmann, Geoffrey-Louis		Nijinsky, Vaslav	Mm
	guillotined	Nourrit, Adolphe	Mm
Edelmann, Jean-Frédéric		Offenbach, Jacques	Mm
	guillotined	Paer, Ferdinando	PL
Enesco, George	PL	Patti, Carlotta and Adelina	PL
Erard, Sébastien	PL	Piaf, Edith	PL
Fauré, Gabriel	Pa	Pierné, Gabriel	PL
Franck, César	Mp	Plessis, Alphonsine	Mm
Galli-Marié	PL	Pleyel, Ignace	PL
Ganne, Louis	SO	Poulenc, Francis	PL
Gaubert, Philippe	PL	Rameau, Jean-Philippe	
Gossec, François-Joseph	PL		Saint-Eustache
Gounod, Charles	Au	Ravel, Maurice	LP
Grétry, André	PL	Reicha, Anton	PL
Guiraud, Ernest	PL	Reszke, Jean de	Mp
Hahn, Reynaldo	PL	Rossini, Gioachino	PL
Haskil, Clara	Mp	Saint-Saëns, Camille	Mp
Heller, Stephen	PL	Satie, Erik	Ar
Hérold, Ferdinand	PL	Sauguet, Henri	Mm
Honegger, Arthur	SV	Sax, Adolphe	Mm
Indy, Vincent d'	Mp	Sor, Fernando	Mm
Inghelbrecht, Désiré-Emile	SV	Taglioni, Marie	Mm
Jolivet, André	Mm	Thill, Georges	SMn
Kosma, Josef	Mm	Thomas, Ambroise	Mm

Vanni-Marcoux   PL
Viardot, Pauline   Mm
Vierne, Louis   Mp
Weber, Louise ("La Goulue")
                                 Mm
Widor, Charles-Marie
                        Saint-Sulpice

8 · Musical Street Names in Paris

Paris has many streets named after musicians, especially composers. By contrast, the Métro system has only three stations with explicit musical associations: Auber (RER line A), named after the composer, and its near-neighbour Opéra (Métro lines 3, 7, and 8, opened in October 1904) are linked by four moving pavements. Carrefour Pleyel (Métro, line 13, opened in June 1952, and the line's northern terminus until the extension to Saint-Denis-Basilique opened in May 1976) is named after the composer, publisher, and instrument maker Ignace Pleyel.

In the Paris region as a whole, musicians are well represented by street names, with Berlioz, Bizet, Debussy, Fauré, Gounod, Massenet, Mozart, and Ravel enjoying the greatest popularity. Among baroque composers, Couperin, Lully, and Rameau are the most frequently encountered. Some districts or towns have particularly strong musical representation, notably Santeny, where almost half the roads are named after composers, and some of the street names do not at present occur elsewhere in the Paris region: rue Ernest-Chausson, rue Olivier-Messiaen, and rue Henri-Sauguet. Other locations have intriguing specialities: Noisy-le-Roi has named several roads after jazz musicians—Louis Armstrong, Sidney Bechet, Fats Domino, Duke Ellington, Errol Garner, Charlie Parker, and Django Reinhardt—as well as the baroque master Michel-Richard Delalande. The streets of Saint-Germain-en-Laye commemorate not only local heroes (Debussy and Jehan Alain), but also most of the great figures of French music over the last three hundred years. Montigny-le-Bretonneux has streets named after every member of Les Six (along with Jean Cocteau).

Among the performers to be honoured with a street name are the cellist Pablo Casals, the conductors Camille Chevillard, Edouard Colonne, Charles Lamoureux, and Charles Münch, the violinist Ginette Neveu, the singer Edith Piaf, the pianist Raoul Pugno, and the violinist Jacques Thibaud.

In addition to Neveu and Piaf, three composers are among the women musicians represented: Lili Boulanger, Augusta Holmès, and Germaine Tailleferre.

As for non-French musicians, a cluster of Russian composers' names appear in the 18e arrondissement (Mussorgsky, Rimsky-Korsakov, and Tchaikovsky). Adjacent streets in Saint-Denis are named after the great Spanish composers Falla and Granados. Apart from the composers who spent a significant part of their working lives in the city and have streets named after them are Bellini, Cherubini, Chopin, Donizetti, Liszt, Pergolesi, Prokofiev, Rossini, Stravinsky, Verdi, and Wagner.

In the index that follows, only musical street names in central Paris (1er–20e arrondissements) are listed. In the region as a whole, such names can be found by consulting the Michelin *Atlas Paris et Banlieue*. Eccentric or inaccurate spellings have been retained for streets, but not for the headings. Thus the street listed in the Michelin *Paris Plan* (Paris, 1997 edition) as rue Pergolèse will be found under "Giovanni Battista Pergolesi." The street names listed here were current in 1998.

Adolphe Adam			*Vincenzo Bellini*	
rue Adolphe-Adam	4e		rue Bellini	16e
Tomaso Albinoni			*Hector Berlioz*	
rue Albinoni	12e		rue Berlioz	16e
Louis Armstrong			*Georges Bizet*	
place Louis-Armstrong	13e		rue Georges-Bizet	16e
Daniel-François-Esprit Auber			*Adrien Boieldieu*	
rue Auber	9e		place Boïeldieu	2e
Georges Auric			*Lili Boulanger*	
rue Georges-Auric	19e		place Lili-Boulanger	9e
Johann Sebastian Bach			*Johannes Brahms*	
rue Jean-Sébastien-Bach	13e		rue Brahms	12e
George Balanchine			*Alfred Bruneau*	
rue George-Balanchine	13e		rue Alfred-Bruneau	16e
Béla Bartók			*Casadesus Family*	
square Béla-Bartok	15e		place des Quatre-Frères-	
Ludwig van Beethoven			Casadesus	18e
rue Beethoven	16e			

Pablo Casals
rue Pablo-Casals   13e
square Pablo-Casals   15e

Emmanuel Chabrier
square Emmanuel-Chabrier   17e

Gustave Charpentier
rue Gustave-Charpentier   17e

Marc-Antoine Charpentier
rue Marc-Antoine-Charpentier
                     13e

Luigi Cherubini
rue Chérubini   2e

Frédéric Chopin
place Chopin   16e

Alexandre Choron
rue Choron   9e

Domenico Cimarosa
rue Cimarosa   16e

Louis-Nicolas Clérambault
rue Louis-Nicolas-Clérambault
                     20e

Edouard Colonne
rue Edouard-Colonne   1er

François Couperin
square Couperin   4e

Nicolas-Marie Dalayrac
rue Dalayrac   2e

Félicien David
rue Félicien-David   16e

Claude Debussy
Jardin Claude-Debussy   16e
rue Claude-Debussy   17e
square Claude-Debussy   17e

Léo Delibes
rue Léo-Delibes   16e

Serge Diaghilev
place Diaghilev   9e

Gaetano Donizetti
rue Donizetti   16e

Paul Dukas
rue Paul-Dukas   12e

Henri Duparc
square Henri-Duparc   17e

Sébastien Erard
impasse Erard   12e
rue Erard   12e

Gabriel Fauré
square Gabriel-Fauré   17e

César Franck
rue César-Franck   15e

George Gershwin
rue George-Gershwin   12e

Christoph Willibald von Gluck
rue Gluck   9e

Benjamin Godard
rue Benjamin-Godard   16e

François-Joseph Gossec
rue Gossec   12e

Charles Gounod
rue Gounod   17e

André Grétry
rue Grétry   2e

George Frideric Handel
rue Georg-Friedrich-Haendel   10e

Reynaldo Hahn
rue Reynaldo-Hahn   20e

Fromental Halévy
rue Halévy 9e

Ferdinand Hérold
rue Hérold 1er

Arthur Honegger
allée Arthur-Honegger 19e

Jacques Ibert
rue Jacques-Ibert 17e

Vincent d'Indy
avenue Vincent-d'Indy 12e

Nicolas Isouard ("Nicolo")
rue Nicolo 16e

Edouard Lalo
rue Lalo 16e

Charles Lamoureux
rue Charles-Lamoureux 16e

Charles Lecocq
rue Charles-Lecocq 15e

Franz Liszt
place Franz-Liszt 10e

Marguerite Long
Jardin Marguerite-Long 17e

Jean-Baptiste Lully
rue Lulli 2e

Albéric Magnard
rue Albéric-Magnard 16e

Victor Massé
rue Victor-Massé 9e

Jules Massenet
rue Massenet 16e

Etienne Méhul
rue Méhul 2e

Felix Mendelssohn
rue Mendelssohn 20e

André Messager
rue André-Messager 18e

Olivier Métra
rue Olivier-Métra 20e

Giacomo Meyerbeer
rue Meyerbeer 9e

Darius Milhaud
allée Darius-Milhaud 19e

Antoine Monsigny
rue Monsigny 2e

Wolfgang Amadeus Mozart
avenue Mozart 16e
square Mozart 16e
villa Mozart 16e

Modest Mussorgsky
rue Moussorgsky 18e

Ginette Neveu
rue Ginette-Neveu 18e

Vaslav Nijinsky
allée Nijinsky 4e

Jacques Offenbach
rue Jacques-Offenbach 16e

Niccolò Paganini
rue Paganini 20e

Paul Paray
square Paul-Paray 17e

Jules Pasdeloup
place Pasdeloup 11e

Giovanni Battista Pergolesi
rue Pergolèse 16e

François-André-Danican Philidor
rue Philidor 20e

Edith Piaf		*Franz Schubert*	
place Edith-Piaf	20e	rue Schubert	20e
Niccolò Piccini		*Déodat de Séverac*	
rue Piccini	16e	rue Déodat-de-Séverac	17e
Gabriel Pierné		*Gasparo Spontini*	
square Gabriel-Pierné	6e	rue Spontini	16e
Robert Planquette		villa Spontini	16e
rue Robert-Planquette	19e	*Johann Strauss*	
Ignace Pleyel		place Johann-Strauss	10e
rue Pleyel	12e	*Igor Stravinsky*	
Francis Poulenc		place Igor-Stravinsky	4e
place Francis-Poulenc	19e	*Piotr Ilyich Tchaikovsky*	
square Francis-Poulenc	6e	rue Tchaikovski	18e
Sergei Prokofiev		*Claude Terrasse*	
rue Serge-Prokofiev	16e	rue Claude-Terrasse	16e
Sergei Rachmaninoff		*Ambroise Thomas*	
Jardin Rachmaninoff	18e	rue Ambroise-Thomas	9e
Jean-Philippe Rameau		*Henri Tomasi*	
rue Rameau	2e	rue Henri-Tomasi	20e
Maurice Ravel		*Charles Tournemire*	
avenue Maurice-Ravel	12e	rue Charles-Tournemire	17e
Ernest Reyer		*Edgar Varèse*	
avenue Ernest-Reyer	14e	rue Edgar-Varèse	19e
Nikolai Rimsky-Korsakov		*Giuseppe Verdi*	
allée Rimsky-Korsakov	18e	rue Verdi	16e
Gioachino Rossini		*Louis Vierne*	
rue Rossini	9e	rue Louis-Vierne	17e
Camille Saint-Saëns		*Antonio Vivaldi*	
rue Saint-Saëns	15e	allée Vivaldi	12e
Pablo de Sarasate		*Carl Maria von Weber*	
rue Sarasate	15e	rue Weber	16e
Erik Satie		*Charles-Marie Widor*	
rue Erik-Satie	19e	rue Charles-Marie-Widor	16e

Index of Locations by Arrondissement

Paris Arrondissements

1er arrondissement

43 rue Cambon (G12, Métro: Madeleine): Delius

5 rue des Capucines, Hôtel de Calais (G12, Métro: Madeleine): Liszt

1 place du Châtelet (J14, Métro: Châtelet): Théâtre du Châtelet

10 rue Coquillière (H14, Métro: Les Halles): Dukas

10 rue Croix-des-Petits-Champs, Hôtel de l'Univers et du Portugal (H13–G14, Métro: Palais Royal): Vaughan Williams

46 rue Croix-des-Petits-Champs (G14, Métro: Palais Royal): Vuillaume

avenue du Général-Lemonnier, Jardin des Tuileries (H12, Métro: Palais Royal): Palais des Tuileries

27 rue de Harlay (J14, Métro: Cité): Berlioz

10 rue Hérold, formerly part of the rue d'Argout (G14, Métro: Palais Royal or Sentier): Hérold

place du Jour (H14, Métro: Les Halles): Saint-Eustache

place du Louvre (H14, Métro: Pont-Neuf): Saint-Germain-l'Auxerrois

8 rue Molière (G13, Métro: Pyramides): Mozart

10 rue des Moulins (G13, Métro: Pyramides): Lully

boulevard du Palais (J14, Métro: Cité): Sainte-Chapelle

45 rue des Petits-Champs, Hôtel Lully (G13, Métro: Pyramides): Lully

corner of rue Radziwill and rue des Petits-Champs (G13, Métro: Palais Royal): F. Couperin

220 rue de Rivoli (G12, Métro: Tuileries): Delibes

69 rue Saint-Honoré (H14, Métro: Châtelet): Debussy

202 rue Saint-Honoré (H13, Métro: Palais Royal): Palais Royal Theatres (i) and (ii)

296 rue Saint-Honoré (G13, Métro: Tuileries): Saint-Roch

43 rue Sainte-Anne (G13, Métro: Pyramides): Lully

3 rue de la Tonnellerie, now 31 rue du Pont-Neuf (H14, Métro: Châtelet): Wagner

rue Traversière, later rue Molière, partly demolished for the avenue de l'Opéra (G13, Métro: Pyramides): Grétry

12 place Vendôme (G12, Métro: Opéra): Chopin

20 avenue Victoria, Hôtel Britannique (J14–J15, Métro: Châtelet): Verdi, Boito

2e arrondissement

19 rue d'Antin (G13, Métro: Opéra): Donizetti

place Boieldieu (F13, Métro: Richelieu-Drouot): Opéra-Comique (Salle Favart)

19–21 rue Feydeau (G14, Métro: Bourse): Théâtre Feydeau

1 rue de Gramont, Hôtel Manchester (G13, Métro: Quatre-Septembre): Donizetti

3 boulevard des Italiens (F13, Métro: Richelieu-Drouot): Hérold

27 boulevard des Italiens, Bains chinois (F13, Métro: Opéra): Bellini

2 rue de Louvois (Métro: Quatre-Septembre): Bibliothèque Nationale (Département de la Musique)

5 rue de Louvois (G13, Métro: Quatre-Septembre): Adam, Donizetti

rue de Louvois (G13, Métro: Quatre-Septembre): Salle Louvois, Théâtre National de la Loi

10 rue du Mail, Hôtel d'Angleterre (G14, Métro: Sentier): Liszt

13 rue du Mail (G14, Métro: Sentier): Salle Erard, Liszt

12 rue Mandar (G14, Métro: Sentier): Martinů

rue Méhul (G13, Métro: Pyramides): Salle Ventadour

4 rue Monsigny (G13, Métro: Quatre-Septembre or Pyramides): Théâtre des Bouffes-Parisiens

7 boulevard Montmartre (F14, Métro: Rue Montmartre): Théâtre des Variétés

22 rue Neuve-Saint-Eustache, now part of rue Aboukir, Hôtel de Strasbourg (G14, Métro: Sentier): Liszt

1 rue Neuve-Saint-Marc, now rue Saint-Marc (F13, Métro: Richelieu-Drouot): Berlioz

82 rue des Petits-Champs (G13, Métro: Pyramides or Opéra): Stravinsky

place des Petits-Pères (G14, Métro: Sentier or Bourse): Notre-Dame-des-Victoires

27 boulevard Poissonnière (F14, Métro: Rue Montmartre): Chopin

21 rue Poissonnière (G15, Métro: Bonne-Nouvelle): Grétry

6 rue Rameau (G13, Métro: Quatre-Septembre): Rossini

52 rue de Richelieu (G13, Métro: Quatre-Septembre): Grétry

59 rue de Richelieu (G13, Métro: Quatre-Septembre): Rameau

83 rue de Richelieu (F13, Métro: Richelieu-Drouot): Viardot

96 rue de Richelieu (F13, Métro: Richelieu-Drouot): Berlioz

10 rue du Sentier (G14, Métro: Sentier): Mozart

27 rue Vivienne (G14, Métro: Bourse): Salle de la Bourse

3e arrondissement

58 rue des Archives, formerly rue du Chaume, Hôtel de Clisson (H16, Métro: Rambuteau): M.-A. Charpentier

rue du Bourg-l'Abbé (H15, Métro: Etienne-Marcel): Mozart

1 rue de Braque (H16, Métro: Rambuteau): Alkan

6 rue Charlot (H16, Métro: Saint-Sébastien-Froissart): Saint-Jean–Saint-François, now Cathédrale Sainte-Croix

3–5 rue Papin (G15, Métro: Réaumur-Sébastopol): Théâtre de la Gaîté Lyrique

23 rue de Sévigné (Métro: Saint-Paul): Musée Carnavalet

70 rue de Turbigo (G16, Métro: Arts et Métiers or Temple): Satie

4e arrondissement

2 place du Châtelet (J15, Métro: Châtelet): Théâtre Lyrique (ii), Théâtre de la Nation, Théâtre Sarah-Bernhardt

2–4 rue François-Miron (J15, Métro: Hôtel-de-Ville): Couperin

68 rue François-Miron (J16, Métro: Saint-Paul): Mozart

place Igor-Stravinsky (H15, Métro: Rambuteau): IRCAM

parvis Notre-Dame (K15, Métro: Cité): Notre-Dame-de-Paris

65 rue Rambuteau (H15, Métro: Rambuteau): Messiaen

place Saint-Gervais (J15, Métro: Hôtel-de-Ville): Saint-Gervais

78 rue Saint-Martin (H15, Métro: Hôtel-de-Ville): Saint-Merry

square Sainte-Croix-de-la-Bretonnerie (J15, Métro: Hôtel-de-Ville): Sainte-Croix-de-la-Bretonnerie

5e arrondissement

26 rue des Boulangers (Métro: Cardinal-Lemoine): Koechlin

32 rue Denfert-Rochereau, now rue Henri-Barbusse (M13, RER: Luxembourg): Séverac

rue Descartes (L15, Métro: Cardinal-Lemoine): Varèse

58 rue de la Harpe (K14, Métro: Cluny-Sorbonne): Berlioz

41 rue Monge (L15, Métro: Cardinal-Lemoine): Varèse

6 place du Panthéon (L14, Métro: Cardinal-Lemoine): Duruflé

rue des Prêtres-Saint-Séverin (K14, Métro: Saint-Michel): Saint-Séverin

104 (later 71 and 79) rue Saint-Jacques (K14, Métro: Cluny-Sorbonne): Berlioz

269 rue Saint-Jacques (M14, RER: Luxembourg): Schola Cantorum

95 boulevard Saint-Michel (L13–L14, RER: Luxembourg): Franck

place Sainte-Geneviève (L15, Métro: Cardinal-Lemoine): Saint-Etienne-du-Mont

6e arrondissement

3 rue de l'Abbaye (J13, Métro: Saint-Germain-des-Prés): Widor

83 rue d'Assas (L13, Métro: Notre-Dame-des-Champs): Lekeu

116 rue d'Assas (M13, RER: Port-Royal): Séverac

3 rue Coëtlogon (K12, Métro: Sèvres-Babylone): Vierne

rue de l'Eperon (K14, Métro: Odéon): Gounod

8 rue Garancière, Hôtel de Sourdéac (K13, Métro: Mabillon or Saint-Sulpice): Widor

20 rue des Grands-Augustins (J14, Métro: Saint-Michel): Gounod

Institut de France, place de l'Institut (J13, Métro: Pont-Neuf or Saint-Michel): Académie des Beaux-Arts, Widor

14 rue Jacob (J13, Métro: Saint-Germain-des-Prés): Wagner

44 rue Jacob, Hôtel Jacob (J13, Métro: Saint-Germain-des-Prés): Varèse

3 rue du Jardinet (K14, Métro: Odéon): Saint-Saëns

23 rue Le Verrier (M13, Métro: Vavin): Canteloube

5 rue de Médicis (K13–K14, Métro: Odéon; or RER: Luxembourg): Poulenc

5 rue Michelet (L13, Métro: Vavin): Séverac

14 rue Monsieur-le-Prince (K13, Métro: Odéon): Saint-Saëns

22 rue Notre-Dame-des-Champs, Collège Stanislas (L12, Métro: Notre-Dame-des-Champs): Roussel

86 rue Notre-Dame-des-Champs (M13, Métro: Vavin): Varèse (Léger's studio)

place de l'Odéon (K13, Métro: Odéon): Théâtre de l'Odéon

12 rue de l'Odéon (K13, Métro: Odéon): Antheil

146 rue de Rennes (L12, Métro: Saint-Placide): Canteloube

11 place Saint-André-des-Arts (J14, Métro: Saint-Michel): Gounod

rue Saint-André-des-Arts (Métro: Saint-Michel): Varèse

place Saint-Germain-des-Prés (J13, Métro: Saint-Germain-des-Prés): Saint-Germain-des-Prés

11 place Saint-Michel (J14, Métro: Saint-Michel): Villa-Lobos

place Saint-Sulpice (K13, Métro: Saint-Sulpice or Mabillon): Saint-Sulpice

49 rue de Seine (J13, Métro: Mabillon): Varèse

9 rue Serpente (K14, Métro: Cluny-Sorbonne): Séverac

19 rue Servandoni (Métro: Saint-Sulpice): Chausson (Mme Rayssac's house)

19 rue Taranne, now 167 boulevard Saint-Germain (Métro: Saint-Germain-des-Prés): Fauré

48 rue de Vaugirard (K13, Métro: Odéon): Massenet

94–96 rue de Vaugirard (L12, Métro: Saint-Placide): Cavaillé-Coll

21 rue du Vieux-Colombier (K12, Métro: Saint-Sulpice): Cavaillé-Coll

7e arrondissement

97 rue du Bac (J11, Métro: Rue du Bac): D'Indy

1(?) rue de Beaune (H12–J12, Métro: Rue du Bac): Massenet

1 rue de Bellechasse (Métro: Solférino, RER: Musée d'Orsay): Musée d'Orsay

31 rue de Bourgogne (J11, Métro: Varenne): Varèse

Hôtel des Invalides (J10, Métro: Latour-Maubourg or Varenne): Saint-Louis-des-Invalides

Institution des Jeunes Aveugles, 56 boulevard des Invalides (L10, Métro: Duroc): Vierne

23 bis rue Las-Cases (J11, Métro: Solférino): Sainte-Clotilde

6 place Saint-François-Xavier, now place du Président-Mithouard (K10, Métro: Saint-François-Xavier): Duparc

243 boulevard Saint-Germain (J11–H11, Métro: Solférino): Viardot

31 rue Saint-Guillaume (J12, Métro: Rue du Bac): Liszt

60 rue des Saints-Pères (K12, Métro: Sèvres-Babylone): Vierne

23 (subsequently 40) rue Vaneau (K11, Métro: Vaneau): Chabrier

31 rue Vaneau (J11, Métro: Saint-François-Xavier): Scriabin

59 rue de Varenne (J11, Métro: Varenne): Jolivet

7 avenue de Villars (K10, Métro: Saint-François-Xavier): Duparc, D'Indy

11 quai Voltaire (H12, Métro: Rue du Bac): Cavaillé-Coll

19 quai Voltaire, Hôtel du Quai Voltaire (J12–H12, Métro: Rue du Bac): Wagner

8e arrondissement

9 rue Alfred-de-Vigny (E9, Métro: Courcelles): Hahn

17 rue de l'Arcade, Bedford Hôtel (F11, Métro: Madeleine): Villa-Lobos

27 rue de Berlin, now rue de Liège (E12, Métro: Liège): Debussy

28 rue Boissy-d'Anglas (G11, Métro: Madeleine): Lully

67 avenue des Champs-Elysées (F9, Métro: Franklin D. Roosevelt): Verdi

2 rond-point des Champs-Elysées (G10, Métro: Franklin D. Roosevelt): Meyerbeer

6 avenue Chateaubriand, now rue Arsène-Houssaye (F8, Métro: Charles de Gaulle–Etoile): Donizetti

18 rue de Chateaubriand (F8, Métro: George V): Scriabin

6 rue du Cirque (G10–F10, Métro: Champs-Elysées–Clemenceau): Hahn

13 rue Clapeyron (D11, Métro: Rome): Debussy

28 rue de Constantinople (E11, Métro: Villiers): Debussy (Vasnier house)

29 rue Daru (E9, Métro: Courcelles): Alkan

25 rue du Faubourg-Saint-Honoré (G11, Métro: Madeleine): Stravinsky

35 rue du Faubourg-Saint-Honoré, British Embassy (G11, Métro: Madeleine): Berlioz (who married Harriet Smithson here)

154 rue du Faubourg-Saint-Honoré (F10, Métro: Saint-Philippe-du-Roule): Saint-Philippe-du-Roule

168 rue du Faubourg-Saint-Honoré (F9, Métro: Saint-Philippe-du-Roule or Ternes): Saint-Saëns

252 rue du Faubourg-Saint-Honoré (E8, Métro: Ternes): Salle Pleyel (iii)

46 rue du Général-Foy (E10, Métro: Villiers): Massenet

7 rue Greffulhe (F12, Métro: Madeleine): Hahn

157 boulevard Haussmann (F9, Métro: Saint-Philippe-du-Roule): Messager

45 rue La Boétie (F10, Métro: Miromesnil): Salle Gaveau

51 rue de Londres (E12, Métro: Europe): Alkan

16 rue Lord-Byron (F8, Métro: Charles de Gaulle–Etoile): Scriabin

9 place de la Madeleine (G11–G12, Métro: Madeleine): Rossini

place de la Madeleine (G11, Métro: Madeleine): Madeleine

14 rue de Madrid (E12, Métro: Europe): Conservatoire

4 avenue Matignon (G10–F10, Métro: Franklin D. Roosevelt): Wagner

6 avenue Matignon (G10, Métro: Franklin D. Roosevelt): Messager

83 rue de Monceau (E10, Métro: Villiers): Poulenc

13 avenue Montaigne (G9, Métro: Alma-Marceau): Théâtre des Champs-Elysées

13 rue Mosnier, now rue de Berne (E11, Métro: Europe): Fauré, Messager

23 rue Mosnier, now rue de Berne (E11, Métro: Europe): Chabrier

5 rue de la Néva (E8, Métro: Ternes): Scriabin

3 cité Odiot (F9, Métro: George V): Satie

14 rue Pierre Charron (Métro: George V): Koechlin

rue Rembrandt (E9, Métro: Monceau): Koechlin

place Saint-Augustin (E11, Métro: Saint-Augustin): Saint-Augustin

2 place des Saussaies (F11, Métro: Miromesnil or Saint-Augustin): Poulenc

5 rue Tronchet (F12, Métro: Madeleine): Chopin

41 rue Washington (F9, Métro: George V): Dukas

9e arrondissement

3 rue d'Aumale (E13, Métro: Saint-Georges): Wagner

36 rue Ballu, now 1 place Lili-Boulanger (D12, Métro: Place de Clichy): N. and L. Boulanger

4 cité Bergère (F14, Métro: Rue Montmartre): Chopin

2 rue Bergère (F15, Métro: Bonne-Nouvelle): Salle du Conservatoire

15 rue Blanche (E12, Métro: Trinité): Salle du Nouveau Théâtre

45 rue Blanche (E12, Métro: Trinité or Blanche): Franck

69 rue Blanche (E12, Métro: Blanche): Franck

19 rue de Boursault, now rue La Bruyère (E13, Métro: Saint-Georges): Berlioz

24 rue Buffault (E14, Métro: Cadet): Adam

9 rue Cadet (F14–E14, Métro: Cadet): Salle Pleyel (i)

4 rue de Calais (D12, Métro: Blanche or Place de Clichy): Berlioz

2 boulevard des Capucines (F13, Métro: Opéra): Théâtre du Vaudeville

8 boulevard des Capucines (F13, Métro: Opéra): Offenbach

12 boulevard des Capucines, Grand Hôtel (F13, Métro: Opéra): Verdi

18 bis rue de Châteaudun, Paris 9 (E13, Métro: Notre-Dame-de-Lorette): Notre-Dame-de-Lorette

2 rue de la Chaussée-d'Antin (F13, Métro: Opéra): Rossini

4 rue de la Chaussée-d'Antin (F13, Métro: Opéra): Grétry

5 rue de la Chaussée-d'Antin (F13, Métro: Opéra): Chopin, Mozart

10 boulevard de Clichy (D13, Métro: Pigalle): Milhaud

71 boulevard de Clichy (D13, Métro: Blanche): Honegger

26 rue de Clichy (E12, Métro: Trinité): Enesco

50 rue Condorcet (E14, Métro: Anvers or Pigalle): Satie

corner of rue Condorcet and rue Rochechouart (E14, Métro: Cadet): Massenet

38 rue Coquenard, renamed rue Lamartine in 1848 (E14, Métro: Cadet): Liszt

22 rue de Douai (D13, Métro: Blanche): Bizet

40 bis rue de Douai (D12, Métro: Blanche): Ravel

46 rue de Douai (D12, Métro: Blanche): Mustel

50 rue de Douai (D12, Métro: Blanche): Viardot

6 rue Drouot, Hôtel d'Augny (F14, Métro: Richelieu-Drouot): Rossini

21 rue Duperré (D13, Métro: Pigalle): Honegger

place d'Estienne-d'Orves (E12, Métro: Trinité): Trinité

25 rue du Faubourg-Poissonnière (F15, Métro: Bonne-Nouvelle): Cherubini

7 avenue Frochot (D13, Métro: Pigalle): Lamoureux

7 rue Fromentin (D13, Métro: Blanche or Pigalle): Ravel

5 rue Gaillard, now rue Paul-Escudier (E12, Métro: Blanche): Milhaud

11 bis rue Geoffroy-Marie (F14, Métro: Rue Montmartre): Vierne

41 boulevard Haussmann (F12, Métro: Havre-Caumartin): Rachmaninoff

25 rue du Helder (F13, Métro: Opéra): Wagner

2 boulevard des Italiens (F13, Métro: Richelieu-Drouot): Milhaud

32 boulevard des Italiens, Hôtel de Bade (F13, Métro: Opéra): Verdi

16 rue Jean-Baptiste-Pigalle (E13, Métro: Trinité): Chopin

73 rue Jean-Baptiste-Pigalle (D13, Métro: Pigalle): Ravel

11 rue La Bruyère (E13, Métro: Saint-Georges): Alkan

15 rue La Bruyère (E13, Métro: Saint-Georges): Franck

30 rue La Bruyère (E13, Métro: Saint-Georges): N. and L. Boulanger

15 rue de La Rochefoucauld (E13, Métro: Trinité): Berlioz

17 rue de La Rochefoucauld (E13, Métro: Trinité): Gounod

26 rue de La Tour-d'Auvergne (E14, Métro: Cadet): Bizet

11 rue Laffitte (F13, Métro: Richelieu-Drouot): Offenbach

23 rue Laffitte, Hôtel de France (F13, Métro: Le Peletier): Liszt, Sand

51 rue Laffitte (F13, Métro: Le Peletier): Massenet

18 rue de Laval, rue Victor-Massé since 1887 (E13, Métro: Pigalle): Bizet

5 rue Le Peletier (F13, Métro: Richelieu-Drouot): Mendelssohn

12 rue Le Peletier (F13, Métro: Richelieu-Drouot): Salle Le Peletier

34 (later 35 and 31) rue de Londres (E12, Métro: Saint-Lazare): Berlioz

36 rue des Martyrs (E14, Métro: Saint-Georges): Wagner

40 rue des Martyrs (E14, Métro: Saint-Georges or Pigalle): Ravel

10 rue des Mathurins (F12, Métro: Saint-Augustin): Liszt

35 rue de Mauberge (E14, Métro: Cadet or Poissonnière): N. Boulanger

7 rue de Montholon (F14–F15, Métro: Cadet or Poissonnière): Liszt

22 rue de Montholon (E14, Métro: Cadet): Franck

10 boulevard Montmartre, now passage Jouffroy (F14, Métro: Richelieu-Drouot): Boieldieu, Rossini, Carafa

10 rue Neuve-Fontaine-Saint-Georges, now rue Fromentin (D13, Métro: Blanche or Pigalle): Fauré

32 rue Neuve-Fontaine-Saint-Georges, now rue Fromentin (D13, Métro: Blanche or Pigalle): Bizet

20 rue Neuve-des-Mathurins, now rue des Mathurins (F12, Métro: Havre-Caumartin): Verdi

95 rue Neuve-des-Mathurins, now rue des Mathurins (F11–F12, Métro: Havre-Caumartin): Adam

42 rue Notre-Dame-de-Lorette (E13, Métro: Saint-Georges): Cavaillé-Coll

place de l'Opéra (F12, Métro: Opéra): Opéra (including Bibliothèque-Musée)

5 square d'Orléans (F13, Métro: Trinité): Sand

9 square d'Orléans (F13, Métro: Trinité): Chopin

square d'Orléans (F13, Métro: Trinité): Viardot, Taglioni

7 rue de Parme (D12, Métro: Liège or Place de Clichy): Fauré

41 rue de Provence (F13, Métro: Le Peletier): Berlioz

61 rue de Provence (F13, Métro: Chaussée-d'Antin): Liszt

4 rue Richer (F14–F15, Métro: Cadet): Verdi

22 rue de Rochechouart (E14, Métro: Cadet): Salle Pleyel (ii), Stravinsky

8 rue Saint-Georges (F13, Métro: Le Peletier): Thomas (and birthplace of Degas)

22 rue Saint-Georges (E13, Métro: Notre-Dame-de-Lorette): Auber

24 rue Saint-Georges (F13, Métro: Le Peletier): Verdi

50 rue Saint-Georges (E13, Métro: Notre-Dame-de-Lorette): Sax

40 (then 34) rue Saint-Lazare (E13, Métro: Trinité): Alkan

50 bis rue Saint-Lazare (E13, Métro: Trinité): Auber

64 rue Saint-Lazare (E13, Métro: Trinité): Lamoureux

4 bis rue Sainte-Cécile (F14, Métro: Bonne-Nouvelle): Saint-Eugène

rue Say (D14, Métro: Pigalle): Honegger

8 rue Taitbout (F13, Métro: Richelieu-Drouot): Thomas

14 rue Taitbout (F13, Métro: Chaussée-d'Antin): Massenet

28 rue Taitbout (F13, Métro: Chaussée-d'Antin): Rossini

33 rue Taitbout (F13, Métro: Chaussée-d'Antin): Boieldieu

13 avenue Trudaine (D14, Métro: Anvers): Chabrier

13 rue de la Victoire (F13–F14, Métro: Le Peletier): Verdi

48 rue de la Victoire (F13, Métro: Le Peletier): Salle Herz

11 rue de Vintimille (D12, Métro: Place de Clichy): Debussy

17 rue de Vintimille (D12, Métro: Place de Clichy): Berlioz

10e arrondissement

place Franz-Liszt (E15, Métro: Poissonnière): Saint-Vincent-de-Paul

66 boulevard de Magenta (F16, Métro: Gare de l'Est): Satie

6 rue de Marseille (F17, Métro: Jacques-Bonsergent): Satie

9 rue des Petits-Hôtels (E15, Métro: Poissonnière): Dukas

16 boulevard Saint-Martin (G16, Métro: République): Théâtre de la
Porte Saint-Martin

12 rue de Strasbourg, now rue du Huit-Mai 1945 (E16, Métro: Gare de
l'Est): Varèse

11e arrondissement

30 rue Faubourg-du-Temple (G17, Métro: République): Adam

5 rue Ménilmontant, renamed rue Oberkampf in 1864 (H17, Métro:
Filles-du-Calvaire): Massenet

place Pasdeloup, rue Amelot (H17, Métro: Filles-du-Calvaire): Cirque
d'Hiver

72 boulevard du Temple, now part of place de la République (G17,
Métro: République): Théâtre Lyrique (i)

12e arrondissement

120 rue de Lyon (K18, Métro: Bastille): Opéra Bastille

14e arrondissement

villa d'Alésia (P11, Métro: Alésia): Copland

3 villa des Camélias (P9, Métro: Porte de Vanves): Varèse

Cimetière de Montparnasse (M12, Métro: Raspail or Edgar-Quinet)

33 rue du Couédic (P12, Métro: Mouton-Duvernet): Delius

11a rue Delambre (M12, Métro: Vavin): Martinů

77 rue des Plantes (P11–R11, Métro: Alésia): Messiaen

207 boulevard Raspail (M12, Métro: Raspail): Copland

place Victor-et-Hélène-Basch (P12, Métro: Alésia): Saint-Pierre-de-Montrouge

15e arrondissement

12 avenue du Maine (L11, Métro: Faulgière): Varèse

13–15 avenue du Maine (L11, Métro: Faulgière): Cavaillé-Coll

60 boulevard Montparnasse, Hôtel de Versailles (L11, Métro: Montparnasse-Bienvenue): Varèse

66 boulevard Pasteur (M10, Métro: Pasteur): Copland

5 rue Valentin-Haüy (L10, Métro: Ségur): Prokofiev

16e arrondissement

10 avenue Alphand (F6, Métro: Argentine): Debussy

17 rue d'Ankara, Dr. Blanche's clinic (J6, Métro: Passy): Gounod

20 rue de l'Assomption (J4, Métro: Ranelagh): Dukas

31 rue de l'Assomption (J4, Métro: Ranelagh): Stravinsky

Cimetière d'Auteuil (M3, Métro: Exelmans)

7 rue Bellini (H6, Métro: Trocadéro): Varèse

3 rue de Belloy (G7, Métro: Boissière): Widor

80 avenue du Bois de Boulogne, now avenue Foch—no. 24 in the square (F6, Métro: Porte Dauphine): Debussy

Palais de Chaillot (H7, Métro: Trocadéro): Trocadéro

74 rue de Chaillot (G8, Métro: Iéna): Chopin

Cimetière de Passy (H6, Métro: Trocadéro)

11 place des Etats-Unis (G7, Métro: Boissière): Weill

43 avenue Georges-Mandel (H6, Métro: Rue de la Pompe): Polignac

1 place d'Iéna (Métro: Iéna): Koechlin

avenue Ingres (Métro: Ranelagh): Rossini

19 avenue Kléber, Hôtel Majestic (F7, Métro: Kléber): Gershwin

17 rue de Longchamp (G7, Métro: Iéna): Saint-Saëns

1 rue Louis-David (H6, Métro: Rue de la Pompe): Vierne

24 rue des Marronniers (J5, Métro: La Muette): Martinů

30 villa Molitor (Métro: Chardon-Lagache): Koechlin

16 rue Newton (F8, Métro: Kléber): Wagner

84 rue de Ranelagh (J4, Métro: Ranelagh): Dukas

38 rue Singer (J5, Métro: La Muette): Dukas

10 avenue des Tilleuls, villa Montmorency (K3, Métro: Jasmin): Koechlin

24 rue de la Tour (H6, Métro: Passy): Scriabin

place Victor-Hugo (G6, Métro: Victor-Hugo): Saint-Honoré-d'Eylau

32 rue des Vignes (J5, Métro: La Muette): Fauré

rue de l'Yvette (K4, Métro: Jasmin): Koechlin

17e arrondissement

17 rue Brey (Métro: Charles de Gaulle–Etoile): Séverac

58 rue Cardinet (D9, Métro: Malesherbes): Debussy

78 rue Cardinet (D9, Métro: Malesherbes): Ecole Normale de Musique

1 bis avenue Carnot, Hôtel Splendide (F7–E7, Métro: Charles de Gaulle–Etoile): Stravinsky, Weill

4 avenue Carnot (F7–E7, Métro: Charles de Gaulle–Etoile): Ravel

Cimetière des Batignolles (B10–A11, Métro: Porte de Clichy)

22 boulevard de Courcelles (E10, Métro: Villiers): Chausson

83 bis rue de Courcelles (E9, Métro: Courcelles): Saint-Saëns

1 square Emmanuel-Chabrier (D10, Métro: Villiers): Honegger

2 square Gabriel-Fauré (D10, Métro: Villiers): Roussel

10 rue Gustave-Doré (D9, Métro: Wagram): Debussy

103 rue Jouffroy-d'Abbans (D8–D9, Métro: Courcelles): Messager

26 rue Lecluse (D12, Métro: Place de Clichy): Chabrier (Verlaine's house)

154 boulevard Malesherbes (D9, Métro: Malesherbes): Fauré

174 boulevard Malesherbes (D9, Métro: Wagram): Messager

20 place Malesherbes, now place du Général-Catroux (D10, Métro: Malesherbes): Gounod

4 rue Milne-Edwards (D7, Métro: Péreire): Tournemire

93 avenue Niel (D8, Métro: Péreire): Fauré

15 boulevard Péreire (C9, Métro: Wagram): Casella

19 boulevard Péreire (C9, Métro: Wagram): Ravel

rue Pierre-Demours (E7–D8, Métro: Péreire): Vuillaume

37 rue Saint-Ferdinand (E6, Métro: Porte Maillot): Vierne

11 bis rue Viète (D9, Métro: Wagram): Roussel

21 rue Viète (D9, Métro: Wagram): Stravinsky

53 avenue de Villiers (D9, Métro: Malesherbes): Liszt

157 avenue de Wagram (D9, Métro: Wagram): Roussel

39 avenue de Wagram (E18, Métro: Ternes): Salle Wagram

18e arrondissement

Cimetière de Montmartre (C12–D12, Métro: La Fourche or Place de Clichy)

Cimetière Saint-Vincent (C13, Métro: Lamarck-Caulaincourt)

6 rue Cortot (C14, Métro: Lamarck-Caulaincourt): Satie, Musée Erik Satie

12 rue Cortot (Métro: Lamarck-Caulaincourt): Musée de Montmartre

4 place Dancourt, now place Charles-Dullin (D14, Métro: Anvers): Vierne

4 passage de l'Elysée-des-Beaux-Arts, now rue André-Antoine (D13, Métro: Pigalle): Vierne

place Jules-Joffrin (B14, Métro: Jules-Joffrin): Notre-Dame-de-Clignancourt

29 avenue Junot, Maison de Santé (C13, Métro: Lamarck-Caulaincourt): Stravinsky

230 rue Marcadet (B12, Métro: Guy-Môquet): Messiaen

66 boulevard de Rochechouart (D14, Métro: Anvers): G. Charpentier

10 rue Saint-Denis, now rue du Mont-Cenis; demolished in 1925 (C14, Métro: Lamarck-Caulaincourt): Berlioz

19e arrondissement

13 villa du Danube (D21, Métro: Danube): Messiaen

110 rue de Flandre, now avenue de Flandre (C18–C19, Métro: Crimée): Erard

221 avenue Jean-Jaurès (C21, Métro: Porte de Pantin): Cité de la Musique (including Musée de la Musique)

20e arrondissement

Cimetière du Père-Lachaise (H20–H21, Métro: Père-Lachaise)

Paris Region

Arcueil

22 (now 34) rue Cauchy, Arcueil (RER: Arcueil-Cachan): Satie

Cimetière d'Arcueil-Cachan (RER: Arcueil-Cachan)

Bellevue

17 bis rue des Capucins, Bellevue (SNCF: Bellevue): Laloy, Stravinsky

Croissy-sur-Seine

8 boulevard de la Mairie, Croissy-sur-Seine (RER: Chatou-Croissy): Delius

Levallois-Perret

Cimetière de Levallois-Perret (A7, SNCF: Clichy-Levallois; or Métro: Pont de Levallois–Bécon)

16 bis rue Louis-Rouquier, formerly rue Chevalier, Levallois-Perret (C6, Métro: Anatole-France): Ravel

Louveciennes

9 bis place Ernest-Dreux, Louveciennes (SNCF: Louveciennes): Weill

Maisons-Laffitte

Saint-Nicolas, Maisons-Laffitte (RER and SNCF: Maisons-Laffitte): Alain

Meudon
3 avenue de Meudon, now 27 avenue du Château, Meudon (SNCF: Belle-vue): Wagner

Montfort-l'Amaury
Musée Maurice Ravel, Le Belvédère, 5 rue Maurice-Ravel, Montfort-l'Amaury (SNCF: Montfort-Lamaury–Méré): Ravel

Neuilly
Villa Borghese, 29 boulevard Victor-Hugo, Neuilly-sur-Seine (Métro: Louise-Michel or Les Sablons): Stravinsky

Le Port-Marly
17 rue de Paris, Le Port-Marly (SNCF: Marly-le-Roi): Bizet

Puteaux
19 bis rampe de Neuilly, Puteaux (SNCF: Puteaux): Bellini

Saint-Cloud
Montretout, 3 rue Gounod, Saint-Cloud (SNCF: Saint-Cloud): Gounod

Saint-Germain-en-Laye
38 rue au Pain, Saint-Germain-en-Laye (RER: Saint-Germain-en-Laye): Debussy

87 rue Péreire, Saint-Germain-en-Laye (RER: Saint-Germain-en-Laye): Alain

Saint-Mandé
Cimetière de Saint-Mandé (Cimetière Nord), 24 avenue Joffre, Saint-Mandé (Métro: Saint-Mandé-Tourelle)

Saint-Ouen
Cimetière Parisien de Saint-Ouen, avenue Michelet, Saint-Ouen (Métro: Mairie de Saint-Ouen or Porte de Clignancourt)

Le Vésinet

8–10 route des Cultures, Le Vésinet (RER: Le Vésinet–Centre): Bizet

Ville d'Avray

Chalet des Lilas à la Chaumière, Ville d'Avray (SNCF: Sèvres–Ville d'Avray): Delius

Paris Streets Listed in the Gazetteer

Former street names are given in *italics* followed by the current name in square brackets.

rue de l'Abbaye, 6e
rue Aboukir, 2e
villa d'Alésia, 14e
rue Alfred-de-Vigny, 8e
avenue Alphand, 16e
rue Amelot, 11e
rue André-Antoine, 18e
rue d'Ankara, 16e
rue d'Antin, 2e
rue de l'Arcade, 8e
rue des Archives, 3e
rue Arsène-Houssaye, 8e
rue d'Assas, 6e
rue de l'Assomption, 16e
rue d'Aumale, 9e
rue du Bac, 7e
rue Ballu, 9e
rue de Beaune, 7e
rue de Bellechasse, 7e
rue Bellini, 16e
rue de Belloy, 16e
cité Bergère, 9e
rue Bergère, 9e
rue de Berlin [now rue de Liège], 8e
rue de Berne, 8e
rue Blanche, 9e
place Boieldieu, 2e

avenue du Bois de Boulogne [now avenue Foch], 16e
rue Boissy-d'Anglas, 8e
rue des Boulangers, 5e
rue du Bourg-l'Abbé, 3e
rue de Bourgogne, 7e
rue de Boursault [now rue La Bruyère], 9e
rue de Braque, 3e
rue Brey, 17e
rue Buffault, 9e
rue Cadet, 9e
rue de Calais, 9e
rue Cambon, 1er
villa des Camélias, 14e
boulevard des Capucines, 9e
rue des Capucines, 1er
rue Cardinet, 17e
avenue Carnot, 17e
rue de Chaillot, 16e
avenue des Champs-Elysées, 8e
rond-point des Champs-Elysées, 8e
place Charles-Dullin, 18e
rue Charlot, 3e
avenue Chateaubriand [now rue Arsène-Houssaye], 8e

rue de Chateaubriand, 8e

rue de Châteaudun, 9e

place du Châtelet, 1er, 4e

rue de la Chaussée-d'Antin, 9e

rue du Cirque, 8e

rue Clapeyron, 8e

boulevard de Clichy, 9e

rue de Clichy, 9e

rue Coëtlogon, 6e

rue Condorcet, 9e

rue de Constantinople, 8e

rue Coquenard, 9e

rue Coquillère, 1er

rue Cortmabert [now rue Pasteur-Marc-Boegner], 16e

rue Cortot, 18e

rue du Couédic, 14e

boulevard de Courcelles, 17e

rue de Courcelles, 17e

rue Croix-des-Petits-Champs, 1er

place Dancourt [now place Charles-Dullin], 18e

villa du Danube, 19e

rue Daru, 8e

rue Delambre, 14e

rue Denfert-Rochereau [now rue Henri-Barbusse] 5e

rue Descartes, 5e

rue de Douai, 9e

rue Drouot, 9e

rue Duperré, 9e

passage de l'Elysée-des-Beaux-Arts [now rue André-Antoine], 18e

square Emmanuel-Chabrier, 17e

rue de l'Eperon, 6e

place d'Estienne-d'Orves, 9e

place des Etats-Unis, 16e

rue du Faubourg-Poissonnière, 9e

rue du Faubourg-Saint-Honoré, 8e

rue Faubourg-du-Temple, 11e

rue Feydeau, 2e

rue de Flandre [now avenue de Flandre], 19e

avenue Foch, 16e

rue François-Miron, 4e

place Franz-Liszt, 10e

avenue Frochot, 9e

rue Fromentin, 9e

square Gabriel-Fauré, 17e

rue Gaillard [now rue Paul-Escudier], 9e

rue Garancière, 6e

place du Général-Catroux, 17e

rue du Général-Foy, 8e

avenue du Général-Lemonnier, Jardin des Tuileries, 1er

rue Geoffroy-Marie, 9e

avenue Georges-Mandel, 16e

rue de Gramont, 2e

rue des Grands-Augustins, 6e

rue Greffulhe, 8e

rue Gustave-Doré, 17e

rue de Harlay, 1er

rue de la Harpe, 5e

boulevard Haussmann, 8e, 9e

rue du Helder, 9e

avenue Henri-Martin [now avenue Georges-Mandel], 16e

rue Hérold, 1er

rue du Huit-Mai 1945, 10e

place d'Iéna, 16e

place Igor-Stravinsky, 4e

avenue Ingres, 16e

place de l'Institut, 6e

boulevard des Invalides, 7e

esplanade des Invalides, 7e

boulevard des Italiens, 2e, 9e

rue Jacob, 6e

rue du Jardinet, 6e

rue Jean-Baptiste-Pigalle, 9e

avenue Jean-Jaurès, 19e

rue Jouffroy-d'Abbans, 17e

place du Jour, 1er

place Jules-Joffrin, 18e

avenue Junot, 18e

avenue Kléber, 16e

rue La Boétie, 8e

rue La Bruyère, 9e

rue Las-Cases, 7e

rue de La Rochefoucauld, 9e

rue de La Tour-d'Auvergne, 9e

rue Laffitte, 9e

rue de Laval [now rue Victor-
     Massé], 9e

rue Le Peletier, 9e

rue Le Verrier, 6e

rue de Liège, 8e

place Lili-Boulanger, 9e

rue de Londres, 8e, 9e

rue de Longchamp, 16e

rue Lord-Byron, 8e

rue Louis-David, 16e

rue de Louvois, 2e

place du Louvre, 1er

rue de Lyon, 12e

place de la Madeleine, 8e

rue de Madrid, 8e

boulevard de Magenta, 10e

rue du Mail, 2e

avenue du Maine, 15e

boulevard Malesherbes

place Malesherbes [now place du
     Général-Catroux], 17e

rue Malesherbes [now rue du
     Général-Foy], 8e

rue Mandar, 2e

rue Marcadet, 18e

rue des Marronniers, 16e

rue de Marseille, 10e

rue des Martyrs, 9e

rue des Mathurins, 9e

avenue Matignon, 8e

rue de Mauberge, 9e

rue de Médicis, 6e

rue Méhul, 2e

rue Ménilmontant [now rue
     Oberkampf], 11e

rue Michelet, 6e

rue Milne-Edwards, 17e

rue Molière, 1er

villa Molitor, 16e

rue de Monceau, 8e

rue Monge, 5e

rue Monsieur-le-Prince, 6e

rue Monsigny, 2e

avenue Montaigne, 8e

rue du Mont-Cenis, 18e

rue de Montholon, 9e

boulevard Montmartre, 2e, 9e

boulevard Montparnasse, 15e

rue Mosnier [now rue de Berne], 8e

rue des Moulins, 1er

rue Neuve-Fontaine-Saint-Georges
     [now rue Fromentin], 9e

rue Neuve-des-Mathurins [now rue
     des Mathurins], 9e

rue Neuve-Saint-Eustache [now part of rue Aboukir], 2e

rue Neuve-Saint-Marc [now rue Saint-Marc], 2e

rue de la Néva, 8e

rue Newton, 16e

avenue Niel, 17e

parvis Notre-Dame, 4e

rue Notre-Dame-des-Champs, 6e

rue Notre-Dame-de-Lorette, 9e

rue Oberkampf, 11e

place de l'Odéon, 6e

rue de l'Odéon, 6e

cité Odiot, 8e

place de l'Opéra, 9e

square d'Orléans, 9e

boulevard du Palais, 1er

place du Panthéon, 5e

rue Papin, 3e

rue de Parme, 9e

place Pasdeloup, 11e

boulevard Pasteur, 15e

rue Paul-Escudier, 9e

boulevard Péreire, 17e

rue des Petits-Champs, 1er, 2e

rue des Petits-Hôtels, 10e

place des Petits-Pères, 2e

rue Pierre-Charron, 8e

rue Pierre-Demours, 17e

rue des Plantes, 14e

boulevard Poissonnière, 2e

rue Poissonnière, 2e

rue des Prêtres-Saint-Séverin, 5e

rue de Provence, 9e

rue Radziwill, 1er

rue Rambuteau, 4e

rue Rameau, 2e

rue de Ranelagh, 16e

boulevard Raspail, 14e

rue Rembrandt, 8e

rue de Rennes, 6e

place de la République, 11e

rue de Richelieu, 2e

rue Richer, 9e

rue de Rivoli, 1er

boulevard de Rochechouart, 18e

rue de Rochechouart, 9e

place Saint-André-des-Arts, 6e

rue Saint-André-des-Arts, 6e

place Saint-Augustin, 8e

rue Saint-Denis [now rue du Mont-Cenis], 18e

rue Saint-Ferdinand, 17e

place Saint-François-Xavier, 7e

rue Saint-Georges, 9e

boulevard Saint-Germain, 7e

place Saint-Germain-des-Prés, 6e

place Saint-Gervais, 4e

rue Saint-Guillaume, 7e

rue Saint-Honoré, 1er

rue Saint-Jacques, 5e

rue Saint-Lazare, 9e

rue Saint-Marc, 2e

boulevard Saint-Martin, 10e

rue Saint-Martin, 4e

boulevard Saint-Michel, 5e

place Saint-Michel, 6e

place Saint-Sulpice, 6e

rue Sainte-Anne, 1er

rue Sainte-Cécile, 9e

square Sainte-Croix-de-la-Bretonnerie, 4e

place Sainte-Geneviève, 5e

rue des Saints-Pères, 7e

place des Saussaies, 8e

rue Say, 9e

rue de Seine, 6e

rue du Sentier, 2e

rue Serpente, 6e

rue Servandoni, 6e

rue de Sévigné, 3e

rue Singer, 16e

rue de Strasbourg [now rue du Huit-Mai 1945], 10e

rue Taitbout, 9e

rue Taranne [now part of boulevard Saint-Germain], 6e

boulevard du Temple [now part of place de la République], 11e

avenue des Tilleuls, 16e

rue de la Tonnellerie, 1er

rue de la Tour, 16e

rue Traversière [later part of rue Molière, partly demolished for avenue de l'Opéra], 1er

rue Tronchet, 8e

avenue Trudaine, 9e

rue de Turbigo, 3e

rue Valentin-Haüy, 15e

rue Vaneau, 7e

rue de Varenne, 7e

rue de Vaugirard, 6e

place Vendôme, 1er

rue de la Victoire, 9e

place Victor-et-Hélène Basch, 14e

place Victor-Hugo, 16e

rue Victor-Massé, 9e

avenue Victoria, 1er

rue Viète, 17e

rue du Vieux-Colombier, 6e

rue des Vignes, 16e

avenue de Villars, 7e

avenue de Villiers, 17e

rue de Vintimille, 9e

rue Vivienne, 2e

quai Voltaire, 7e

avenue de Wagram, 17e

rue Washington, 8e

rue de l'Yvette, 16e

Bibliography

This bibliography is a selective list of books, exhibition catalogues, and articles which have been of particular value in the compilation of the gazetteer; many can also be recommended for further reading.

A. Adam: *Lettres sur la musique française, 1836–1850* (Geneva, 1996)

G. Aitken: *Artistes et théâtres d'avant-garde: Programmes de théâtre illustrés, Paris, 1890–1900* (Pully, 1991) [exhibition catalogue]

E. Anderson: *The Letters of Mozart and His Family*, 3 vols. (London, 1938)

G. Antheil: *Bad Boy of Music* (Garden City, N.Y., 1945)

L. Archbold and W. J. Peterson, eds.: *French Organ Music from the Revolution to Franck and Widor* (Rochester, N.Y., 1995)

J.-M. Bailbé: "Mendelssohn à Paris en 1831–1832," in *Music in Paris in the Eighteen-Thirties*, ed. Peter Bloom (Stuyvesant, N.Y., 1987), 23–39

C. Bailey, L. Nochlin, and A. Distel: *Renoir's Portraits: Impressions of an Age* (New Haven, Conn., 1997) [exhibition catalogue]

P. Barbier: *Opera in Paris, 1800–1850: A Lively History* (Portland, Ore., 1995)

J. Barraqué: *Debussy*, rev. ed. (Paris, 1994)

J. Barzun, trans. and ed.: *New Letters of Berlioz, 1830–1868* (New York, 1954)

C. Bauer: *Les hauts lieux de la musique en France* (Paris, 1990)

P. Beaussant: *François Couperin* (Portland, Ore., 1990)

H. Berlioz: *The Memoirs of Hector Berlioz*, trans. and ed. D. Cairns (London, 1969)

E. Blom, ed.: *Grove's Dictionary of Music and Musicians*, 5th ed. (London, 1954), especially the entries on Conservatoire de Musique, Paris, and Prix de Rome

P. Bloom, ed.: *Music in Paris in the Eighteen-Thirties* (Stuyvesant, N.Y., 1987)

J. Bonnerot: *C. Saint-Saëns, 1935–1921: Sa vie et son oeuvre*, 2nd ed. (Paris, 1922)

F. Bournon: *Paris-Atlas* (Paris, 1900, repr. 1991)

F. Bowers: *Scriabin: A Biography*, 2nd ed. (New York, 1996)

E. Brodie: *Paris: The Musical Kaleidoscope, 1870–1925* (New York, 1987)

J. Brooks: "Nadia Boulanger and the Salon of the Princesse de Polignac," *Journal of the American Musical Society*, 46 (1993), 415–68

J.-M. Bruzon and M. Kahane: *Rossini et Paris* (Paris, 1993)

S. Buckland, trans. and ed.: *Francis Poulenc, Echo and Source: Selected Correspondence, 1915–1963* (London, 1991)

E. Burger: *Franz Liszt: A Chronicle of His Life in Pictures and Documents* (Princeton, N.J., 1989)

D. Cairns: *Berlioz, 1803–1832: The Making of an Artist* (London, 1989)

M.-D. Calvocoressi: *Musician's Gallery: Music and Ballet in Paris and London* (London, 1933)

L. Carley: *Delius: The Paris Years* (London, 1975)

————: *Delius: A Life in Letters, 1862–1908* (Cambridge, Mass., 1983)

L. Carley and R. Threlfall: *Delius: A Life in Pictures* (Oxford, 1977)

A. Casella: *Music in My Time: The Memoirs of Alfredo Casella* (Norman, Okla., 1955)

"César Franck," *L'Orgue: Cahiers et Mémoires*, no. 44 (1990)

C. Cessac: *Marc-Antoine Charpentier* (Portland, Ore., 1995)

"Charles Koechlin: Correspondance," *Revue Musicale*, nos. 348–50 (1982)

"Charles Koechlin: Koechlin par lui-même," *Revue Musicale*, nos. 340–41 (1981)

"Charles Tournemire," *L'Orgue: Cahiers et Mémoires*, no. 41 (1989)

D. Charlton: *Grétry and the Growth of Opéra-Comique* (Cambridge, England, 1986)

L. Chassin-Dolliou: *Le Conservatoire de Paris, ou les voies de la création* (Paris, 1993)

F. Chopin: *Chopin's Letters*, ed. H. Opieński (New York, 1931)

M. Conati: *Encounters with Verdi* (Ithaca, N.Y., 1984)

A. Copland and V. Perlis: *Copland: 1900 Through 1942* (London, 1984)

A. Coquis: *Léo Delibes: Sa vie et son oeuvre* (Paris, 1957)

F. Cougniaud-Raginel: *Joseph Canteloube: Chantre de la terre* (Béziers, 1988)

R. Craft: *Stravinsky: Selected Correspondence*, 3 vols. (New York, 1982, 1984, 1985)

M. Curtiss: *Bizet and His World* (London, 1959)

H. de Curzon: *L'histoire et la gloire de l'ancienne salle du Conservatoire de Paris, 1811–1911* (Paris, [1916])

L. Davies: *César Franck and His Circle* (London, 1970)

W. Dean: *Bizet: His Life and Work* (London, 1965)

R. Delage: *Chabrier: Iconographie musicale* (Geneva, 1982)

A. Devriès and F. Lesure: *Dictionnaire des éditeurs de musique français*, vol. 2, *De 1820 à 1914* (Geneva, 1988)

Diaghilev: Les Ballets Russes (Paris, 1979) [exhibition catalogue]

M. Dietschy: *A Portrait of Debussy* (Oxford, 1990)

A. Distel: *Renoir: A Sensuous Vision* (New York, 1995)

D. Drew: *Kurt Weill: A Handbook* (London, 1987)

G. Dulong: *Pauline Viardot: Tragédienne lyrique*, 2nd ed. (Paris, 1987)

M. Dupré: *Recollections*, trans. and ed. R. Kneeream (Melville, N.Y., 1975) [foreword by O. Messiaen]

K. Ellis: *Music Criticism in Nineteenth-Century France: La Revue et Gazette Musicale de Paris, 1834–1880* (Cambridge, England, 1995)

P. Fauré-Fremiet: *Gabriel Fauré* (Paris, 1929)

G. Ferchault: "Géographie musicale de Paris," *Le Guide du Concert et Le Guide Musical*, Numéro spécial de l'Exposition 37 (1937), viii–xv

A. FitzLyon: *Maria Malibran: Diva of the Romantic Age* (London, 1987)

————: *The Price of Genius: A Life of Pauline Viardot* (London, 1964)

B. François-Sappey, ed.: *Charles-Valentin Alkan* (Paris, 1991)

Y. Fromrich: *Musique et caricature en France au XIXe siècle* (Geneva, 1973)

J. J. Fuld: *Harmonizing the Arts: Original Graphic Designs for Printed Music by World-Famous Artists* (New York, 1986) [exhibition catalogue]

M. Gaillard: *Paris au XIXe siècle* (Marseille, 1991)

J. Gallois: *Franck* (Paris, 1966)

B. Gavoty: *Louis Vierne: La vie et l'oeuvre* (Paris, 1943)

————: *Reynaldo Hahn: Le musicien de la Belle Epoque* (Paris, 1976)

C. Girdlestone: *Jean-Philippe Rameau: His Life and Work,* 2nd ed. (New York, 1969)

C. Goubault: *Claude Debussy* (Paris, 1986)

C. Gounod: *Autobiographical Reminiscences* (London, 1896)

R. S. Grover: *Ernest Chausson: The Man and His Music* (London, 1980)

P. Guillot: *Déodat de Séverac: Ecrits sur la musique* (Liège, 1993)

B. Häger: *Ballets Suédois* (London, 1990)

H. Halbreich: *L'oeuvre d'Arthur Honegger* (Paris, 1994)

J. Harding: *The Ox on the Roof* (London, 1972)

————: *Gounod* (London, 1973)

————: *Jacques Offenbach* (London, 1980)

————: "Paris: Opera Reigns Supreme," *The Late Romantic Era: From the Mid-19th Century to World War I,* ed. J. Samson (London, 1991), 99–125

A. Hedley, ed.: *Selected Correspondence of Fryderyk Chopin* (London, 1962)

"Henri Duparc," *Zodiaque,* no. 152 (1987)

P. Hill, ed.: *The Messiaen Companion* (London, 1995)

J. Hillairet: *Dictionnaire historique des rues de Paris* (Paris, 1993 ed.)

D. K. Holoman: *Berlioz* (London, 1989)

W. Horwood: *Adolphe Sax: His Life and Legacy* (Bramley, England, 1980)

J. House and A. Distel: *Renoir* (London, 1985) [exhibition catalogue]

V. d'Indy: *César Franck* (London, 1910)

D. Irvine: *Massenet: A Chronicle of His Life and Times* (Portland, Ore., 1994)

E. Jablonski and L. D. Stewart: *The Gershwin Years*, 2nd ed. (Garden City, N.Y., 1973)

V. Jankélévitch: *Ravel*, rev. ed., J.-M. Nectoux (Paris, 1995)

H. Jourdan-Morhange: *Ravel et nous* (Paris, 1945)

M. Kahane: *L'ouverture du nouvel Opéra*, Musée d'Orsay, 1986 (Paris, 1986) [exhibition catalogue]

————: *Le Foyer de la danse*, Musée d'Orsay, 1988 (Paris, 1988) [exhibition catalogue]

M. Kahane and N. Wild: *Wagner et la France* (Paris, 1983) [exhibition catalogue]

————: *Les Ballets Russes à l'Opéra* (Paris, 1992)

R. Kimball and A. Simon: *The Gershwins* (New York, 1973)

H. Koegler: *The Concise Oxford Dictionary of Ballet* (Oxford, 1987)

S. Kracauer: *Jacques Offenbach, ou le secret du Second Empire* (Paris, 1994)

D. W. Krummel and S. Sadie, ed.: *The New Grove Handbooks in Music: Music Printing and Publishing* (London, 1990), especially entries on Ballard, Brandus, Choudens, Durand, Erard, Heugel, La Sirène, Pleyel, Schlesinger, Troupenas

N. Labelle, ed.: *Albert Roussel: Lettres et écrits* (Paris, 1987)

L. Laloy: *La musique retrouvée, 1902–1927* (Paris, 1928)

B. Large: *Martinů* (London, 1975)

M. Le Clère: *Guide des cimetières de Paris* (Paris, 1990)

F. Lesure: *Debussy: Iconographie musicale* (Geneva, 1980)

————: *Paul Dukas* (Paris, 1965) [exhibition catalogue]

F. Lesure, ed.: *Stravinsky: Etudes et témoignages* (Paris, 1982)

F. Lesure, ed., and R. Langham Smith, ed. and trans.: *Debussy on Music* (London, 1977)

C. Levisse-Touzé: *Paris libéré, Paris retrouvé* (Paris, 1994)

R. P. Locke: "Paris: Centre of Intellectual Ferment," *The Early Romantic Era: Between Revolutions, 1789 and 1848,* ed. A. Ringer (London, 1990), 32–83

E. Lockspeiser: *Debussy: His Life and Mind* (London, 1962, 1965)

A. Loewenberg: *Annals of Opera, 1597–1940,* 3rd ed. (London, 1978)

R. Machart: *Poulenc* (Paris, 1995)

Gustav Mahler: Un homme, une oeuvre, une époque (Paris, 1984) [exhibition catalogue]

J. and F. Maillard: *Vincent d'Indy: Le maître et sa musique* (Paris, 1994)

N. Malcolm: *George Enescu: His Life and Music* (London, 1990)

A. Marès: *L'Institut de France: Le parlement des savants* (Paris, 1995)

C. Martinů: *My Life with Bohuslav Martinů* (Prague, 1978)

C. Massip, ed.: *Portrait(s) d'Olivier Messiaen* (Paris, 1996) [exhibition catalogue]

"Maurice Duruflé," *L'Orgue: Cahiers et Mémoires,* no. 45 (1991)

O. Messiaen: *Conversations with Olivier Messiaen,* ed. C. Samuel (London, 1976)

P. Migel: *Great Ballet Prints of the Romantic Era* (New York, 1981)

D. Milhaud: *My Happy Life* (London, 1995)

Y. Millon and T. Renaut: *Maurice Ravel à Montfort l'Amaury* (Paris, 1997)

J. Mongrédien: "Paris: The End of the Ancien Régime," *The Classical Era: From the 1740s to the End of the 18th Century,* ed. N. Zaslaw (London, 1989), 61–98

S. Monneret: *L'Impressionisme et son époque* (Paris, 1978–81)

B. de Montgolfier: *Le Musée Carnavalet* (Paris, 1992)

Mozart à Paris (Paris, 1991) [exhibition catalogue]

Musée de la Musique: Guide (Paris, 1997)

Musée d'Orsay: Catalogue sommaire illustré des peintures (Paris, 1990)

"La Musique dans l'Exposition de 1937," *Revue musicale,* no. 175 (1937)

R. Myers: *Emmanuel Chabrier and His Circle* (London, 1969)

J.-M. Nectoux: *Gabriel Fauré: His Life Through His Letters* (London, 1984)

————: *Gabriel Fauré: A Musical Life* (Cambridge, England, 1991)

J.-M. Nectoux, ed.: *Camille Saint-Saëns et Gabriel Fauré: Correspondance (1862–1920)*, 3rd ed. (Paris, 1994)

J.-M. Nectoux et al.: *1913: Le Théâtre des Champs-Elysées* (Paris, 1987) [exhibition catalogue]

R. Nichols: *Debussy Remembered* (London, 1992)

————: *Ravel Remembered* (London, 1987)

C. Noisette de Crauzat: *Cavaillé-Coll* (Paris, 1984)

O. Ochse: *Organists and Organ Playing in Nineteenth-Century France and Belgium* (Bloomington, Ind., 1994)

Offenbach (Paris, 1996) [exhibition catalogue]

A. Orenstein: *Ravel: Man and Musician* (New York, 1975)

————: *A Ravel Reader* (New York, 1990)

R. Orledge: *Gabriel Fauré* (London, 1979)

————: *Satie the Composer* (Cambridge, England, 1990)

————: *Satie Remembered* (London, 1995)

P. Ory: *1889: L'Expo universelle* (Paris, 1989)

R. Osborne: *Rossini,* rev. ed. (London, 1993)

F. Ouellette: *Edgard Varèse: A Musical Biography* (London, 1973)

Paris et banlieue: Atlas, Michelin no. 25 (Paris, 1997 ed.)

Paris Plan, Michelin no. 11 (Paris, 1997 ed.)

A. Pâris: *Dictionnaire des interprètes,* 2nd ed. (Paris, 1985)

J. Passler: "Paris: Conflicting Notions of Progress," *The Late Romantic Era: From the Mid-19th Century to World War I,* ed. J. Samson (London, 1991), 389–416

L. M. Peppercorn: *Villa-Lobos: Collected Studies* (Aldershot, 1992)

A. Périer: *Messiaen* (Paris, 1979)

Petite encyclopédie illustrée de l'Opéra de Paris, 2nd ed. (Paris, 1978)

M. J. Phillips-Matz: *Verdi: A Biography* (Oxford, 1993)

Hommage à la Princesse E. de Polignac née Winaretta Singer, 9 novembre 1988 (Paris, 1989)

"Poulenc: Dialogues des Carmélites," *L'Avant-Scène Opéra*, no. 52 (1983)

F. Poulenc: *Emmanuel Chabrier* (Paris, 1961)

S. Prokofiev: *Soviet Diary 1927 and Other Writings*, trans. and ed. O. Prokofiev (London, 1991) [includes *Autobiography*]

M. Proust: *Chroniques* (Paris, 1927)

T. Reff: *Degas: The Artist's Mind* (Cambridge, Mass., 1987)

Regards d'écrivains au Musée d'Orsay (Paris, 1992)

H. Robinson: *Sergei Prokofiev: A Biography* (London, 1987)

G. Roland: *Stations de Métro* (Paris, 1986)

J. Roselli: *The Life of Bellini* (Cambridge, England, 1996)

L. Rosenstiel: *The Life and Works of Lili Boulanger* (London, 1978)

————: *Nadia Boulanger: A Life in Music* (New York, 1982)

Rossini à Paris (Paris, 1992) [exhibition catalogue]

J. Rougerie: *Paris insurgé: La Commune de 1871* (Paris, 1995)

J. Russell: *Paris* (London, 1983)

J. A. Sadie: "Paris and Versailles," *The Late Baroque Era: From the 1680s to 1740*, ed. G. Buelow (London, 1993), 129–89

S. Sadie, ed.: *The New Grove Dictionary of Music and Musicians* (London, 1980), especially entries on: Adam, Alkan, Auber, Boëly, Bordes, Campra, Charpentier (Gustave), Charpentier (Marc-Antoine), Chopin, Couperin, David (Félicien), Delibes, Dukas, Franck, Gounod, Grétry, Hérold, d'Indy, Koechlin, Léonin, Lully, Marais, Messager, Mulet, Offenbach, Paris, Pérotin, Pleyel, Rameau, Saint-Saëns, Viardot

————: *The New Grove Dictionary of Opera* (London, 1992), especially the entry on Paris

C. Saint-Saëns: *Musical Memories* (Boston, 1919)

H. Schauerte: "Jehan Alain, 1911–1940: L'homme et l'oeuvre," *L'Orgue*, dossier 3 (1985)

G. Servières: *Gabriel Fauré* (Paris, 1930)

N. Slonimsky: *Music Since 1900*, 5th ed. (New York, 1994)

J. Spycket: *Nadia Boulanger* (Lausanne, 1987)

M. Stegemann: *Camille Saint-Saëns and the French Solo Concerto from 1850 to 1920* (London, 1991)

V. Stravinsky and R. Craft: *Stravinsky in Pictures and Documents* (London, 1979)

A. Sutcliffe: *Paris: An Architectural History* (New Haven, Conn., 1993)

L. Symonette and K. Kowalke: *Speak Low (When You Speak Love): The Letters of Kurt Weill and Lotte Lenya* (London, 1996)

A. Thomson: *The Life and Times of Charles-Marie Widor, 1844–1937* (Oxford, 1987)

Toulouse-Lautrec: Prints and Posters from the Bibliothèque Nationale (Brisbane, 1991) [exhibition catalogue for "Les Lautrec de Lautrec"]

L. Vallas: *Claude Debussy: His Life and Works* (Oxford, 1933)

————: *Vincent d'Indy*, vol. 2, *La maturité, la vieillesse, 1886–1931* (Paris, 1950)

T. Vallois: *Around and About Paris*, 3 vols. (London, 1995–97)

U. Vaughan Williams: *R. V. W.: A Biography of Ralph Vaughan Williams* (Oxford, 1964)

L. Verdebout, ed.: *Guillaume Lekeu: Correspondance* (Liège, 1993)

L. Vierne: "Mes souvenirs et journal," *L'Orgue: Cahiers et Mémoires*, nos. 3–4 (1970)

O. Vivier: *Varèse* (Paris, 1973)

O. Volta: *Erik Satie* (Paris, 1997)

————: *Satie Seen Through His Letters* (London, 1989)

T. J. Walsh: *Second Empire Opera: The Théâtre Lyrique Paris, 1851–1870* (London, 1981)

W. Weaver: *Verdi: A Documentary Study* (London, 1977)

H. Weinstock: *Donizetti and the World of Opera in Italy, Paris, and Vienna in the First Half of the Nineteenth Century* (London, 1964)

————: *Rossini: A Biography* (New York, 1968)

————: *Vincenzo Bellini: His Life and His Operas* (London, 1972)

E. W. White: *Stravinsky: The Composer and His Works,* 2nd ed. (London, 1979)

A. Williams: *Portrait of Liszt by Himself and His Contemporaries* (Oxford, 1991)

W. Wiser: *The Crazy Years: Paris in the Twenties* (London, 1983)

Envoi

The frontispiece shows Renoir's *Yvonne et Christine Lerolle au piano* (Paris, Musée de l'Orangerie: Collection Walter-Guillaume), a painting which evokes a network of important musical and artistic associations. Renoir completed this portrait of Yvonne Lerolle (on the left) and her younger sister Christine by October 1897. When Julie Manet saw the finished picture in Renoir's studio, she described it in her diary: "It's ravishing! Christine has a delicious expression, Yvonne is not a very good likeness but her white dress is beautifully painted. The background, with Degas's little Dancers in pink with their plaits, and the Races, is lovingly painted." The setting is the spacious Lerolle apartment at 20 avenue Duquesne, 7e (K10, Métro: Ecole Militaire or Saint-François-Xavier).

Yvonne and Christine were the daughters of Henri Lerolle (1848–1929), a successful salon painter, musician, and collector. Like Degas, he studied at the studio of Louis Lamothe, and Lerolle and Degas were friends from at least 1883. Lerolle studied the violin with Colonne and was a gifted and enthusiastic player. His interest in both music and the visual arts was a consuming one, and his friends included Chausson (Lerolle's brother-in-law), Dukas, Debussy, Degas, Renoir, Denis, Mallarmé, and Gide. All were regular visitors to musical evenings at 20 avenue Duquesne, where they could also admire his excellent collection of paintings (two of which are charmingly illustrated in the background of the present picture). Surprisingly, this picture was never in his collection (nor was the portrait of Christine Lerolle embroidering, now in the Columbus Museum of Art, Ohio). Lerolle later had two sons, Jacques (who became a music publisher) and Guillaume.

Debussy first met Yvonne (born 16 April 1877) in 1893. In February 1894 he dedicated a Japanese fan to her, on which he wrote out nine bars (in piano score) from Act 1, scene 3, of *Pelléas et Mélisande,* the introduction to the scene, where Mélisande's theme is heard. To this he added an inscription: "to Mademoiselle Yvonne Lerolle, in memory of her little sister Mélisande." Yvonne was also the dedicatee of Debussy's 1894

Images, first published complete in 1977 as *Images (oubliées),* including the "Sarabande" which later reappeared in a revised form as the second movement of *Pour le piano.* The dedication reads: "May these *Images* be accepted by Mademoiselle Yvonne Lerolle with a little of the pleasure that I have had in dedicating them to her."

It is clear that Debussy was very fond of Yvonne, whom he perhaps imagined as an elder sister to his Mélisande (he had started work on the opera in 1893). At the time when Debussy was closest to Yvonne, he was also on the point of marrying Thérèse Roger (though the engagement was broken off in March 1894). Marcel Dietschy (1990, 90) has speculated on Debussy's feelings for this highly cultured sixteen-year-old girl at a particularly turbulent time in his life: "His dedication [of the fan] to Yvonne Lerolle seems to take on the meaning of a farewell. Maybe he was saying farewell to a dream that she personified, farewell to what was perhaps his feminine ideal, from the purest and deepest layer of his being. ... Those who knew Yvonne Lerolle have testified to her grace, her transparent air, her 'unattainability.'"

The following year (1895), Chausson dedicated his piano piece *Paysage* to Christine Lerolle (born 13 November 1879), who was two years younger than her sister.

Photographic Credits

Grateful acknowledgement is made to the following for permission to reproduce photographs:

Figures 1.5, 1.7, 1.8, 1.11, 1.12, 1.14, 1.22, 1.23, 1.24, 1.30, 1.31, 1.33, 1.34, 1.36, 1.41, 1.42, 1.44, 1.54, 2.1, 2.3, 2.4, 2.5, 2.7, 2.8, 2.9, 2.10, 2.11, 3.2, 3.9, 3.15, 7.1, 7.2, 7.3, 7.5, 7.6, 7.7, 7.8, 7.9, 7.10. 7.11, 7.12, 7.13, 7.14, 7.16, 7.17, 7.18, 7.19, 7.20: Stephen Cornell and Karen Sturt; Figure 1.3: Princeton University Library; Figures 1.38, 1.39, 1.40: Fondation Singer-Polignac.

Other photographs and illustrations are from the author's collection.